Native Wildflowers and Other Ground Covers for Florida Landscapes

UNIVERSITY PRESS OF FLORIDA

Florida A&M University, Tallahassee
Florida Atlantic University, Boca Raton
Florida Gulf Coast University, Ft. Myers
Florida International University, Miami
Florida State University, Tallahassee
New College of Florida, Sarasota
University of Central Florida, Orlando
University of Florida, Gainesville
University of North Florida, Jacksonville
University of South Florida, Tampa
University of West Florida, Pensacola

D1607747

University Press of Florida

Gainesville

Tallahassee

Tampa

Boca Raton

Pensacola

Orlando

Miami

Jacksonville

Ft. Myers

Sarasota

Native Wildflowers

and Other Ground Covers for Florida Landscapes

Craig N. Huegel

Library of Congress Cataloging-in-Publication Data
Huegel, Craig Norman.
Native wildflowers and other ground covers for Florida landscapes /
Craig N. Huegel.
p. cm.
Includes bibliographical references and index.
ISBN 978-0-8130-3980-0 (alk. paper)
1. Native plant gardening—Florida. 2. Ground cover plants—Florida.
3. Landscape plants—Florida. 4. Landscape gardening—Florida. I. Title.
SB439.24.F6H84 2012
712.09756—dc23   2011037510

The University Press of Florida is the scholarly publishing agency
for the State University System of Florida, comprising Florida A&M
University, Florida Atlantic University, Florida Gulf Coast University,
Florida International University, Florida State University, New College
of Florida, University of Central Florida, University of Florida, University
of North Florida, University of South Florida, and University of West
Florida.

University Press of Florida
15 Northwest 15th Street
Gainesville, FL 32611-2079
http://www.upf.com

This book is dedicated to my number one supporter, my wife and best friend, Alexa Wilcox-Huegel, and to the memory of a truly free spirit, role model, and inspiration, my godmother, Adelaide Wilke. One of my earliest childhood memories involves driving out into the countryside with my grandfather John J. Huegel to purchase cut black-eyed susans and purple coneflowers for her. I had promised her this book and I wish she could have seen it published.

Contents

Preface and Acknowledgments

In 1512, Ponce de Leon, the Spanish adventurer and fortune seeker, is said to have named our state "La Florida," the Land of Flowers, for the only real wealth he ever discovered. Though he never found the fabled Fountain of Youth or the gold he was seeking, de Leon could not fail to notice the great riches of flowering plants that surrounded him. His name for this land persists.

Florida is a treasure trove of beautiful ground covers, but this wealth has been largely undervalued. While many states have learned to use their native wildflowers, ferns, and grasses for landscape purposes, Florida has not. The vast majority are not readily available in the trade, and even specialized native plant nurseries carry very few. It is sadly ironic that the state named for its wildflowers has lagged so far behind nearly everywhere else in their use within home landscapes.

The reasons we have ignored our native ground covers are difficult to pinpoint, but we have done so from the beginning. As our state legislature debated the selection of a state flower on May 15, 1909, all three choices under consideration were non-natives that originated in Asia: camellia, gardenia, and oranges. Florida has always stirred exotic images in the minds of those who've moved here from the north, and the residents fostered that image as a way to sell the state. We have tried hard to make this place something it isn't and ignored virtually everything it is. In doing so, we destroyed the sense of place that makes us unique and created a bizarre caricature of nothing. It was not only Walt Disney who made Florida a fantasyland. He had help from nearly everyone else.

Because so many of us arrived to an already altered landscape, few know to yearn for the natural Florida that once was. We do not have a yardstick by which to measure the losses of our youth, the way folks in New England, Texas, or the Midwest might—areas where the movement to use wildflowers is almost legendary. Few of us understand real Florida enough to try to put some of it back, and many of us simply seem resigned to "go with the flow" and fit in with the neighbors. Our lethargy and our general disinterest have left many hundreds of beautiful and functional native wildflowers, ferns, and grasses by the roadside—literally. Without demand, there is no market, and without a market, no demand is created. It is a classic catch-22.

There are signs that more of Florida's native ground covers will be used in future landscapes. Water restrictions and a rekindling of environmental awareness have spawned an interest in landscaping with native plants. A greater longing to create a sense of place has made many of us reevaluate our use of non-natives, and a desire for butterflies and other wildlife near our homes has created an understanding that natives have far greater value than we have given them. And for some, simply planting our landscapes to ensure we can witness the passage of the seasons and rekindle the anticipation and excitement this passage provides is reason enough. Regardless, there is much to gain and little to sacrifice in adding more natives to the places where we live and work.

Florida has the third-richest palette of native plants of any state in the nation, and many of these are spectacular. Unlike many regions of the country, we have hundreds of beautiful wildflowers from which to choose from and plants of every color and texture with which to weave our landscapes. To the novice native plant gardener, the problem is not finding the starting point, but selecting one from which to begin. Our choices are many and varied. This diversity of choices can be confusing, but it should not cause us to hesitate about getting started.

The purpose of this book is to help you make those choices, to help you whittle down your possibilities to a workable number and select species that will fit well together. It is directed at the home gardener and landscaper, not the field naturalist. I have purposely avoided most of the woody species (trees, shrubs, and vines) and taken an in-depth look at the herbaceous ones. Many of the plants I have included are commercially available from a wide variety of retail sources, some are difficult to find, and some are simply unavailable unless you grow them yourself. I do not see that as a hindrance, however. Perhaps it is time we took some responsibility for expanding the number of species available to us.

My purpose is to rebel a bit against the status quo, expand our knowledge base, and create demand for something new. I believe that far too few of Florida's best species are currently available, and my fervent hope is that more will become available when we realize what is missing. As development gobbles up what is real of Florida, it is in our hands to replace some of what has been lost. We should be proud of the vision apparent to Ponce de Leon more than 400 years ago. Use this book to add native wildflowers, ferns, and grasses effectively into your landscape. Then take the message to your neighbors and retail nurseries. Good luck with your gardening endeavors.

All authors write from a vantage point created by standing on the shoulders of others. I am no exception, and I wish to acknowledge the teachers whose willingness to listen and share made it possible for me to write this book. My parents, Jack and Louise Huegel, put me in a garden at a very early age and instilled a love of plants. I learned that putting my nose into flowers often has its rewards, and that getting dirty with a trowel in hand is a blessed experience. My life would have been far poorer without their encouragement. I owe them greatly, and I miss them even more.

I was introduced to the science of biology by my high school biology teacher, LeRoy Lee. Mr. Lee taught me to see what was in front of me and to collect data to test hypotheses. He saw something in me that others missed and encouraged me in ways others never had. In graduate school, I learned how to question both the unbelievable and the commonly accepted. I am most indebted to Robert McCabe and Orrin Rongstad at the University of Wisconsin, and to Louis Best and Robert Dahlgren at Iowa State University.

This book has greatly benefited from the knowledge and assistance of Gil Nelson and Daniel Austin. Their initial reviews of the manuscript were on target and invaluable. My editors at the University Press of Florida, Lucinda Treadwell and Nevil Parker, finalized those editorial changes and made my words correct. They did an exceptional job. Barbara and Lyle Hoffman converted a number of my 35-mm color slides to digital images, and Cathy Vogelsong, Zachary Grogg, and Alexa Wilcox-Huegel assisted in selecting the images ultimately used to illustrate this book. Though most of those images are mine, the book has been enormously enhanced by the photography of others: Christina Evans, Shirley Denton, Roger Hammer, and Gil Nelson. Finally, I am indebted to the many wonderful friends and mentors I have met since coming to Florida. As a Midwest transplant, I would have been lost without their knowledge and patience. Those especially significant were Michael Kenton, Nancy and Bill Bissett, Brightman Logan, David Drylie, Steve Riefler, Gil Nelson, Walter K. Taylor, Richard Wunderlin, Bruce Hansen, Peggy and Don Lantz, Richard Workman, Rick Joyce, Richard Moyroud, and Dick Deuerling. My Florida Native Plant Society friends, Judith Buhrman, Candy Weller, Marcia Warren, Barbara Hoffman, Chuck Parsons, Debbie Butts, Greg Howe, Debra Davies, Cathy Vogelsong, and Bruce Turley, were there nearly from the start and have always been valuable sounding boards. For more than two decades, I have been encouraged by the great many people I have met and spoken to and by the dedication they have exhibited in managing their home landscapes in ecological ways. Perhaps this book will help in some small way.

Defining the Plants

Native Plants

By most counts, Florida has approximately 3,000 species of native plants. Of these, about 115 are ferns and fern relatives, approximately 500 are grasses and grasslike plants (graminoids), and nearly 825 are trees, shrubs, and woody vines. Most of the remaining 1,560 species could be considered native wildflowers, though for some that would be a stretch.

As defined by the Florida Native Plant Society, plants are native if they occurred in Florida at the time of European contact. The early Spaniards

The Wade Tract, near Thomasville, Georgia, existed in this condition when early European settlers arrived more than 200 years ago.

brought oranges and other agricultural crops with them when they arrived; because of this, citrus are not considered native. Some confusion will always exist as to what is native and what is not because the Spaniards did not take exhaustive notes on the plants they encountered. Therefore, much of what we accept as native is based on assumptions that are, in turn, based on ecology and the notes of later botanists.

Transporting plants around the world for aesthetic and agricultural purposes is not something invented by Europeans. Native peoples also traded plants and introduced species to Florida. Some of these took hold without husbandry and persist in the present-day flora. By definition, these are native, although their introduction was just as contrived.

Plants introduced from elsewhere are often referred to as "exotics," "aliens," or simply non-natives. I prefer the last term, as introducing plants from elsewhere does not seem exotic or alien to me. It seems like human nature. Plants have been crossing our border since the dawn of time. It is nothing new. It's just the number of recent introductions that is staggering. Over the past several centuries, Florida has been bombarded by new species brought in for agricultural and ornamental purposes. Since before statehood, we have tried to reshape our flora with new plants that seemed

Mexican wild petunia (*Ruellia tweediana*) is listed as a Class I Invasive Pest Plant by the Florida Exotic Pest Plant Council and is a good example of a non-native flower that has escaped cultivation and invaded natural areas.

better somehow. Some have behaved themselves. Many have escaped our management and invaded natural areas. It is these plants that have caused irrefutable harm and enormous expense to control.

There is a renewed interest in using Florida's native plants. For one thing, the correct native plants, used in the right place, exist without the need for supplemental assistance. They were here before humans felt the need to design landscapes, and they would persist if we simply packed up and went back to the places from where we came. In a world of rapidly declining resources, it makes sense to simplify the amount of work it takes to keep our landscapes up. By choosing the right native for the right place, we can significantly reduce the amount of water, fertilizer, and pesticides commonly used in the traditional Florida landscape. Reducing these types of inputs will save valuable natural resources and money. Who is not in favor of that?

Native plants are also better at providing habitat for wildlife. Most of us desire more butterflies and songbirds around us. Native plant landscapes are the key to creating the conditions where such animals can thrive. The decline in Florida's wildlife populations is directly tied to habitat loss caused by development. We can put some of that lost habitat back by landscaping appropriately.

Using natives within our home landscape also gives us back a sense of place. By making landscapes look like Florida, we return them to a simpler place in time. We eliminate the tropicals in neon colors that never change and replace them with native plants that flower and fade at their appointed times each year. We can then follow the seasons through our landscapes and look forward to the changes each week brings. I find it exciting to have new things to look forward to over the course of the year and am bored otherwise. What is the point of exploring your landscape when you already know what you will find there?

Although natives have a great deal going for them, do not be fooled into thinking you can plant them and walk away. All newly planted species will need care as they become established, and some may need a bit of extra help during periods of extreme conditions even after they are established. One of the greatest mistakes I see is letting plants fend for themselves too soon. Even adaptable plants take time to adjust to life in the ground. Do not abandon them once they are planted and watered in. While some natives are extremely tough and adaptable to a great many

Many songbirds, like this common yellowthroat, benefit from landscapes designed with native plants. Photo by Christina Evans, with permission.

growing conditions, many others are not. Some native plants can be extremely sensitive and demanding. Many of our rarest species are adapted to a very narrow range of growing conditions. If you create these conditions in your landscape, or are fortunate enough to have them already, you may be able to include these plants in your landscape plan, but the secrets to native plant landscaping are to use the right plants for the right location and to combine plants that share similar growing requirements. In a way, you are looking to create a community of plants that function together under the same growing conditions. If you achieve that, you will find that much of your gardening energy can then be devoted to the part that is most enjoyable: watching your garden grow. I spend far more time now in my native garden than I ever did under the old model, but it is time I choose to spend and time I would not trade for something else.

The plants I have chosen to include in this book are typically lumped together as ground covers: plants that grow close to the ground beneath the trees and shrubs. As a group, they form the lowest layer of a typical plant community.

Given Florida's great plant diversity, our choices are overwhelming, so I have imposed a few more restrictions to make the number of plants discussed in this book a bit more manageable. As this book is about landscaping, I generally have not included species so difficult to grow they are impractical for all but the most experienced gardener. Some species, regardless of their beauty, will simply never be realistic garden subjects. Either they are extremely difficult to propagate or they are nearly impossible to provide for in the home landscape. I have made a few exceptions, however, for certain showy species, such as the lupines (*Lupinus* spp.), that are garden favorites in other states. In Florida, lupines are not easily mastered.

Sky blue lupine (*Lupinus diffusus*) is a beautiful native wildflower but extremely difficult to propagate and use in home landscapes.

I generally have not included species that are exceedingly rare unless they are being propagated by the nursery trade and/or experience has shown that they can be fairly easily grown outside their narrow natural ranges. Some of the scrub mints, such as the genera *Conradina* and *Calamintha*, can be wonderful additions to a home landscape despite their limited geographic ranges. Others, like the genus *Dicerandra*, are far less practical and not included despite their great beauty.

I also have avoided the great many species whose aesthetics are limited or are only an acquired taste. Although beauty is said to be in the eye of the beholder, many herbaceous plants simply do not have much going for them as garden subjects and are unlikely ever to be the subject of consumer demand. I have avoided most species I consider "weeds." My wife, Alexa, believes that a weed is simply a plant in the wrong place, but I use a different definition. To me, weediness is more a character trait. Weeds are plants of disturbed places, capable of quickly establishing themselves, often short lived with rapid growth, and quick to reach maturity. Weeds colonize areas quickly following a disturbance, spread rapidly, and often outcompete other plants as long as conditions are favorable for them. Sunny, open gardens are ideal places for weeds—even native ones. Many are nearly impossible to control once they are introduced. Spanish needles (*Bidens alba*) is one such weed. Thistles (*Cirsium* spp.) are another. Although both have value to the butterfly garden, their behavior makes them nuisances in most home landscapes. The few exceptions I've included are generally plants that can easily be weeded from the places they are not wanted. Dotted horsemint (*Monarda punctata*) is a "weed" I have planted everywhere I have lived in Florida.

What I've included are ferns, grasses, and wildflowers that have aesthetic beauty and growing requirements that can be met in the home landscape. Sometimes, as with black-eyed susans (*Rudbeckia* spp.), the genus includes common garden species as well as others that are rarely grown. In these situations, I have included many of the lesser-known species if they have qualities that warrant a better look. I have lumped species if they are nearly impossible to distinguish from one another without a botany degree. This is especially true for many of the ferns and grasses. If they look alike and grow alike, I have lumped them under one heading.

But before we get too detailed, it might be best to define what constitutes

Spanish needles (*Bidens alba*) and yellow thistle (*Cirsium horridulum*) are wonderful nectar sources for pollinators, but very weedy and difficult to control in a typical landscape.

Spanish needles (*Bidens alba*) with nectaring pearl crescent butterfly.

Yellow thistle (*Cirsium horridulum*).

a fern, grass, or wildflower. It may seem a simple thing on the surface, but understanding these three very different groups is important to your future success in the landscape. Failing to understand their needs and the way they grow and multiply can make it very difficult to either combine them or have them thrive.

Ferns

Ferns are a very ancient group of plants and were present well before the dinosaurs. They preceded the flowering plants by millions of years and have been successful enough to persist in many forms into our present-day flora. These forms have mystified humans since at least the Middle Ages. Medieval peoples ascribed all kinds of mystical and superstitious qualities to ferns. Today, ferns are mostly admired and loved for their simple, elegant beauty.

Ferns are an important understory component in moist shady locations.

For the most part, ferns are a component of shady forest floors. Few of them are adapted to full sunlight, and perhaps fewer can be grown in soils that are droughty. Most do best when planted in shady locations or in areas of dappled sunlight. When given more sun, most need to be grown in soils that are wet or fully saturated. Most also prefer soils with ample organic matter resulting from decaying leaves.

There are exceptions, but many of these are rather rare and not widely available. Some of the most beautiful exceptions are adapted to growing on limestone outcrops or very thin soils in areas with limestone on the surface. A few others are epiphytes: so-called air plants that attach themselves to the branches and trunks of woody species to get up off the forest floor. Epiphytes do not draw their nutrition from their hosts as parasites do, so epiphytic ferns can be added to a landscape without negative impact on the plants they attach to. But finding epiphytic ferns in a nursery is often difficult, because they don't grow in pots with soil.

Ferns are not flowering plants. They produce microscopic spores in specialized bodies (sori) that usually develop on the underside of their fronds (leaves). Mature fronds develop sori at specific times of the year, just as flowering plants have distinct flowering seasons. Each sorus contains a number of capsules or sacs known as sporangia. Sporangia are the fertile part of the overall structure, and they produce the spores. At just the right time each year, depending on the fern species, the covering of each sporangium opens up and many dustlike spores are released into the air. On a shady forest floor, with little air movement, these spores may travel only a few feet before settling back down, but when air currents are right, they might travel miles from their parent.

Most spores die before they ever have a chance to develop further. When they land in an area where conditions are right, they develop quickly into tiny heart-shaped plants known as prothallia. The prothallia stage is so small that ferns in this stage usually go undetected, even by the most watchful gardener. Prothallia remain tiny but quickly develop male and female organs on the heart-shaped leaf. When fertilization eventually occurs, the resulting "egg cells" begin developing into recognizable fern plants. Ferns, therefore, have two stages in their life cycle when they are one-celled organisms. In both stages, they are extremely vulnerable to environmental conditions and at high risk of not surviving.

The ripe sporangia of ferns release thousands of spores into the air to complete their life cycle, and their pattern on the underside of the fronds is like a fingerprint for identifying them to species.

Swamp fern (*Blechnum serrulatum*).

Shield fern (*Thelypteris interrupta*).

Cinnamon fern (*Osmunda cinnamomea*).

Virginia chain fern (*Woodwardia virginica*).

Some ferns also spread asexually by underground rhizomes. The common bracken fern (*Pteridium aquilinium*) and the often-planted sensitive fern (*Onoclea sensibilis*) are both well known for their tendency to spread through the landscape when conditions are to their liking.

For the most part, ferns will be added to your landscape by purchases of potted specimens grown by a nursery, and they will spread slowly over time from the spot where initially planted. It is unlikely that you will have much success in propagating them on your own, and it may be years before those you plant have offspring large enough to notice. Ferns are plants for specialized locations. You will be adding them to the understory of moist shady areas. If you are fortunate enough to have an open wet area in your landscape, or diligent enough to create one, you may add ferns to these areas as well.

Grasses

Grasses belong to the group of flowering plants known as monocots, a group that gets its name from the fact that the sprouting seed initially produces only one (mono) leaf (cotyledon). Most gardeners are familiar with the difference between a sprouting kernel of corn (monocot) and that of a green bean (dicot). We do this experiment often in grade school.

The monocots include plants that I have included in my wildflower section, groups such as the lilies, amaryllises, spiderworts, and irises. Many of the remaining monocots are grasses and grasslike plants, typically lumped into the group known as "graminoids." I will refer to these graminoids as grasses for the purpose of this book, though a few are more correctly called sedges or rushes.

Grasses, sedges, and rushes have different flowering structures and slightly different stems and leaf shapes, but they share the characteristic of having a simple leaf blade, and root and growth forms that are virtually identical. To most gardeners, lumping them together makes sense since they function in the landscape very similarly.

Although some grasses are found in the understory of shady habitats, the vast majority are common to open sunny ones. Grasses often grow as clumps from a central root mass, whether they are evergreen or deciduous. These types are referred to as bunchgrasses. From their central root mass, numerous single-bladed leaves are produced by a central bud. Bunchgrasses are "well behaved" in a landscape setting because they stay close to where they are planted. Others spread by runners; a well-known example is St. Augustine grass (*Stenotaphrum secundatum*), but other native grasses behave this way as well.

Grasses are either annuals or perennials. By definition, annual grasses die back each year and persist in an area by reseeding themselves. Perennial grasses often die back each year and resprout in the spring from the bud located in the root mass beneath the soil surface. Even perennial grasses do not live forever. Every few years, the central bud dies and is replaced by one that forms in the younger roots. Because of this, perennial grasses slowly "migrate" in a garden.

Grasses also fall into two distinct groups: "warm-season" or "cool-season," based on whether their active growth occurs during the heat of

Native grasses provide the foundation for all of Florida's sunny wildflower areas. Most, like this native foxtail (*Setaria* sp.), are quite beautiful when used correctly. Photo by Christina Evans, with permission.

summer or during the cooler months of late winter and spring. Most of Florida's non-native lawn grasses are warm-season grasses; hence the reason they look so disheveled during the winter despite our best attempts to lure them into growth with fertilizers and water. Annual rye-grass (*Lolium perenne*) is a non-native cool-season grass, which is why it looks good during the winter months but declines in the late spring. The vast majority of native grasses described in this book are warm-season species and dormant during the winter.

Most grasses produce large numbers of seeds and rapidly colonize bare ground. While this can be a problem during the early years when your landscape is first developing, it can be managed by controlled weeding and the use of a light layer of mulch. Grasses are an extremely important part of a wildflower meadow as they provide structure and habitat to the landscape, but they should be incorporated cautiously and planted with sufficient spacing if it is important to your plans to have more than just grasses. Your bunchgrasses will expand outward from their central core once established. As they do, they will take up more space and fill in some of the bare ground around them.

Wildflowers

For the purposes of this book, wildflowers are herbaceous flowering plants, nearly everything that is not a "grass." They can have showy or rather inconspicuous blooms, but they all belong to the large group of plants that reproduce sexually from seed produced by flowers.

Because they are herbaceous, many die back to the ground during the winter and spend those months as roots and tubers beneath the soil surface until spring. For the purposes of this book, I call these types of

Florida has approximately 1,560 native species of wildflowers, more than any state or province in North America except California and Texas.

wildflowers "deciduous." Others become dormant and spend the winter as basal leaves near the soil surface. I refer to these wildflowers as "evergreen." Very few stay green and bloom year-round. The exceptions are those species resident to southernmost Florida, where winter temperatures do not dip below freezing, but even many of these have distinct resting and growing phases.

Wildflowers can be annuals, biennials (two years), or perennials. Annuals, by their nature, are especially adept at colonizing sites that are frequently disturbed, and they reproduce by scattering large numbers of seeds before they die. In the conventional landscape, we use masses of flowering non-native annuals (e.g. petunias, marigolds, and zinnias) and replace them when they die. That is not the approach I suggest for native plant landscapes. Annuals in our wildflower garden should be adapted so they reseed and do not need to be replaced each year.

Biennials are really annuals that take two years to mature, flower, and set seed. During their first year, they produce foliage and establish their root systems, but produce no blooms. In their second, they go for broke, flower extensively, set seed, and die. Early in my gardening life, I could not understand why some of my plants did so well only to die after flowering. While a few of these were simply gardening mistakes, most turned out to be biennials. Because of their nature, it is best to plant biennials annually for the first several years so that some are always scheduled to bloom and set seed. If conditions are to their liking and they reproduce, they will persist. If not, they will die out. In my opinion, it is not worth the time and effort to keep a plant that takes two years to bloom if it then dies and disappears.

Perennials are not really perennial; no plant lives forever. Some persist for decades, but most do not. Short-lived perennials live and bloom for only two or three seasons before they expire. The difference between these and the biennials is that they bloom for more than one season.

Perennials will be the most dependable segment of your wildflower garden. Regardless of whether they die back to the ground or not, they can be counted on to come up each year in the spot they were planted. Some sucker and spread, and others set viable seed, but the parent plant stays put. Perennials form the foundation of a landscape plan because of this. You can count on them season after season, and you can plant around them with species that are less dependable. Unlike annuals and biennials, perennial plants do not *have* to produce viable seeds to persist in the landscape.

Most perennials are well behaved. When conditions are right, they cast their seeds annually, and some of these sprout and survive. Over time, if you have selected plants appropriate to your conditions, your landscape will fill in and become everything you had hoped it would. If not, even your perennials will slowly expire, your planted areas will grow thinner, and you will be faced with the need to either replant or try something different. I do not mind replacing a few plants from time to time, but our goal is a landscape that persists without a lot of additional planting effort.

Most native wildflowers reproduce easily by seed and multiply if allowed to ripen in the landscape and not mulched too heavily.

2

The Natural Landscape

I am not a proponent of using native ground covers in the same way we traditionally have used non-natives. Although it can be done, it requires a great amount of work to make plants behave in such rigid order and rarely achieves the same level of success as landscapes based on more naturalistic approaches. Most of us are familiar with the traditional "cottage garden" design. These are the gardens we see in magazines, and we are urged to emulate them, but they are fantasy. Our fascination with cottage gardens has brought us to the point where we are today: using vast amounts of energy and valuable resources to force nature to behave in an organized manner. Albert Einstein once said that the definition of insanity is doing the same thing over and over and expecting different results. He could have been talking about our approach to the home landscape. It is time we abandon the cottage garden and seek designs that provide function as well as beauty.

We have ignored the concept of planting a functional landscape for far too long. In nature, it is clear what landscapes provide. Most of us understand the ecological importance of natural areas. For some reason, we do not often see the same need to preserve those functions in developed ones. We have come to accept the fallacy that landscapes are meant only as window dressings to our homes. Conventional landscapes are a symbol of our success at conquering nature. The natural landscape is an acceptance that we are part of it.

Landscapes that rely on well-chosen natives will do far more than conventional landscapes in providing services back to us. Just as native lands enrich our soils, filter toxins and chemicals, and reduce runoff and capture water for our aquifer, so will landscapes designed on the principles

We have come to accept the formal garden, composed of non-native plants, as "normal," even though it requires great effort to maintain and frequently fails to survive over time. In South and Central Florida, we have taken this to extremes by using tropical plants that often freeze.

of nature do the same. Using plants adapted to our sites and combining them properly will reduce our need to fertilize, water, and spray with insecticides. It should also reduce runoff and slowly enrich our soils.

One other major function of a landscape is to provide habitat for the

A native wildflower landscape is diverse, persists over time, and provides habitat for wildlife. Deer tongue (*Carphephorus paniculatus*) is a good nectar source for pollinating insects like this gulf fritillary.

rest of the earth's creatures. Some of our most interesting wildlife are in decline because of habitat loss. We lose habitat when we strip it away in preparation for each and every development, but we can restore it by purposeful landscaping that replaces the native plants and plant communities. Native landscapes have an overstory of trees and shrubs and an understory of herbaceous plants. Of the two, it is the understory that is most radically altered in the traditional developed landscape.

I have devoted an entire earlier book (Huegel, C. N., 2010, *Native Plant Landscaping for Florida Wildlife*, University Press of Florida) to the concept of landscaping to provide wildlife habitat. I will not repeat that discussion here, except to state that landscapes can be aesthetically beautiful and still provide habitat. Plants provide food for wildlife with their seeds, fruit, and foliage and by the insects they attract. Their foliage provides structure for nests and concealment for hiding. If you travel through Florida, you will find native landscapes that are relatively open in structure and those that are dense and shady. Each provides habitat for certain types of wildlife, and none is better than another. It simply depends on the types of wildlife for which you wish to create habitat.

My earlier book focused on woody species, but the herbaceous understory is equally important. Many species of songbirds, small mammals, and other wildlife spend time on the ground and rely on the food and cover provided there. Replacing turf with native grasses and wildflowers in sunny locations will produce profound changes in the value of your yard to wildlife. The same is true of replacing woody mulches in shady locations with ferns and shade-tolerant grasses and wildflowers.

Abandoning the cottage garden does not mean creating a "wild" yard or that everything will be growing willy-nilly wherever it happens to come up. We can maintain whatever degree of order our aesthetic tastes require, but our plant choices will be for purposes greater than mere looks. Those of us who need a high degree of order can weed out the

Creating a native wildflower prairie from former turfgrass lawn takes time and energy, but it has many rewards.

seedlings and plants that spread to the "wrong" places. Some of us like to weed; it's good therapy and relieves tension, but my personal goal in my own landscape is to spend more time watching and less time performing real work.

A natural landscape approach does not necessarily mean abandoning all use of non-native plants. If there are species you simply can't live without, use them. Just put them in areas where they are adapted and limit them to species that are truly able to thrive without excessive inputs of energy, harsh chemicals, and natural resources. There are non-natives that are adaptable and not invasive. Some even have value to butterflies and other wildlife. Use them without guilt if they are important to you. Our goal in plant selection is to avoid species that are invasive or likely to pass away if we stop nurturing them for a week or two. Mixing natives and non-natives is fine, but it is best done with a desire to create function, not solely for aesthetics.

Mixing native wildflowers with cultivated non-natives can have positive ecological benefits. Here, native blanket flower (*Gaillardia pulchella*) has been added to a bed of orange mule marigolds.

Planting a natural landscape does not release you from management responsibilities. You cannot let everything go. There is a big difference between active gardening and slothfulness. What I espouse are designs that mimic elements of nature: selecting a plant palette and directing the landscape's succession, not letting things develop on their own. Our yards will never mimic nature unless we take an active part in their genesis and their continued management. We must choose what we want from the beginning if we are ever to be in harmony with nature, and that endpoint comes with its own price. It takes thoughtful planning to be successful, and it will take work to put it on the right path.

A natural landscape provides many benefits, but it is not without some of the headaches of traditional landscaping. While the challenges may be different, they are challenges nonetheless, and they need to be accepted and taken head-on to be successful.

Myth Number 1 is that using native understory plants will result in a need for less landscape maintenance. While this seems plausible, it is not true. What I have found is that you trade one set of maintenance needs for another. Some things are definitely easier with a native yard, but some things require more work.

While it is true that a well-manicured lawn requires supplemental irrigation and fertilizer to do its best, and that it often falls victim to disease and pests that require chemicals, it is a very simple thing to hire a lawn-maintenance company to do all the work for you. How can life get much easier than that? Even if you do it yourself, most homeowners spend fewer than a couple hours per week turning on an irrigation system, walking behind a self-propelled mower or riding a tractor mower, and scattering granules of something with a spreader. There are significant costs associated with maintaining plants poorly adapted to our growing conditions, but there is a certain ease in this approach that is hard to argue.

A naturalistic understory has its own set of maintenance challenges. While properly selected native plants are better adapted to Florida's growing conditions and thrive without many supplemental inputs once they are established, getting it all established requires a significant amount of work. If you believe (or are told) that you can simply remove your turf and ornamental beds, plant natives, and sit back and enjoy it all, you will have a rude awakening once reality sets in. Removing your monoculture

Old fields, stripped of native vegetation and left alone, will be colonized by weedy species and may never recover their original diversity unless purposely restored. This area is within a nature preserve and has remained in this condition for more than 20 years.

of turfgrass will expose your soil to every weed seed in the region. Some may have been lying dormant in the soil, but the vast majority will arrive on the breeze or be deposited by birds, raccoons, or other far-ranging wildlife. You cannot roll out a carpet of native ground cover the way you can sod an open field, and you cannot plant your new native landscape so dense as to prevent patches of bare soil from remaining.

Establishing an area of native ground covers will take several years, and during that time you will have to weed. Do not get lazy and let "nature take its course," assuming that everything will eventually sort itself out and come to balance. It won't. Weeds will outcompete your native species if left alone. Over time, they will become dominant, and everything will become a weedy mess, not the natural nirvana you once may have envisioned. Pull the weeds as soon as they appear and well before they can set seed or sucker. The same is true of your native species. Some will be more aggressive than others. Let your plantings develop and reproduce, but never get complacent and let the more aggressive ones get too dominant and crowd the others out. Things will come to a balance, as in nature, but it may take several years before you can sit back a bit. Until then, be prepared to pull weeds. And, unlike the situation with your former turfgrass areas, you are unlikely to find someone to do the work for you who has any idea of what he or she is doing.

Because of this, never take on a new planting area larger than you can manage. One of the biggest mistakes you can make is trying to do everything at once. Be patient and it will pay off immensely. When Alexa and I converted our yard to natives, we did it in distinct patches. Each year, we picked a new area, killed the grass, ripped out the non-natives, and planted. We were particularly vigilant in the front yard, where everything is visible to our neighbors. We then took on the side yard, where we have a deck where we entertain, and then the back, where everything is generally screened by privacy fencing. Develop a set of landscape priorities and spend more time on the areas that are most important to you.

Although it has taken us nearly a decade, the time was well spent. Our yard is finally filled with birds and other wildlife, and we are at the point where we can spend more time bird watching than hunched over, pulling weeds. But we still pull them when we need to.

I have touched on *Myth Number 2* in various passages already, the myth that a native/natural landscape is simpler than the more traditional one. Nothing can be further from the truth. Native landscapes are very complex communities. Creating one from scratch is not simple. Frankly, it is much easier to add natives to an already established ornamental bed than it is to create a native wildflower meadow from a turfgrass lawn.

Open natural areas are a mixture of wildflowers and native grasses comprising many different species. Grasses provide important benefits. They provide the structure necessary to hold taller wildflowers upright, and they fill the holes that would otherwise be bare during the winter, providing openings for weed establishment. Many of Florida's native grasses have great ornamental value, and some produce seeds, foliage, and cover important to wildlife. And, since most Florida wildflowers become dormant during the winter, grasses add interest when little else is happening.

Native landscapes are diverse. In this photo at the Nature Conservancy's Tiger Creek Preserve in Polk County, it is easy to see how small changes in elevation change plant communities in Florida.

Combining a diversity of wildflowers ensures something will be blooming and/or setting seed most months. Although it is spectacular to have everything in flower at one time, that approach also means that you will have nothing but green leaves the rest of the year. I like to plan for a burst of color during one season and a trickling of color every other month. Even in southernmost Florida, where freezing temperatures are not in the equation, most wildflowers and native grasses have distinct blooming seasons that should be planned for. Shadier understories are often less diverse but still composed of more than one type of fern and several wildflowers and grasses.

The image of simplicity in a natural understory is a mirage. Interesting understories are complex, and adding the diversity you need takes planning and a good deal of maintenance during the early years. It will be a juggling act to keep all the parts thriving together. Be patient in the early years, do not be afraid of altering your planting plan, and strive to maintain diversity. Do not succumb to the temptation to let the few strongest take over and win. The first few years will require work, but the years following will reward you for your efforts.

That takes me to *Myth Number 3*, one to which I have also alluded previously: that a natural landscape can be managed by nature. While naturalistic landscapes mimic nature, the natural forces that would shape them are lost post-development, and it takes active intervention to replace their function. You likely can't burn your landscape on a natural cycle, for example, but fire is an integral part of most native systems in Florida. You will not have grazing animals pruning your plants and dropping fertilizer behind them. The hydrology of your site will have been inexorably altered

Recurring fire is a natural process in Florida and important for maintaining the diversity of understory communities. The understory of this longleaf pine forest is dependent on fire and quickly recovers its natural complexity.

during development, and water flow and rainfall patterns will likely be altered from predevelopment conditions.

Your developed landscape will also be surrounded by more invasive and non-native species than any area of nature. Look under any shrub or tree in your landscape where birds regularly perch and see if you don't find seedlings of invasive non-native species. Our landscaping goal is to work with nature, but the "new nature" of developed areas requires us to intervene, because natural processes are altered by development, and our yards are simply too small to be immune from these alterations.

Because most of us cannot burn our grasses, we should be prepared to clip them back from time to time. Native bunchgrasses cannot be mowed to less than about 6 inches without damaging them, but letting them grow unchecked will eventually lead to overgrown conditions and problems. Clip them back in late winter or early spring.

Be prepared to water your new plantings for at least several months to get them established, and do not be afraid to water them during droughty periods if they need it. Native plants, planted in the right location, may never need additional water once they are fully established, but they will need plenty of it to get to that point. Rainfall patterns have changed in Florida with the rapid rise of development. We do not get rain as often, in the same locations, or in the same amounts as we did historically. While I advocate the strictest and wisest use of water possible, having a native landscape does not necessarily mean that it will not need additional irrigation from time to time.

Last, be prepared to weed out invasive plant seedlings and other undesirable plants until the end of time. In my yard, the neighboring live and laurel oaks (*Quercus virginiana* and *Q. laurifolia*, respectively) drop a constant rain of acorns on my yard every fall. If I did not pull the seedlings, my entire yard would be nothing but an oak forest. I pull invasive carrotwood (*Cupaniopsis anacardioides*) and Brazilian pepper (*Schinus terebinthifolius*) seedlings from beneath my shrubs almost monthly. You will need to "play God" in your landscape and decide who will live and who will leave. This necessity does not go away just because you have adopted a naturalistic landscape approach.

Whether you choose to take a more naturalistic approach with your native understory or a more traditional one by simply adding natives to your existing mix, it is critical that you put the right plants together for the

Landscapes in developed areas are constantly bombarded by the seed of invasive plants. These seedling carrotwood (*Cupaniopsis anacardioides*) appear constantly in my landscape beneath roost sites frequented by birds.

location you are planting. Our goal is to create beautiful landscape areas that function together as a community with a minimum of inputs of water, fertilizer, pesticides, and labor. Regardless whether all your landscape material is native or not, you do not want your plants fighting each other. Choose wisely to match your conditions.

It is very difficult to significantly alter the overall growing conditions found naturally in your landscape. Augmenting the soil around your new plants by adding "potting soil" or "garden soil" is usually a waste of time and money. If your plants survive your landscape, their root mass will quickly outgrow the area you initially augmented. It is best to live with what you have and plan your planting areas accordingly.

But it is possible to make changes to small areas of the landscape that allow you to use plants that would fail otherwise. Alexa and I have done these types of alterations several different ways in our own yard. In the backyard, we wanted to create a woodland setting around some large live oaks that were left post-development. We had envisioned a setting of ferns and spring-blooming wildflowers beneath the trees, but the soils were simply too dry and inorganic for that to work, and the evergreen canopy limited the types of wildflowers we could use. We altered this site by extending the tree canopy with deciduous trees and by annually adding

I was able to increase the understory diversity in this portion of my yard by adding leaf mulch to the surface and deciduous canopy trees to the overstory.

layers of oak and maple leaves as mulch. As the canopy developed and created moister and shadier conditions and as the organic mulch broke down and fed the soil, we eventually reached the point where many of our desired plants could thrive.

We also wanted to grow herbaceous wetland plants in a sunnier part of our landscape for the butterflies and the diversity. Our yard is well drained, so adding these species was not possible without altering a portion of it. We did this by digging a hole approximately three feet deep and six feet in diameter, lining it with a thick plastic pond liner, refilling the hole with the dirt we excavated, and directing the runoff water from our roof to the new wetland. Now, every time it rains, the water runs directly to our wetland and saturates the soil. Except in periods of extreme drought, our plants do not need extra water from our hose. When they do, it takes very little, and it is not wasted because the liner traps it.

You may not have the same growing conditions in every part of your yard. Many of us have areas where soil was brought in as fill. We may have spots that are lower and moister or higher and better drained. Spots that are shadier may be very different from areas in the sun. Develop different planting plans for those different parts of your landscape. Just make sure that everything in your planting palette has similar needs for each distinct area.

3

Landscape Maintenance

As I've discussed in the previous chapters, your native plant understory will require maintenance whether you use a naturalistic approach or not. Maintenance is especially critical during the early years while your plant community is developing, but routine care will always be important.

Annuals vs. Perennials

Most native ferns and grasses are perennials, but some of your wildflowers may be annuals. Annuals tend to survive in nature by taking advantage of disturbances of one kind or another. When conditions are stable, vacant spots of ground are taken over by long-term tenants. Such situations are not conducive to annual plants. Disturbances are natural occurrences, even in stable sites. Animals rooting up the soil, hurricanes, trees dying and falling over are all part of a natural landscape. In these conditions, annuals gain a foothold, produce seed, and thrive until the gap is lost. By then, a new gap has opened up somewhere nearby.

You can keep annuals thriving in your landscape by maintaining gaps and providing places for the seeds to reach your soil. If your plantings are too thick or if you are using a deep layer of mulch, annuals will not be able to reseed, and the only way to maintain them is to replant them each year. In our landscape, Alexa and I keep our annuals such as common tickseed (*Coreopsis leavenworthii*) and blanket flower (*Gaillardia pulchella*) by leaving some bare soil around them.

Annuals such as this marsh pink (*Sabatia stellaris*), need some bare soil nearby to reseed the landscape. Do not mulch such plants heavily or they will not persist.

Deciduous vs. Evergreen

Another plant selection consideration is whether they are deciduous or evergreen. The majority of grasses are evergreen, whereas most ferns and wildflowers are not. Using only deciduous plants will result in your landscape being a patch of dirt or mulch during winter and early spring. This is not aesthetically interesting. The problem is that many of the most beautiful understory plants are deciduous. Obviously, this requires compromise and planning.

To achieve balance, use evergreens throughout your planting beds. In the shady garden, use ferns that do not die back to the ground. Christmas fern (*Polystichum acrostichoides*), for example, is so named because it is green throughout the winter. Violets (*Viola* spp.) and partridgeberry (*Mitchellia repens*) also stay green. Surround these plants with patches of low-growing evergreen woody plants, such as dwarf wild coffee (*Psychotria nervosa*), so that the areas comprising only leaf mulch are reduced and scattered. In the spring, these "holes" fill in once more with deciduous species.

In sunnier areas, make sure to add grasses for structure and a few wildflowers that never seem to totally quit. Although most native grasses are dormant during the winter, they never turn completely brown. Cut some of the dead leaves back at this time, but leave clumps of vegetation to

Wildflower areas are best designed to include grasses and provide color over the greatest number of months possible. This is done by using a diversity of species whose flowering times overlap a little, but peak at different times.

break up the monotony. Use wildflowers, such as white beardtongue (*Penstemon multiflorus*), *Carphephorus* spp., and skullcaps (*Scutellaria* spp.), that spend the winter as rosettes of leaves. Although they do not bloom during the winter, their foliage provides interest. Then, incorporate some of the standbys, such as red salvia (*Salvia coccinea*), blanket flower, and dune sunflower (*Helianthus debilis*), that simply never stop until there is a hard freeze. In North Florida, you have far fewer choices of wildflowers that do not die back during a hard freeze. In southernmost Florida, you have more.

Mulches

As I've alluded earlier, mulching your native ground covers should be done carefully. Mulches applied too thickly do not allow wildflowers and native grasses to reseed and may create conditions that favor certain fungi that will kill them. In nature, few locations experience a deep buildup of leaf litter. Our Florida weather, lightning-caused fires, and soil fauna tend to promote their rapid disappearance, providing essential nutrients and opening the soil surface to better evaporation and oxygen transfer. We need to look past the idea that mulches are decorative weed barriers to seeing them as valuable parts of the living landscape. Mulches are supposed to decay and add nutrients, and they are supposed to keep the surface of the soil cooler and retard evaporation. To do this effectively, they cannot be applied so deeply as to prevent water from easily reaching the soil or prevent good oxygen exchange with the atmosphere.

Leafy mulches are superior to wood-based ones in improving soil fertility. Bark and chipped wood contain few nutrients and break down slowly, requiring termites and soil-borne fungi and bacteria to decompose them. Native soil contains almost no nitrogen, phosphate, or sulfate. Plants in nature rely on the decomposition of plant material to get these essential nutrients. In developed landscapes, we are faced with adding them in the form of commercial fertilizer or through mulching. Most of us have access to leaf and pine needle mulch at little or no cost, and these release ample nutrition to the plants.

In my neighborhood, my neighbors spend inordinate amounts of time and energy each fall and spring raking and bagging oak leaves and pine

Leaf mulches decompose slowly over time, adding essential elements to the soil and im-proving its fertility. This photograph shows an area in my backyard. The wildflowers include blooming lanceleaf tickseed (*Coreopsis lanceolata*), large numbers of woodland sunflower (*Helianthus strumosus*), and the basal rosette of a vanilla plant (*Carphephorus odoratissimus*).

needles, which they then carry to the curb for trash collectors to haul away. Each year, repeated throughout neighborhoods across Florida, millions of pounds of valuable mulch are hauled away and deposited in landfills, and millions of pounds of commercial fertilizer are manufactured at great cost to the environment, sold at greater cost to the family budget, and spread across the now sterile landscape. It's a ludicrous cycle that needs to be broken.

Alexa and I collect the free curbside mulch our neighbors set out and use it to mulch our native plantings. What we cannot use each year, we give to our friends. Over the past years, we have watched our poor sandy soil become more fertile because of it.

In our landscape, I prefer to use mulches that mimic those that would occur naturally. I like the look of everything seeming as though it was taken from nature, and I like the function that mulching provides to the plantings. My front yard is landscaped in harmony with the pines

Pine needles make a wonderful mulch because they decompose slowly and allow water to easily reach the soil surface. This area is in our front yard, where we grow grasses and wildflowers that require sunny conditions.

we planted, while our back and side yards are designed around an oak-dominated woodland. I use pine needles as mulch in the front and oak and maple leaves in the other areas. These are very different mulches, and they should be used differently.

I love pine needles as mulch. They break down slowly, allow water and oxygen to easily pass through the soil surface, and generally stay put. When applied thinly across the soil surface, they also allow wildflower and native grass seeds to germinate. While some of my neighbors bemoan how "messy" their pines are, Alexa and I look forward each year to the needle drop and the opportunity this provides to replenish our mulched areas. Pine needles should not be applied more than ½ inch deep, or you will lose much of the benefit described above. If you keep the excess needles dry, they will keep for a great many months, and you can use them as needed throughout the year.

The leaves of broad-leaved trees, on the other hand, are not as good at letting water reach the soil surface and can make it difficult for your soil to breathe. For this reason, I use them mostly in shady locations where it is easier to keep the soil surface moist. If the soil surface becomes dusty dry, you may find that water runs off the leaf mulch and away from the plants that need it. But once the soil is moist, it tends to remain that way longer beneath a leaf mulch layer. Forest floor understory plants are adapted to leaf litter that is ½ inch or more deep. Most spread by root suckers and runners as opposed to small seeds that would be smothered by the mulch. I generally apply deciduous leaf mulch annually, letting it break down as it does in nature before applying a new layer in the late winter or early spring. And, I prefer not to use thick leathery leaves, such as those of live oak and southern magnolia (*Magnolia grandiflora*), that break down more slowly. The thinner leaves of hickories (*Carya* spp.), sugarberry (*Celtis laevigata*), and maples (*Acer* spp.) make better choices.

Unlike wood-based mulches, leaves and needles also attract a wealth of detritus consumers: worms and other invertebrates that, in turn, play an important role within the wildlife food web. Once you make the switch to organic mulches, you will be astounded by the life this layer supports.

Watering

While it is true that established native plants in the "right" location adapt to your landscape conditions and require little additional water, all plants, whether native or not, require water to become established and supplemental water during periods of abnormal drought. No plant can survive having its roots dry out. No matter how long a plant has been established, extreme drought can kill it. This is true for every plant regardless of its origin and is especially true for plants that have spent time confined to a pot. In nature, seedling plants develop extensive root systems that seek out the soil layer that has the right amount of moisture to supply its needs. If you allow your native wildflowers and grasses to reproduce by seed in your garden, you may well find that the seedlings are the toughest specimens during periods of prolonged drought, not the adults that you planted from a pot. Potted plants quickly send roots to the bottom of the container and then develop extensive root systems that wind around that depth. In a typical 1-quart or 1-gallon specimen, this root mass is less than 1 foot in

Plants kept too long in pots eventually become pot-bound. Roots this tightly wound around the pot are best cut with a sharp knife or clippers before planting, and extra watering may be needed to get the plant established in the landscape.

depth. When such plants are put in the ground, it may take months for those roots to leave the comfort of that root ball and venture deeper into the soil. This situation is compounded if the soil beneath these roots is drier than the soil currently surrounding them.

New plants need to be watered regularly and watered deep to encourage the roots to go deeper into your landscape soil. Make sure that you thoroughly water the hole into which you are planting before putting the new plant into it. You want your new plants to seek a deeper soil layer than the one where their roots are starting from. If you allow the deeper soil to dry out, you may well be watering only to the depth of the existing root mass each time, and this will ensure that the roots remain shallow and that the plant never adapts to your site.

While our goal is to create a landscape using natives adapted to our growing conditions, extremes are part of nature, and you shouldn't feel guilty about watering when these extremes occur. Alexa and I have turned off our irrigation system and shut down our shallow well, but I water by hand when the situation requires it. If I didn't, my landscape would consist of about four or five species, and my conservation goal of providing diversity would lose out to my goal of conserving water. In my opinion, the value of diversity outweighs the other as long as my supplemental watering is rarely required.

Reclaimed water is available to some communities and can provide a valuable conservation benefit if used wisely. It has a different chemistry than drinking water, however, and has higher salt levels. Some native plants do not respond well to long-term or frequent use of reclaimed water. Generally, salt-tolerant plants do better under reclaimed water than those that aren't. Take this into account as you plan your landscape if you intend to use reclaimed water and conserve its use to those times when it is really needed.

Water is a vital component of any landscape, even native ones. Try to add plants during months when rain is most predictable and water new plants thoroughly every few days until they are established.

4

Where to Get Plants

The availability and use of native plants has changed dramatically since I arrived in Florida more than 20 years ago. More species are now being propagated, and more nurseries than ever are making them available to the homeowner. Even some of the larger commercial chains have a few native plants in their regular offerings, and many retail garden centers carry some as well. We could encourage a greater diversity if we simply asked for it. I believe in the power of supply and demand, so if you have a favorite garden center that does not typically carry mostly natives, give them a chance and ask them if they might carry a larger selection.

For the most part, you will have the most success by patronizing native plant nurseries. They will already have made the commitment to native plants and will carry the largest selections. And, they are likely to be much more sympathetic if you are looking for something they do not routinely carry.

In Florida, most native plant nurseries are members of FANN, the Florida Association of Native Nurseries. This is the best place to begin your search for native plants. FANN is composed of wholesale growers as well as retail nurseries and publishes a catalog each year that includes contact information for all their members as well as a detailed listing of who sells what. If you are looking for black-eyed susan, for example, you can look this plant up in the catalog and see a listing of every nursery propagating it. Some of these nurseries sell directly to the public, but all sell to the retailers also listed. The catalog, and a whole host of other information, is accessible online: www.floridanativenurseries.org.

Learn to patronize the retail native plant centers nearest you. Generally, these businesses carry a wide range of products other than native plants and are run by folks who are extremely knowledgeable about the plants in which you are interested. Most of the time, they are thrilled to be able to "talk plants" with you, and they are wonderful sources of information.

You may also wish to contact your local chapter of the Florida Native Plant Society. More than forty local chapters now exist, and they all host monthly meetings where programs are offered free to the public and plants are offered in silent auctions and the like. You may find some interesting plants not generally available from commercial sources, and you are very likely to find members who can steer you toward someone locally who is growing plants. As you get involved with your local chapter, you are bound to learn a great deal about native plants and how to use them in your landscape.

Though the number of retail native plant centers has grown exponentially in recent years, there may not be one close to you, or there may be none near you carrying a plant you really wish to try. The age of the Internet has made some of this situation moot. Over the past few years, a number of Web sites have made it easy to locate native plants and information of interest to the home gardener. Never underestimate the power of simply Googling the name of the plant you are looking for followed by words such as "nursery" or "retail." Just be careful to note the location of any retail sources that result from your online searches. Plants originating from growers outside the Deep South are often unlikely to thrive in our Florida climate. There are exceptions, but I caution against trying them unless you have no other option and are willing to experiment a bit with a few plants first.

Last, you can always try propagating your own. I have always loved growing my own plants, usually from seed but occasionally from cuttings, and over the years, I have added dozens of species to my landscape that were not commercially available. One word of caution: collecting seed from plants you do not own without permission or a permit may be illegal depending on where and what you collect. I have written more on this topic later in this chapter.

Most of you will someday want to add plants to your landscape you have propagated yourself. While some species will easily reseed and multiply in the landscape, a great many others will be best added as seedlings. Most are easy to grow when you are armed with some very basic information.

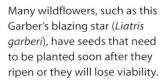

Many wildflowers, such as this Garber's blazing star (*Liatris garberi*), have seeds that need to be planted soon after they ripen or they will lose viability.

As I stated previously, many of Florida's native wildflowers and grasses produce seed that loses its viability rather quickly. Exceptions include species adapted to harsh growing conditions such as scrub and beach dunes. The seed of these species may remain dormant for months or even years before favorable conditions arrive that allow them to germinate.

Most, however, should be sown within a month after ripening, even those that require cold or heat stratification. For that reason, be careful about purchasing wildflower seed sold in packets here. A few firms are currently making the effort, but do not purchase seed too long after the harvest date or you are likely to get very low germination rates.

Wildflower and grass seed contain moisture. Because of this, they will rot if stored in plastic bags or any other container that does not breathe. I use brown paper lunch bags to store the seed I collect. I fold the top over to keep the seed inside should the bag tip over, but I do not seal it shut. Paper bags are ideal for storing seed, and they allow new seed to dry sufficiently before planting. Make sure you record which species is in each bag, as well as the collection date and location, even if you collected it from your own garden. I use pencil and reuse my bags over several seasons.

For species that require cold stratification to germinate, I transfer the dried seed into sealable plastic bags partially filled with moist (not wet) builder's sand. I add the seed to the bag, gently massage the sand to make sure the seed get evenly distributed, and then keep the bags in my refrigerator for several months. Sealable bags can be easily stored on their side and take up relatively little space. They are also sturdy and not likely to spring a leak. With the seed in the moist sand, its viability is well maintained and it is easier to sow once it is stratified. After the seed has been in my refrigerator for two or three months, I spread the sand out on top of the flat and cover it lightly with potting soil. There is no need to take each seed out and sow it individually.

Some species, such as the prairie clovers, require heat stratification to germinate with any success. Put the seed in a heat-resistant cup and pour a small amount of boiling water over them. Let them stand until everything is room temperature, and then sow the seed into potting soil.

A few wildflowers in the pea/bean family do best when the seed coat is nicked by a knife or file, a process called scarification. In nature, these types of seed pass through the gut of an animal before they can germinate. File the seed coat lightly with a metal file, rub it with sandpaper, nick it with a knife, or crack it gently with a hammer to weaken the seed coat.

For large-seeded wildflowers like lupines and milkweeds, I often germinate the seed before transferring them to their own pot. Spread the seed uniformly (try to keep them from touching each other) on a moist (not wet) paper towel inside a sealable plastic container. Mark the top of the container and shut it. The conditions inside the container allow the seed to remain uniformly moist for months (if necessary), and you can check on their progress daily and pot each seed as it germinates.

For most of the wildflowers and grasses I propagate, I sow the seed in standard plastic flats with a good potting soil. I use potting soil that contains a time-release fertilizer, and I pack the soil down firmly both before sowing the seed and after I have covered it. It is important not to plant the seed too deeply when you sow it and to water it well until it germinates. I generally do not cover the seed with more soil than the length/diameter

Large seeds, such as swamp rose milkweed (*Asclepias incarnata*), can be sprouted on a moist paper towel inside in a tightly closed container and then planted individually.

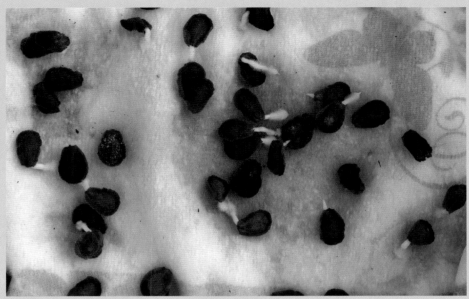

Sprouting swamp rose milkweed seeds.

Individual milkweed plants can be more easily transplanted as they mature.

of the seed itself. Flats or pots of seed should be watered daily or at least every day that the soil surface feels dry. Remember that the seed is not buried deeply, and the new developing root system is very shallow at first. For the same reason, do not water forcibly. Using a sharp stream of water may well expose the seed and reduce your germination rate.

If you grow seed in flats, it will be important to transfer them to pots individually before planting them. Flats have shallow soil, and your thriving collection of seedlings will soon take up all the space available and the roots will become hopelessly intertwined. Before you get to this stage, separate the individual plants and pot them individually. It is impossible not to damage the root systems a bit during this process, so pot them quickly, water them well, and keep them well watered for at least the first week after transplanting. Separate the plants carefully and plant them so they are neither deeper nor shallower than they were in the flat, and make sure you do not let their root systems dry out during the transfer. If you take care of their roots, most will survive and perk up immediately. It is also helpful to add a root-stimulating fertilizer when you initially water them. Your newly potted plants will be ready to transfer into the landscape when you can see evidence of their recovered root system at the bottom of the pot.

Getting plants to grow from cuttings is an art, and one that only experienced gardeners are likely to have much luck at. I use it mostly on woody wildflowers and prefer it for these because it is a much quicker way to get flowering-sized specimens. To be effective, cuttings should be small and taken to include the active growing tip of a stem. Just as herbivorous wildlife crop a plant by biting, judicious cuttings will stimulate the plant to produce new growth. For the vast majority of wildflowers, do not take cuttings as the plant is entering its blooming period, while it has mature seed ready to be dispersed, or when it is dormant.

Cuttings should be kept moist and quickly transferred to the propagation area. Lightly rub the surface of the cut stem, dip it in a root-stimulating hormone, and place it carefully in the rooting medium. I often use sterile play sand, but I have also had luck using perlite. It is important to slip your hormone-coated cuttings into the medium without brushing the hormone off. Include only a small amount of foliage with each cutting to reduce the need to maintain unnecessary leaves while also trying to generate roots. Cuttings that wilt within 24–48 hours are unlikely to root,

Cuttings of false rosemary (*Conradina canescens*) in perlite.

but if they don't and develop new foliage in the early weeks, it is a good sign. Check the bottom of the container after the second week on a regular basis. If you see new roots working their way toward the drainage holes, it is likely time to carefully pot them. Then, keep them well watered until it is obvious that a good root system is developing. Growing plants from cuttings has advantages, but it takes commitment to do well. If you cannot make the commitment, you should not attempt it.

Some plants spread naturally by root suckers. Species in the sunflower family, for example, are notorious for this trait, and it often becomes necessary to thin them out. You may desire to add the surplus to another region of your landscape. Most suckering plants are easily propagated by gently digging up these suckers after they are about one-quarter to one-half their height at maturity. At this time, they generally have developed their own root system and can be planted immediately into individual pots until that root system recovers and is firmly reestablished. Again, initially water them with a root-stimulating fertilizer to help them along.

Some plants, like this pinebarren goldenrod (*Solidago fistulosa*), produce suckers from their root systems and form extensive colonies.

While propagating your own wildflowers can be very rewarding and allow you to fill areas of your landscape at less cost, there is a set of ethics that must be maintained as well as laws to be obeyed if you want to collect material from anywhere other than your own landscape. There is no sense in harming the natural world if we are seeking to improve it.

The Laws

While wildlife are owned by the general public and wildlife laws are written to protect them regardless of where they reside, plants are considered the property of the property owner. If you own the property, you own the plants and can take whole plants, seeds, and cuttings of even the rarest species without fear of legal repercussions.

Plants listed as "Threatened," "Endangered," or "Commercially Exploited" by the state of Florida cannot be harvested on private or public lands and taken home to your propagation area without permission of the property owner and a permit issued by the Florida Department of Agriculture and Consumer Services, Division of Plant Industry (FDACS). The permit is required for Threatened and Commercially Exploited species only if the plant is to be eventually offered for sale, but having to go to court to prove that the plants are being grown only for your personal use is not something you would want to go through. This prohibition includes seeds and cuttings, not only the whole plant. In Florida, that is a long list (more than 420 species) and one with which you should be familiar if you wish to get into propagating plants you find off your property boundary. If you do not know the identity of the plant you are hoping to collect, you should not collect it.

All native plants, whether or not they are listed, cannot be harvested without the permission of the property owner. Even common species are the property of someone or something, and private property law makes it a trespass issue to be there without permission and theft if you remove something. Most public lands have very specific rules that prohibit the collection of any plant without written permission by the agency in charge. There are few places where simply collecting a few seeds or taking a few cuttings is permissible without first obtaining permission.

If you have obtained the necessary permission and permits to collect and transport off-site, there are a few ethical issues to also address so your zeal to propagate something does not end up causing more harm than good. For one, never collect more than a small percentage of the

Collecting seeds, cuttings, and plants requires permission from the landowner. Even common plants are protected on public lands.

seed on-site or more than you need for your personal growing purposes—whichever is smaller. Just because the seed seems plentiful does not mean that taking it will have no impact. Leave the vast majority behind as part of the ecosystem. If you truly need more, look for more at a second site and collect a little from both.

Never remove more than a few cuttings from any individual plant. An ethical collector, even with all the necessary permissions, will remove only a few cuttings and in such a way that such removal will be nearly impossible to detect.

Finally, never take material from plants that are not familiar to you or that you are not fully prepared to grow. It is tempting to collect things that catch our eye, but it is unethical to remove those things we are not sure we can properly care for. When in doubt, take a deep breath, leave it alone, and spend some time researching the species to see what growing conditions it requires.

There are good conservation reasons to propagate native plants, and the state has established clear guidelines for you to follow. Because of this, even many of the rarest species are commercially available—legally. This approach is a far better one than going through the hoops to obtain permission and a license. Commercial nursery people have the experience and the knowledge to propagate these species effectively. If you wish to add more of a particular plant once you have made your initial purchases, speak to them to gain some of their insights. Once the plant is in your landscape, it becomes your property, and you can propagate it freely from that point onward as long as you are doing so for your own personal landscape uses and not planning to sell it.

5

Ferns

This chapter and the two that follow provide the information you need to evaluate ferns, grasses, and wildflowers for your landscape. It is intended for gardeners and home landscapers. Because of this, I have included the information I feel is most needed from a gardening perspective.

Each plant has merit in the home landscape and aesthetics that make it a worthy addition. I have tried to include information on both its merits and its aesthetic qualities. If the plant has special wildlife uses, I have described these as well. Gardeners also need to know cultural information: what conditions each plant needs to prosper, how easy it is to maintain, and whether it spreads. I have based this information, whenever possible, on my more than twenty years of personal gardening experience in Pinellas County. During this time, I have grown nearly every plant included in this book. I also have drawn from the experiences of friends who have hands-on gardening experience.

I have arranged the species alphabetically first by the non-Latin family name and then by the Latin species name. Even though some of these plants do not have widely accepted common names, I have used the names most widely used. Most avid gardeners eventually learn the value of learning Latin names, but few of us know the names well enough to recall them without first looking them up. Therefore, I have decided on the common family names for purposes of organization, but then used the Latin ones for purposes of precision. Latin names are specific and universal worldwide. Whether you travel to India, to Sweden, or across Florida, the Latin name is the same, and everyone knows exactly what species you are referring to. Become familiar with the Latin names even if you use the common ones in conversations with your friends and neighbors. They are important.

Bracken Fern (*Pteridium* spp.)

Bracken ferns are some of the world's most widely distributed species and are exceedingly common. We have only one native but somewhat variable species in Florida (*P. aquilinum*), and it is found statewide. Bracken fern is a common component of open sandy uplands and one of the few ferns adapted to such conditions. It thrives with frequent fire and land disturbances. Bracken fern will freeze back after below-zero temperatures, rebounding quickly once warmer temperatures return.

In the landscape, bracken fern rapidly spreads to all areas except those that are deeply shaded or excessively wet. Because of this, it can often be more of a nuisance than a treasured addition, especially in landscapes confined to relatively small areas and ones where some order is desired.

Bracken fern (*Pteridium aquilinum*).

Bracken fern spreads by its deeply rooted rhizomes that traverse the land-scape in all directions. The 2–3-foot-tall stiff, upright fronds are widely spaced in the understory, especially in well-drained uplands. In moister sites, however, bracken fern will get taller and denser and may outcompete all the more diminutive species planted with it. In the wild, bracken fern provides valuable cover in open areas subject to frequent fire. Because it is so deeply rooted, it is one of the first plants to green up and recolonize the open understory. This feature is far less valuable in the home landscape where such need is rarely a concern.

Brake Ferns (*Pteris* spp.)

The genus *Pteris* is found worldwide, but only two species are considered native to Florida. An additional species, Chinese brake fern (*P. vittata*) is a very common ornamental that has escaped cultivation and become es-tablished in a wide variety of locations. Many species of non-native brake ferns are offered for sale in garden catalogs, but these should be grown as indoor potted plants and not added to Florida landscapes.

Bahama brake fern (*Pteris bahamensis*). Photo by Shirley Denton, with permission.

Of the two native species, only the Bahama brake fern (*P. bahamensis*) is generally cultivated and available from native plant nurseries. Bahama brake fern is an erect terrestrial species with stiff upright fronds that generally are 3–5 feet tall. It is resident to shady and partly sunny locations, often in areas of limestone outcroppings. It is native only to southernmost Florida but can be used further north in areas where freezing temperatures are uncommon. In its normal range, Bahama brake fern is evergreen.

Because it grows well in alkaline soils, it is a good choice for shady areas near the foundation of the home. Its durability and tolerance of occasional droughty soils also aids in its ability to survive. Grow Bahama brake fern in protected areas, away from open northern exposure in Central Florida or nearly anywhere in shady to partly sunny locations in South Florida. Plant individual specimens no closer than 3 feet apart. Individual plants will slowly expand by their underground rhizomes. Divide them if they become too numerous.

Chain Ferns (*Woodwardia* spp.)

The chain ferns are distributed worldwide, but only two species are native to Florida. Their name is derived from the way the scalelike areoles line up, chainlike, along the central leaf vein on the underside of the fronds. Chain ferns are resident to moist forests and wetland edges. If given ample

Chain ferns (*Woodwardia* spp.) are so named because of the rectangular cells or "chains" that run along the main rachis of the frond.

water, they can tolerate a great amount of sunlight, but they are most common in shadier conditions. Both our native species tend to be deciduous except in southernmost Florida, where warmer temperatures allow them to maintain their fronds through the winter.

Although both are beautiful additions to the landscape, they are rather aggressive and tend to spread rather rapidly by underground rhizomes. Use chain ferns to fill in large open areas in shady locations where the soils are normally moist. In confined locations, they may become too dominant and prevent other species from adding to the diversity. I have found them to be relatively forgiving of soils that occasionally dry out if they are kept shaded. They may need supplemental watering, however, during prolonged drought or to get established. Chain ferns are not clumping ferns. They produce individual fronds that are evenly spaced from the underground rhizome.

Netted Chain Fern (*W. areolata*)

Netted chain fern is the smaller of the two species and the one most likely to be encountered in the nursery trade. At maturity, it rarely exceeds 1 foot in height. It is easily distinguished from its close relative, and from other

Netted chain fern (*Woodwardia areolata*).

ferns, by the distinct "wing" that runs along both sides of the stem (i.e., rachis) below the frond and by the fact that the fertile and infertile fronds are distinctly different in shape.

This species is found nearly statewide but is more common to Central and North Florida. Infertile fronds appear in very early spring, but the fertile ones are produced during the summer and early fall. Individual fronds are closely spaced from the underground rhizome. As such, they form dense colonies that tend to shade out smaller plants around them. This is not a problem for understory trees and shrubs, but it makes maintaining ephemeral woodland wildflowers difficult without regular weeding.

Virginia Chain Fern (*W. virginica*)

Virginia chain fern is a much more robust species and often reaches 3–4 feet in height. It is a vigorous grower with a strong stout underground rhizome and is very difficult to remove once established. For this reason, it should be planted in the landscape only after careful consideration determines that it is truly the fern you desire. Individual fronds are produced at 3–6-inch intervals along the rhizome, leaving some noticeable gaps between them in the landscape, but the overlapping nature of the rhizomes,

Virginia chain fern (*Woodwardia virginica*).

once the plant is firmly established, eventually leads to this plant's becoming dense and firmly dominant.

Virginia chain fern is a common resident of swamps and wet forests throughout Florida. It can tolerate some drought, but such conditions will slow its growth. Use this fern in large expansive areas where soils are often moist to wet. It is not a good choice for typical landscape settings unless there is a well-defined wet area surrounded by uplands that may limit its spread.

Christmas Fern (*Polystichum acrostichoides*)

This wonderful well-behaved fern is evergreen, hence its name. It is the only member of this genus native to Florida, though a great many others occur throughout North America and worldwide. In Florida, it is found naturally in moist forest understories from North Florida south to around Hernando County, but I have grown it in my home landscape in Pinellas County for many years with good results and suspect it is adaptable to much of Central Florida if planted in the proper conditions.

Christmas fern (*Polystichum acrostichoides*).

Christmas fern retains its older fronds through the winter months and provides interesting texture to woodland plantings at a time of year when most other species are dormant. During the winter, these fronds droop gracefully and touch the forest floor. A new flush of growth is produced in early spring. The tightly coiled crosiers (the "fiddleheads" of new fronds) are partially covered by silvery-white scales before they burst upward. Few leaves are produced later in the year, so this new spring growth is largely all that occurs. The leaves rarely stand taller than 3 feet.

Christmas fern is best used in moist woodland plantings. It is not especially adaptable to drought and declines if not given additional water during extended periods with no rainfall. For best interest, use this fern in scattered clumps of 3–5 plants with each clump no closer than 4–5 feet apart and concentrate it in the middle section of the beds so it is noticeable. If it adapts well to its surroundings, it will slowly spread outward by its underground rhizome. If it multiplies more than desired, it can be easily divided and the divisions planted elsewhere or shared with friends.

Golden Polypody (*Phlebodium aureum*)

Golden polypody is a fern of tropical America and found throughout much of peninsular Florida but rarely in the Panhandle. It is cold sensitive and

Golden polypody (*Phlebodium aureum*).

should not be used in landscapes that regularly dip into the low 20s F. This is one of the "rabbit's foot"-type ferns, and its distinct aboveground rhizome is densely covered with golden hairlike scales; hence its common name. In nature, golden polypody fern often occurs as an epiphyte, growing above ground nestled in the "boots" of cabbage palms (*Sabal palmetto*). It also does well in moist forest soil if located in areas where flooding is not common.

Golden polypody creeps slowly outward by its rhizome, and its single leaves arise from it at regular intervals. Each leaf may be several feet in length, blue green in color, and deeply lobed. This is an evergreen fern when moisture and temperature conditions are favorable, but individual leaves will turn yellow and drop off the golden rhizome when conditions are severe or as they age past 6–9 months. In ideal conditions, a well-grown specimen will have numerous leaves arising from its snaky golden "foot," itself several feet long.

Golden polypody is best used as an accent fern in moist shady areas. It can be grown in a pot or hanging basket, much the way that staghorn (*Platycerium* spp.) ferns are sometimes used in the landscape, but I prefer them grown naturally. If you have cabbage palms, attach the ferns inside the boots of the spent lower or midstory leaves. Such conditions are ideal for this fern as they provide additional moisture and nutrients around the rhizome. If you wish to use a different type of tree, pack some sphagnum moss around the rhizome when you attach it, and keep it moist while the fern becomes established. You also can try planting it directly into the understory. This is a shallow-rooted species, so take care to plant it no deeper than ½ inch, and give it plenty of moisture while it is becoming established.

Southern Lady Fern (*Athyrium filix-femina*)

Another well-behaved beautiful fern for Florida landscapes is the southern lady fern. Although this genus contains a number of commonly grown species, this is the only one native to Florida. It is native to moist forest understories and naturally occurs in North Florida, south to the Gainesville/Ocala area. I have grown it in Pinellas County, however, for a number of years, and it seems adaptable to landscapes in Central Florida if provided proper conditions.

Southern lady fern (*Athyrium filix-femina*).

Southern lady fern is a wonderful addition to the woodland landscape as it does not overwhelm adjacent plants, and the graceful lacy texture of the fronds adds an element of elegance not quite matched by other species. The early fronds are light green in color, but this deepens to a richer green as they mature. At maturity, southern lady fern is rarely taller than 3 feet and much more likely not to exceed 2 feet in height. It spreads outward very slowly from its underground rhizome, and individual clumps may eventually reach several feet across. This is a deciduous species that dies back each fall and reappears in late spring. It is not the first to makes its appearance in the landscape, so have some patience.

Lady fern is best used in scattered groupings with 3–5 ferns per group. Because of its stature, make sure at least some of the clusters are planted near the front and along walkways. This fern has limited tolerance of extended drought and would need supplemental water should the soil become too dry for any length of time. Therefore, it is best used in areas that stay moist naturally and in forest soils higher in organics and nutrients. Southern lady fern is popular among commercial growers, and numerous cultivars have been developed.

Leather Ferns (*Achrostichum* spp.)

There are two species of leather fern in Florida: the relatively common giant leather fern (*A. danaeifolium*) and the rarer golden leather fern (*A. aureum*). Both species are members of a small genus of evergreen tropical ferns, confined primarily to South and South Central Florida. Giant

Giant leather fern (*Achrostichum danaeifolium*).

leather fern has more cold tolerance and can be found throughout the peninsula. Golden leather fern has a much more restricted natural distribution and far less cold tolerance. Both species are very similar in appearance and growing requirements.

Leather ferns are the largest ferns native to Florida, and their size is one factor that limits their use in developed landscapes. Mature specimens of both species may stand 6–9 feet tall with a circumference nearly that great. The other factor that limits their use is their growing requirements. Leather ferns are found most commonly at the edges of mangrove forests, along the edges of brackish water streams, and occasionally in freshwater wetlands. They prefer soggy saturated soils and are less adapted to typical landscapes. Despite this, I have seen them used quite dramatically as specimen plants in home landscapes, but only in shady areas.

Plant them at the edges of streams or ponds where the soil is saturated and in areas where their large size will not be detrimental. They grow well under full sunlight if given sufficient moisture, but with less water they do best in partial sun. Give them at least 4 feet between neighboring plants.

Maidenhair Ferns (*Adiantum* spp.)

Few ferns are more beloved landscape additions than the maidenhairs, and they are used across the country to create an impact in shady woodland

Southern maidenhair fern (*Adiantum capillus-veneris*).

plantings. Two species are rather widely distributed in Florida: southern maidenhair (*A. capillus-veneris*), and brittle maidenhair (*A. tenerum*), though the brittle maidenhair is listed as an endangered species and almost never grown commercially. A third very rare maidenhair fern (also listed as a state endangered species), fragrant maidenhair (*A. melanoleucum*), is confined to a few forests over limestone soil in Dade County.

Maidenhair ferns are recognizable and get their name from the way the tiny leaflets (pinnules) are arranged along the central rachis. These delicate arching fronds seem feminine somehow and appear as braids. Regardless, maidenhair ferns bring a simple beauty to a landscape long recognized by landscape designers as well as homeowners. All our species are best grown in alkaline soils in conjunction with limestone outcroppings. These conditions can sometimes be met in the average landscape near the foundation of the home, but are best achieved in a rock garden built of lime rock and situated in a shady location.

Southern maidenhair fern also requires good moisture to prosper. We have grown this fern for many years in large landscape pots beneath our woodland canopy, but they are the very first fern to show signs of stress if we forget to water them on a regular basis. We keep saucers beneath the pots, and these help keep the soil nearly saturated most days. A mister controlled by a timer can also be used to effectively grow this species in areas that would naturally be too dry.

If you can provide the growing conditions required by this fern, it will reward you greatly with its aesthetic appeal. Mature specimens will reach several feet in height and many feet across. Over time, it expands outward from its underground rhizome. In warmer locations, it is evergreen, but it will die back following a freeze.

Osmunda Ferns (Cinnamon and Royal Ferns; *Osmunda* spp.)

If you are a seasoned orchid grower, you may remember the day when osmunda fiber was a common potting medium. Osmunda is the fibrous material produced by the rhizome and base of the fronds of either the cinnamon (*O. cinnamomea*) or royal fern (*O. regalis*). At one time, this material was harvested on a large scale throughout the native ranges of these two ferns, and the practice had a great impact on their populations. Today, orchid growers use other potting media, and the fern populations

Cinnamon fern (*Osmunda cinnamomea*).

Royal fern (*Osmunda regalis*).

have largely recovered. In Florida, both ferns continue to be protected as "commercially exploited" species, and it is illegal to collect them without a permit and permission of the property owner.

Both species are found statewide and are most abundant in freshwater forested wetlands inundated by shallow water for months at a time. Given sufficient water, both species can tolerate relatively sunny locations. Cinnamon fern tolerates periodic drought better than its close cousin. We have used cinnamon fern near the front of our home in Pinellas County for nearly a decade without supplemental irrigation. This site receives water from the roof during rain events but can become quite dry during periods of extended drought. Although these ferns occasionally wither, they recover quickly following a rain or brief hosing. Our royal ferns have not been as forgiving, and we had to move them to the back of the house to shadier and moister conditions.

Both ferns are well behaved and grow as defined clumps, spreading very slowly by their underground rhizomes. They are robust and make wonderful accent ferns given the right growing conditions. Mature specimens produce erect fronds that reach 2–3 feet in height. Plant them in small clusters to provide interest or as isolated specimens in a mixed forested wetland setting. Both species are evergreen in areas not subjected to freezing temperatures, but they will die back when temperatures are cold.

Cinnamon fern is perhaps the best landscape choice of the two species. Its tall, bright green foliage is attractive throughout the year, but it gets its name from the narrow fertile fronds produced in late spring and early summer. These are a bright copper in color and produce a showy display that is quite appealing.

Royal fern has very distinctive foliage, somewhat lacy in appearance and quite attractive, especially when planted in small clusters. The foliage is blue green in color. Royal fern produces fertile fronds that are distinctive and completely different in structure from the infertile ones, but they are straw colored and less aesthetically interesting than those of the cinnamon fern.

Resurrection Fern (*Pleopeltis polypodioides*)

Resurrection fern is common throughout Florida, but not commonly used as a landscape plant. For the most part, it is strictly epiphytic, growing high in the branches of mature forest trees. It is frequently associated

Resurrection fern (*Pleopeltis polypodioides*).

with live oak but is not particular to the species of tree, only to its structure and the structure of the habitat surrounding it. As an epiphyte, resurrection fern receives no nutrients directly from its host plant. What it
receives is a vantage point in the canopy that provides the right mix of
dappled sunlight and humidity.

Its common name comes from its tendency to shrivel up during periods of low moisture. At these times, it looks dead, but following a rain
event or periods of dense fog, it unfurls its fronds and takes the moisture
in. It becomes "resurrected."

Resurrection fern makes a wonderful addition to a woodland landscape. In the right setting, it normally arrives on its own by its airborne

spores. We added ours from limbs we found discarded following some pruning in our neighborhood. If you find this fern under similar circumstances, remove the bark with the ferns attached and attach all of it to a large limb on your own tree. Do not remove these ferns from natural areas or from limbs on the forest floor, as the ferns may live under these conditions for many years. Resurrection fern needs light airy locations but should not get much direct sunlight.

Sensitive Fern (*Onoclea sensibilis*)

Sensitive fern is a medium-large robust fern native to moist-soil habitats in the northernmost counties of Florida and most of the eastern half of North America. This widely distributed fern is not used much in Florida landscapes but is a favorite north of us, where its distinctive lobed fronds add character to shady moist landscape settings. Although sensitive fern has a rather restricted natural range in Florida, we have grown it for years in our wooded landscape, and I suspect it could be grown over the peninsula if given the proper conditions.

Sensitive fern (*Onoclea sensibilis*).

Like many wetland ferns, sensitive fern has more drought tolerance than might be guessed. It will take quite a bit of sunlight if grown in wet or shallowly inundated soils, but it will not fare well in these conditions if the soil is more droughty. In the shaded woodland understory, it will prosper if heavily mulched and kept somewhat moist.

Its common name comes from its sensitivity to cold weather. Its leaves shrivel and fall when temperatures dip into the 30s F. It doesn't take a frost for sensitive fern to lose its fronds. It also is one of the last of our deciduous ferns to reappear in the spring, sometimes not making its appearance until early May.

In ideal conditions, sensitive fern can become a nuisance in small gardens because of its tendency to spread by its underground rhizomes. Its rather large size (12–18 inches tall, with each frond 8–12 inches wide) also causes it to crowd out its more diminutive neighbors, but in a more spacious setting, sensitive fern is a beautiful and unique addition. It spreads much less aggressively when grown in less-than-ideal conditions such as those provided by most residential landscapes.

Shield Ferns (*Thelypteris* spp.)

There are a great many shield ferns in Florida (a total of 16 species), and they are common components of most moist forest and wetland settings statewide. Despite this, they are rarely offered by the nursery trade. Most of the shield ferns in our landscape showed up on their own after we created the right conditions for them; their tiny spores were likely brought in on the wind from nearby locations.

To anyone other than a fern specialist or plant taxonomist, shield ferns are difficult to differentiate from each other. They are remarkably similar in general appearance and in the types of conditions they inhabit. For this reason, I have lumped them together. If you are a real collector and wish to add more than one species to your landscape, study and learn to distinguish them. Identify them by the pattern of the sori (the spore-producing organs) on the undersides of the fertile fronds. Each species is unique, like a fingerprint.

Shield ferns are common components of shady woodlands with moist to wet soils, but they adapt well to most typical landscape settings and do

Shield fern (*Thelypteris* sp.).

not require much in the way of supplemental watering once established. We have southern shield fern (*T. kunthii*) in our landscape. It remains evergreen through the winter when we do not get a hard freeze and stays where it is planted. Over time, each plant spreads outward and increases slowly in girth. It also has spread by spores. Some gardeners report shield ferns to be invasive, but ours has been pretty well behaved. Different experiences may be the result of differences between the species, some being more aggressive than others, or differences in growing conditions. This fern will be better behaved in average soils than in wetter ones.

Most shield ferns stand 12–24 inches in height, and individual plants may spread out an equal distance in diameter. They can be used as accents within a woodland understory and are best used in the background so that less robust species can be kept in view.

Spleenworts (*Asplenium* spp.)

The spleenworts are an exceptionally large group of ferns worldwide and include species that are widely used landscape specimens. The genus

Ebony spleenwort
(*Asplenium
platyneuron*).

includes 11 distinct species native to Florida and many hybrids. Some are very rare endemics; six are listed as state endangered. Most require alkaline soils and occur in areas of limestone outcroppings, conditions often difficult to replicate in a landscape.

The spleenworts are only rarely offered by Florida growers, and only one species is likely to be available with any frequency: ebony spleenwort (*A. platyneuron*). This beautiful species occurs statewide in a wide variety of woodland habitats. It is the only Florida species that sometimes grows on the ground, and it can tolerate soils that have an average pH. The others occur either only on lime rock (lithophytes) or on trees as epiphytes.

Ebony spleenwort gets its name because the rachis (the central vein of the frond) is dark brown to black and quite shiny and conspicuous. Well-grown specimens with their contrasting rich green fronds and shiny black rachises make excellent additions to a shade garden. Because this species rarely exceeds 12 inches in height, it is best used in mass plantings near the front of the planting area. Plant 3–5 specimens together, spaced 1 foot apart, and mix these with various woodland wildflowers. A good companion fern would be southern lady fern.

Ebony spleenwort thrives best in fertile moist soils but has good tolerance of periodic short-term drought. It dies back after a winter freeze and returns by early spring. This is a native fern that should be more widely grown and sold in Florida. My personal success with out-of-state stock has been poor. We can only hope that more Florida nursery people will make this fern available.

Strap Ferns (*Campyloneuron* spp.)

The strap ferns are a tropical genus with three (possibly four) species native to Florida. Only the long strap fern (*C. phyllitidis*) occurs outside a limited area of southernmost Florida, and even this species is widely scattered and infrequently encountered.

Long strap fern is native from the central peninsula southward. It

Long strap fern (*Campyloneuron phyllitidis*).

cannot be used in landscapes further north as it is intolerant of colder temperatures. In nature, it occurs on the ground at the edges of forested wetlands, as epiphytes on the trunks of forest wetland trees, and sometimes on limestone boulders in moist forested sinkholes.

Despite its adaptability, long strap fern (and its much rarer cousins) is very rarely offered for sale by the nursery trade. This is regrettable as it makes a striking addition to the landscape. Use long strap fern as a specimen in a mixed woodland understory. Because it may reach 12–18 inches in height and exceed 2 feet in diameter, it should be planted individually in widely spaced locations and not in the front of the planting area. In this situation, the long, evergreen straplike fronds are quite distinctive and add an elegance few other ferns can match.

In our landscape, this fern has done exceptionally well, is surprisingly drought tolerant, and has survived temperatures in the mid-20s F. Long strap fern does not readily spread or multiply in the home landscape. Because of this, it is one of the most behaved ferns for a mixed understory planting and deserves far more attention.

Swamp Ferns (*Blechnum* spp.)

Swamp ferns (sometimes referred to as "deer ferns") are widely distributed in the tropics and subtropics, but only two species are native to Florida,

Swamp fern (*Blechnum serrulatum*).

and only one of these (*B. serrulatum*, swamp fern) is ever likely to be sold commercially. Swamp fern occurs statewide in a variety of wetland habitats (including estuaries) but is reasonably adaptable if given a mostly shady location and soils that are not too droughty.

Swamp fern is an erect upright fern that produces individual fronds from the underground rhizome. Eventually, it spreads and forms rather dense plantings. If planted with other robust species, such as shield fern or chain fern, it often forms a dense mixed community. It will overrun more diminutive and less aggressive species and should be used with caution if that type of planting is desired.

Where appropriate, swamp fern makes an attractive addition. Its shiny, deep-green, 2–3-foot-tall fronds are evergreen unless a hard freeze occurs. Young fronds are coppery red in color and offer a nice contrast to the mature ones. Use this fern at the edge of a wetland or pond where soils are inundated or at the edge of woodland plantings. In our landscape, we've used it to hide the outer edge of a raised deck in our side yard. Its spread is limited by sunny droughty soils beyond the deck and by our occasional weeding.

Sword Ferns (*Nephrolepis* spp.)

The native sword ferns are often the target of mistaken identity and are, because of this, often misused in Florida landscapes. Two commonly encountered sword ferns are highly invasive non-natives (tuberous sword fern, *N. cordifolia*, and Asian sword fern, *N. multiflora*), and the former is frequently referred to as "Boston fern," adding greatly to the confusion. It was actually the common native sword fern (*N. exaltata*) that was first named "Boston fern" after an unusual-looking specimen was discovered in a shipment of these plants sent to a Boston-based plant distributor. Both this and the native giant sword fern (*N. biserrata*) have been important to the nursery trade, the latter often sold as "macho fern." But the extreme invasive character of the two non-native species and their similarity of appearance seem to have made many shy away from using any sword fern in landscapes.

It is not difficult to distinguish the native sword ferns from the invasive non-native ones. An excellent publication by Ken Langland at the University of Florida, titled "Natural Area Weeds: Distinguishing Native

Common sword fern (*Nephrolepis exaltata*).

and Non-Native 'Boston Ferns' and 'Sword Ferns'(*Nephrolepis* spp.)," provides detailed photos and descriptions and is available at no cost from the Internet (UF IFAS Extension leaflet SS-AGR-22, http://edis.ifas.ufl. edu/pdffiles/AG/AG12000.pdf). The best way to tell them apart in nature is by their growth habit: native sword ferns do not normally form an impenetrable carpet across the ground while the non-natives do. Tuberous sword fern is also the only one that produces underground rounded tubers covered by hairy golden scales.

Native sword ferns are excellent ground covers for most shady sites and are very similar except for their size. Both are evergreen. Common sword fern rarely stands taller than 12–18 inches, while giant sword fern

Tuberous sword fern
(*Nephrolepis cordifolia*).

Giant sword fern (*Nephrolepis biserrata*).

produces fronds that exceed 3 feet in length and can stand 6 feet tall in ideal growing conditions. Although both species prefer moist sites, they can withstand a good deal of drought once established and given shady conditions. They also tolerate a high amount of sunlight if provided sufficient moisture. Common sword fern occurs statewide while giant sword fern naturally occurs only in the southern half of the peninsula.

Native sword ferns spread outward from their underground rhizome, but the distance between fronds is normally several inches. This often leaves space between them and allows other plants to coexist in the understory. They are ideal ferns to use in drier shady situations where few other plants can be coerced to grow. Over time, a planting of sword fern fills in and provides lush attractive foliage. Just make sure that the sword ferns you are planning to install are the native ones, as the non-native species are tough to control once established.

Southern Wood Ferns (*Dryopteris ludoviciana*)

Southern wood fern is the only member of this large genus native to Florida and occurs nearly statewide in a variety of moist-soil habitats. It is

Southern wood fern (*Dryopteris ludoviciana*).

most common in shady habitats but will tolerate more sunlight if given enough moisture.

Southern wood fern is a medium-sized fern that behaves well in the landscape. It rarely exceeds 18 inches in height, and individual clumps are about the same diameter. It also is evergreen and lends its texture well to a woodland setting during the winter months, when many other plants are dormant. Use southern wood fern in small clusters scattered throughout the planting area. It has not spread much in our Pinellas County landscape, so you will want to put it directly in the areas you want it to occupy.

At present, southern wood fern is not widely available from Florida native plant nurseries, but you can find it if you look hard enough. As this fern is endemic to the southeastern states, those specimens offered in southern gardening catalogs are normally well adapted to Florida landscapes. You can use these sources if you do not have one closer to your geographic location.

6

Grasses and Graminoids

Basketgrass (*Oplismenus hirtellus*)

Basketgrass is found nearly statewide in the understory of moist forested habitats. As such, it is one of just a few native grasses that will prosper in shady conditions. In fact, basketgrass sometimes does a bit too well when given the right combination of soil moisture and shade, and it may have to be weeded to keep it in check. I have friends who both swear by it and

Basketgrass (*Oplismenus hirtellus*).

swear at it. It is useful for expansive shady areas where other ground covers have proven difficult. It is not the best choice for smaller areas or areas where you are trying to maximize diversity.

Basketgrass is diminutive. Its tiny leaves are normally no more than 1 inch long and about ¼ inch wide. These are evenly spaced along the stems, which run across the ground. These stems eventually go in all directions and form a low mat across the ground surface. Basketgrass is excellent at creating a ground cover to prevent erosion beneath the canopy of oaks and other shade trees. It is not especially hardy to foot traffic, however, and does not make a good substitute for turf. Use walkways or stepping stones to prevent it from getting trampled if you intend to use it in areas where you routinely walk. Basketgrass also is deciduous in the late fall and "disappears" until warmer temperatures return in spring. Because of this, areas where it is used should be mulched to prevent erosion during the winter. Basketgrass is one of several native grasses used by Carolina satyr butterfly caterpillars as food.

Beaksedges (*Rhynchospora* spp.)

The beaksedges are a large genus of mostly perennial grasslike plants in the sedge family. Although a total of 52 species are considered native to Florida, only white-topped sedge or star rush (*R. colorata*) has been widely grown for home landscape use. For the most part, beaksedges are common components of open wet meadows, prairies, and marshes. They rarely stand more than 2 feet tall and are inconspicuous when not in bloom. Even then, they blend in among the other species of grasses and wildflowers, and most have very limited landscape potential. Some species are used by Duke's skipper butterfly caterpillars as food, but white-topped sedge is not listed among these.

White-topped sedge can be effectively used in moist sunny locations when mixed with other low to medium-tall graminoids and wildflowers. This is not a plant to be used in small planting areas or scattered in small groupings. Its beauty is seen best when used in a mass in extensive plantings. White-topped sedge produces long, pointed bracts beneath the developing flower head that turn white and remain that color for several months. This flash of color can add a lot to a mixed meadow planting. It

White-topped sedge (*Rhynchospora colorata*).

has some drought tolerance but should not be used in droughty areas if it is to thrive and look its best.

Bluestems (*Andropogon* spp.)

Bluestem grasses are significant components of the tallgrass prairies that occur to our north and west. They are also some of the most common grasses throughout Florida. Throughout their range, bluestems are important to wildlife both as habitat and as food sources. Many songbirds and grazing mammals eat their seeds and/or foliage, and they are the food of at least six different butterfly caterpillars in the satyr and skipper families.

Bluestems are bunchgrasses. Individual plants grow outward from the

Splitbeard bluestem (*Andropogon ternarius*).

Bushy bluestem (*Andropogon glomeratus*).

Broomsedge (*Andropogon virginicus*).

clump but generally "stay put" and do not rapidly spread throughout the landscape. They are rather robust. Most bluestems stand several feet tall (not counting the flower stalk produced in late summer), and individual clumps are likely to be several feet across. These are ideal grasses to provide structure to a large mixed planting of native grasses and wildflowers, but they should be placed near the back of the planting area to work more as a screen and as support for taller wildflowers that might otherwise fall over, for example, certain blazing stars (*Liatris* spp.) and eastern silver aster (*Symphyotrichum concolor*)

Bluestems are interesting both for their foliage and for their seed heads. The main clump persists through the winter; new shoots emerge from it in early spring. Most bluestems have leaf blades greater than 3 feet long but less than ½ inch wide. Though several common species are bright green in color, a good many are bluish green and quite attractive. Flowering occurs in late summer to early fall, and the seed heads are often fuzzy and colorful. Bluestems are adaptable and thrive in a wide variety of landscape conditions. For best growth, give them ample light and drainage. Several species are common to wetland edges and can tolerate wet soils, but nearly all are very easily grown in an average home landscape.

Eleven species have been described in Florida, some with distinct varieties, and several are commonly offered for sale by native plant nurseries. Some of the best are bushy bluestem (*A. glomeratus*), splitbeard bluestem (*A. ternarius*), and broomsedge (*A. virginicus*). All three of these occur statewide. Splitbeard bluestem is very distinct for its paired, split, silvery white seed heads in the fall. A very attractive blue-green variety of broomsedge known as "chalky bluestem" (*A. virginicus* var. *glaucus*) is commonly available from native plant sources and adds interesting color because of its foliage.

Cordgrasses (*Spartina* spp.)

Five species of cordgrass are native to Florida, and they often take a dominant role in the habitats they occur in. Four species occur nearly statewide and three are commonly sold commercially. Only sand cordgrass (*S. bakeri*), however, is a candidate for typical home landscape settings. Smooth or saltmarsh cordgrass (*S. alternifolia*) and saltmeadow cordgrass (*S. patens*) spread aggressively by underground rhizomes and tend

Sand cordgrass (*Spartina bakeri*).

to form extensive monocultures. They are best used in saltmarsh restoration projects. Saltmarsh cordgrass is the food plant of saltmarsh skipper butterfly caterpillars.

Sand cordgrass is a large bunchgrass with a mounded appearance. Over time, individual clumps grow outward from the center and become several feet across and several feet tall. It is native to wet soils in either freshwater or brackish water marshes and performs best when given extra moisture and plenty of sunlight. It is adaptable, however, and can survive nearly any landscape condition except extreme drought.

Sand cordgrass is best used for its foliage as the flower heads are not particularly showy. The leaves are soft to the touch but appear needlelike. Each thin cordlike leaf may be 4–5 feet long, and each clump contains hundreds of leaves. The leaves are semierect and do not arch over to the extent that most other large bunchgrasses do. Because of this, it makes a nice screen or hedge. It should not be used in small areas, but can add a dramatic touch to more extensive plantings. Use it at the back of the planting bed or as a linear divider between two distinct areas.

Dropseeds (*Sporobolus* spp.)

Although eight species of dropseed grasses are native to Florida (along with two very common invasive non-natives), only the pinewoods or pineywoods dropseed (*S. junceus*) is commonly offered in the commercial trade. As its name suggests, this is a grass common to Florida's pinelands and occurs nearly statewide.

Pinewoods dropseed is one of the very best native grasses for a mixed wildflower meadow. It will grow nearly anywhere except locations that require salt tolerance, and it is exceptionally well behaved. Pinewoods dropseed is a bunchgrass and stays where it is planted. Individual clumps rarely stand taller than 1 foot and are more than 18 inches in diameter. It is just diminutive enough to blend well into a mixed planting of wildflowers, but attractive enough to be noticed. In the right conditions, pinewoods dropseed will bloom and set seed throughout the summer and fall, but heaviest blooming occurs in early summer. Bloom spikes stand 2–3 feet tall and can be numerous at any one time. Although not exceptionally striking, the flowers are an attractive reddish brown in color.

Pinewoods dropseed (*Sporobolus junceus*).

I like to use pinewoods dropseed with wiregrass (*Aristida* spp.) in scattered clumps mixed with wildflowers. It is especially good when used near walkways and near the front of a planting area, but it also provides wonderful structure for wildflower meadows when mixed throughout. Pinewoods dropseed is dormant in the winter, but greens up quickly in the spring.

Fakahatchee Grasses or Gamagrasses (*Tripsacum* spp.)

Two species of grasses, commonly referred to as Fakahatchee grass or gamagrass, are native to Florida and often offered in the native plant nursery trade. These are very different from each other and not interchangeable in landscape settings, though both are quite adaptable to conditions well outside those where they grow naturally.

Fakahatchee Grass or Eastern Gamagrass (*T. dactyloides*)

Fakahatchee grass is native to freshwater marshes, disturbed moist areas, and the edges of forested wetlands throughout Florida. Despite its most commonly used common name in Florida, Fakahatchee grass is native to nearly every state in the eastern half of the nation and not restricted to the Fakahatchee Strand near Everglades National Park.

Despite its natural affinity to wetlands, Fakahatchee grass is adaptable

Fakahatchee grass (*Tripsacum dactyloides*).

to upland landscape settings. For many native plant gardeners, this grass has become a substitute for situations where pampas grass (*Cortaderia selloana*) may have been used in the past. Fakahatchee grass is a large robust species that dominates any setting in which it is placed. Well-grown specimens are often 4–5 feet tall and 3–4 feet in diameter. The leaf blades are nearly 1 inch wide and arch gracefully from the growing center. The leaves are normally bright green in color, but blue-green forms are also offered.

Use this species in areas where their large size does not crowd out or overwhelm what's adjacent to it. Fakahatchee grass makes a wonderful screen, for example, or an easy-to-maintain planting beneath larger trees where sufficient sunlight is present. It is not often effective in mixed-species wildflower meadows because it is simply too large. Do not use Fakahatchee grass in tight spaces.

This grass produces large seed heads in late summer to fall, and they are especially useful to seed-eating birds and other wildlife. It is also the food plant of three skipper butterfly caterpillars: three-spotted, clouded, and byssus. This is normally a well-behaved grass in landscape settings but can be problematic if not maintained, spreading to other parts of the landscape, especially in moist fertile areas.

Dwarf Fakahatchee Grass or Florida Gamagrass (*T. floridanum*)

Dwarf Fakahatchee grass is a very rare grass in nature and found in only two counties in southernmost Florida, in Cuba, and on a few other Caribbean islands. It is listed as a state threatened species. Dwarf Fakahatchee grass has slightly wider leaf blades than its close cousin, but is shorter in stature, rarely exceeding 3 feet in height. It also tends to produce only one flower stalk per plant.

Dwarf Fakahatchee grass is native to pine rockland habitats, where adapting to shallow alkaline soils, occasional drought, and frequent fire is important. In home landscapes, it is adaptable to most settings except extremes of soil moisture—either wet or dry. Despite its natural rarity, this grass is often available from native plant nurseries. Use it in settings where a medium-sized bunchgrass is most appropriate. It could be effectively used in a mixed species planting with other grasses and wildflowers, but its size might overwhelm smaller species. Dwarf Fakahatchee grass is also

Dwarf Fakahatchee grass (*Tripsacum floridanum*).

not especially cold tolerant, so it should be planted only in the southern half of the peninsula.

Indiangrasses (*Sorghastrum* spp.)

Indiangrasses are also dominant components of the Midwest prairie community and the open understories of open woodlands, prairies, and pinelands throughout the Southeastern Coastal Plain into Florida. Like the bluestems with which they often occur, Indiangrasses are tall, robust bunchgrasses that may stand 4 feet tall before blooming and nearly 6 feet tall or more in late summer and fall when in full bloom.

Indiangrasses are native to well-drained sunny habitats and grow best

Lop-sided Indiangrass (*Sorghastrum secundum*).

when given ample sunshine and well-drained soils. They will survive a good deal of shade but perform poorly in this condition and often flop over and fail to bloom properly. All four of our native species share many of the same general attributes and are exceptional grasses for wildlife habitat, but only one, lop-sided Indiangrass (*S. secundum*), is commonly available. Thankfully, it is the most beautiful species and occurs statewide.

Lop-sided Indiangrass derives its name from the way its golden flowers and seeds develop on top of the flower stalk; they hang down on only one side. As they dangle, shining in the breeze, they make a spectacular sight across the open prairie or flatwoods understory. Lop-sided Indiangrass begins this process in mid-September and the seeds are usually gone by late fall. When not in flower or seed, it is a rather coarse-leaved bunchgrass that may be several feet across. This is a grass to add for its golden flowering stalk.

Use lop-sided Indiangrass in a mixed grass and wildflower planting to add character and height. It makes a wonderful addition to the back of a planting, where it can serve a dual purpose as a screen or boundary. If you have enough space, it is beautiful as an accent, mixed in small clusters throughout the landscape. Because of its size, it is not especially attractive in small beds, and I find that it looks out of place in such settings.

Lop-sided Indiangrass is one of the better grasses for wildlife value. The relatively large seeds provide food for a number of seed-eating songbirds and small mammals, while the foliage is important forage for grass-eating species. Lop-sided Indiangrass is also the food of six different skipper butterfly caterpillars and therefore can be effectively incorporated into a butterfly garden.

Inland River Oats (*Chasmanthium latifolium*)

Although several other species in this genus are more widely distributed in Florida, only inland river oats has the aesthetic attributes needed to make it commonly propagated and sold commercially. It is native to the understory of moist, rich woodlands in much of northernmost Florida and throughout most of the eastern two-thirds of the country. Although its range in Florida is restricted, it can be used well south of this latitude if given the appropriate growing conditions.

Individual plants produce more than a dozen ½-inch-wide leaves and stand about 8–12 inches tall. It is grown mostly for its interesting seed heads that look somewhat like those found on true sea oats (*Uniola paniculata*). The arching flower stalks and the green sea-oatlike seeds, which ripen to a golden brown, make this species a very effective accent plant in understory plantings. The seeds are produced over many months and are present for much of the growing season in one form or another. Inland river oats is deciduous and dies back to the ground in early winter.

Inland river oats is not especially drought tolerant and performs best

Inland river oats (*Chasmanthium latifolium*).

when given above-average fertility and moist soils. It also does not perform well if given too much sunlight. Protect it from full sun and provide filtered sunlight or high shade. Too much shade will make it weak and it won't bloom well. If these conditions can be provided, inland river oats can be grown well into South Central Florida. Mix it with some of the medium- to smaller-sized ferns and with shade-tolerant wildflowers such as violets, wild gingers (*Asarum* spp.), and the like. Inland river oats is one of several grasses used by common roadside skipper caterpillars as food.

Little Bluestem (*Schizachyrium scoparium*)

Little bluestem is another major component of the tallgrass prairie and open woodlands throughout eastern North America. Although an impor- tant grass, and found statewide, it has never been commonly propagated here by commercial growers and is often difficult to find at nurseries.

Little bluestem is an exceptionally adaptable species and tolerant of most growing conditions common to home landscapes. Despite its name, it is not little, just a bit more demure than its close cousins in the genus

Little bluestem
(*Schizachyrium scoparium*).

Andropogon. Little bluestem reaches nearly 5 feet in height, and the slender stems are banded in color, alternating between rusty red and bluegreen. This is a bunchgrass that slowly produces clumps of many stems. The seed heads are produced near the top of the stem in late summer and fall. They consist of small silvery white tufts that are attractive in an understated way.

Little bluestem is not a very effective landscape grass when used alone, but makes a wonderful addition to a prairie planting of mixed grasses and wildflowers. Use it in small clusters near the back half of the bed with bluestems and lop-sided Indiangrass in expansive plantings and combine it with taller wildflowers such as many of the blazing stars, rosinweeds (*Silphium* spp.), sunflowers (*Helianthus* spp.), and asters (*Symphyotrichum* spp.).

Lovegrasses (*Eragrostis* spp.)

Eleven species of lovegrasses are considered native to Florida, and nearly twice that number have become established from other countries. This genus comprises both annuals and perennials. Both produce large numbers of seeds each year and spread throughout the landscape, taking advantage of any spots of bare soil. For this reason, they are frequently found in sites that have been disturbed. Lovegrasses may be encountered in nearly every conceivable habitat type, though most reside in open sunny areas.

Lovegrasses often have rather coarse, wide leaf blades and open panicles of flowers that eventually mature into seed heads of varying colors. Flowering tends to occur in late summer to early fall and is well over by late October. They are bunchgrasses and form dense mounds that shade other species around them. Over time, these mounds of vegetation can become substantial and may require occasional pruning to maintain them in the condition desired. It's the flowering stalks that make these grasses so attractive, but also the part that make them difficult to maintain, especially in a small landscape area. Lovegrass seed heads naturally break off when ripe and the breezes blow them about the garden like tiny tumbleweeds.

Elliott's lovegrass (*Eragrostis elliottii*).

For this reason, I like to prune them as soon as flowering is completed and before much of the seed has been dispersed. If you let these species go to seed, you will eventually have to thin the extras out. Many members of this genus are rather weedy, but two species are frequently available through commercial sources. Both are exceptional grasses for the home landscape and extremely adaptable to most conditions. They are not good choices for coastal plantings, but Elliott's lovegrass (*E. elliottii*) has some salt tolerance.

Elliott's lovegrass is found nearly statewide in a wide variety of upland settings. It is sometimes called "silver lovegrass" for its silvery blue-green foliage and seed heads. Elliott's lovegrass is a medium-sized member of this genus and usually measures about 32 inches tall and about that same distance across.

Purple lovegrass (*E. spectabilis*) is also found nearly statewide in Florida and is similar in size and character to Elliott's lovegrass, differing mostly in the color of its flowers and leaves. The flower heads are a rich purplish red in color, and the leaf blades often have a purplish cast. This rich color adds a lot of interest to a mixed grass and wildflower planting in the late summer months.

Use both species in mixed plantings with medium-tall wildflowers

Purple lovegrass (*Eragrostis spectabilis*).

such as black-eyed susan (*Rudbeckia hirta*), wild petunia (*Ruellia caroliniensis*), and narrowleaf silkgrass (*Pityopsis graminifolia*). It is not a good choice for less assertive wildflowers as it will eventually outcompete them for space. Both species perform well in moist to well-drained sites and in full to partly sunny locations.

Muhly Grasses (*Muhlenbergia* spp.)

Although this genus contains two species in Florida, only hairawn muhly grass (*M. capillaris*) is ever likely to be encountered in a nursery or used purposefully in a landscape setting. And, without a doubt, this species is more widely used to accent home and commercial landscapes and roadway median strips than any other native grass in Florida.

Hairawn muhly has much to offer. Its mounding mass of soft, needlelike leaves stay semierect and rich green in color most of the year, and stand about 3 feet tall. Clumps of hairawn muhly are just large enough to make a dramatic statement and small enough to not overwhelm everything else around them. Individual clumps grow slowly outward and eventually become substantial in girth. For this purpose, it may be necessary to thin

Hairawn muhly grass (*Muhlenbergia capillaris*).

them annually if they begin to usurp space needed for other plants. A sharp spade will do the trick especially well. You can then take the spaded piece and repot it to give to a neighbor or friend.

Although you could grow hairawn muhly simply for its wonderful foliage, I suspect no one does. It's the spectacular blooms that truly attract our attention. There is no native grass more aesthetically attractive than a mass of hairawn muhly in full bloom. It blooms across the full width of its crown, and the flowers are a vivid pinkish crimson. Planted in an understory around the base of taller woody species or as a foundation planting, it seems ablaze during the fall season, especially with the sunlight catching it from behind.

Hairawn muhly is technically a wetland grass, but it is exceptionally adaptable and can be used in nearly any landscape setting. It is salt tolerant and can withstand a high degree of drought. Use it in sunny to partly sunny locations, but it will flower much more profusely if planted in areas that receive plenty of sunlight. Use it purely as an accent planting or mixed with taller wildflowers. In a mixed planting, it is most effective in the back half of a planting bed.

Panic and Witch Grasses (*Panicum* and *Dichanthelium* spp., respectively)

At one time, these two genera were all considered panic grasses. Today, it is generally accepted that they are different enough to warrant being split. Generally, the witch grasses are more diminutive, have wider leaf blades that lie closer to the ground, and bloom twice during the year, in spring and fall. Although some witch grasses are aesthetically interesting and a few are adapted to shady locations that are difficult to plant, I am not aware of any grown commercially at this time. This should change someday as commercial nurseries add more species to their inventory and demand increases for additional grasses adapted to lower light situations, but further discussion of this genus does not seem warranted here and at this time.

The panic grasses, on the other hand, are a large genus with several species that are significant to landscapes. Included in this genus are two highly invasive non-natives: torpedo grass (*P. repens*) which was introduced as a cattle forage grass from South America in the late 1800s, and

Witch grass
(*Dichanthelium* sp.).

Guinea grass (*P. maximum*), which was introduced from Africa. Torpedo grass rapidly spreads throughout wetland and upland areas by forming extensive deep underground rhizomes and is extremely difficult to control. Guinea grass is common to roadsides and disturbed upland sites, where it can form dense thickets. At a mature height of more than 6 feet, it tends to overwhelm everything adjacent to it. Thankfully, the rest of the genus is reasonably well behaved and a few of the native species are commonly planted.

Panic grasses tend to be robust, medium-tall perennials or annuals with arching leaves and panicle seed heads. They are important forage grasses for livestock and grass-feeding wildlife and birds, and other seed-eating wildlife are often drawn to them as well. Panic grasses tend to dominate areas where they occur. They are often rhizomatous, spreading by underground rhizomes. Most species stand 1–2 feet tall with flower heads that might add another foot during the late summer to fall. A few species produce flowers that are colorful and somewhat showy, but the vast majority are planted in restoration projects for their habitat value and not in developed landscapes for their aesthetics. The following species are often available commercially and have some application in the home landscape.

Bitter Panic Grass (*P. amarum*)

Bitter panic grass is commonly encountered in coastal dunes throughout Florida in association with sea oats (*Uniola paniculata*). It is a highly adaptable coastal grass and can be found in both upland and wetland sites. This is a somewhat coarse-looking grass that may stand about 3 feet tall. The leaves are blue-green in color and provide some interesting contrast when planted with sea oats in a coastal dune setting. Bitter panic grass tends to die back during the winter and flowers most months from

Bitter panic grass (*Panicum amarum*).

spring through fall. This grass is best used to stabilize dunes and to restore disturbed open coastal areas. It is not particularly valuable in other landscape situations.

Maidencane (*P. hemitomon*)

Maidencane is ubiquitous throughout Florida's freshwater wetland systems. Here, it tends to form dense stands of cover for wetland wildlife, and its seeds are often a staple of some species' diets. It also is the food of three butterfly caterpillars: clouded, Delaware, and Aaron's skippers. Maidencane normally stands 3 feet tall at maturity, with the seed heads adding another foot during the summer months. Although it has some drought

Maidencane (*Panicum hemitomon*).

tolerance, maidencane is not a good choice for the typical home landscape and is best used to improve the habitat value of shallow water areas.

Switchgrass (*P. virgatum*)

Switchgrass is an extremely important component of the tallgrass prairie communities to our north and west, but is also present throughout much of Florida in a wide variety of upland and wetland sites. It is a robust grower. This trait and its adaptability have made it a potential target as a biofuel producer, but it is not a good choice in the typical home landscape. Its large size and energetic growth are inappropriate for all but the most expansive settings. If used, it should be mixed with other tallgrass prairie grasses—bluestems, little bluestems and Indiangrasses—and placed at the very back of the planting bed where it can provide a visual screen.

Switchgrass (*Panicum virgatum*). Photo by Shirley Denton, with permission.

Rushes (*Juncus* spp.)

The rushes differ from grasses by having round stems and a terminal and branched flower cluster that produces three-sided fruit capsules with many tiny seeds. Most of the commonly encountered species form large clumps of round, needlelike leaves and occur in wetlands. A total of 21 species are known to occur in Florida. None are especially drought tolerant or have attributes that make them good candidates for the average home landscape. Nevertheless, rushes are exceedingly important components of natural landscapes, and several are widely grown for restoration projects. Two of these would make interesting and attractive elements within a wetland restoration planting or within an extensive natural landscape approach for wet sites.

Soft Rush (*J. effusus*)

Soft rush occurs statewide in freshwater wetland habitats. As its common name implies, the long needlelike leaves are soft to the touch. Individual plants may stand 4 feet tall or taller and are nearly that large in diameter.

Soft rush (*Juncus effusus*). Photo by Shirley Denton, with permission.

In the summer months, they develop rusty brown flower clusters at the tips of the leaves that are attractive. Soft rush sometimes occurs in the wetter pockets of pine flatwoods and has more drought tolerance than other species in this genus. Despite this, it is best planted at the edges of lakes, ponds, and other similarly wet areas.

Needle Rush (*J. roemerianus*)

Needle rush is also known as black rush and is a very common component of brackish marshes throughout Florida. As its common name implies, it has stiff needlelike leaves and can form impenetrable thickets of cover in the salt marsh areas it inhabits. This makes it a wonderful candidate for large restoration projects, but a very poor choice for the home landscape.

Needle rush (*Juncus roemerianus*).

Sea Oats (*Uniola paniculata*)

Few plants characterize the coastal dune community better than sea oats. This tall robust salt-tolerant grass is found statewide on the leading edge of beach dunes and is extremely important in stabilizing them and in

Sea oats (*Uniola paniculata*).

providing habitat. Because of significance and not because of rarity, sea oats are federally protected and cannot be disturbed or their seeds collected without a permit.

Sea oats are rhizomatous and spread throughout the dune. This network of roots and runners holds the sand in place, and the tall stems tend to capture blowing grains of sand and build the dune crests. Sea oats stand 6 feet tall. The individual stems are not particularly floriferous, and most of the leaves are stiff and surround the stem near the sand. What makes sea oats most distinctive are the seed heads. Seeds are produced from spring through fall. They occur at the top of the grass and form loose panicles of dense "oatlike" seeds. They are an important food source for Florida's rare beach mice. Though sea oats are characteristic of Florida's beach communities, they can be used in any well-drained sandy soil where ample sunlight is available.

Tall Redtop (*Tridens flavus*)

Tall redtop is a perennial bunchgrass native to much of Florida except the most southerly counties. It is most commonly encountered in the edges of shady woodlands where the soils are a bit richer and moister, but it is quite adaptable. We have planted it in our Pinellas County landscape in a wide variety of situations and have found it to be exceptionally drought tolerant and forgiving of high sunlight and varying soil fertility and pH.

Tall redtop produces rich arching foliage that stands about 3 feet tall during the summer and fall. Blooming occurs in summer and early fall. As the name implies, the flowers are purplish red and quite attractive. In the variety *flavus*, as pictured in this book, the flower heads dangle. In a second variety, *chapmanii*, the flower heads stand erect.

Tall redtop is offered only occasionally by commercial sources at this time, which is regrettable as it has much to offer the home landscape. Because of its height, use it to provide an accent at the back of a mixed planting of wildflowers and native grasses, or in a gap of sunlight within a mixed woodland. For the most part, this is a well-behaved grass that remains where it is planted. It does produce rhizomes from its base and will spread outward over time. Like most grasses, it also produces seeds, and the seedlings will germinate some distance away from the parent plants.

Tall redtop (*Tridens flavus*).

All of these are controllable through pruning. Tall redtop is one of a great many coarse grasses used by clouded skipper butterfly caterpillars as food.

Toothache Grass (*Ctenium aromaticum*)

Toothache grass is one of several species of plants in Florida named for the fact that chewing on its leaves will leave you with a slight tingling in your mouth, tongue, and gums. Reputedly, Native Americans used this to their advantage when they had toothaches, but I have not found it to be very effective for this purpose. The Latin name is derived from this grass's distinctive comblike seed heads; the word *ctenium* is Greek for "little comb."

Toothache grass is native to most of Florida and occurs in the understory of moist pinelands, glades, and savannas. In these habitats, it is not particularly noticeable until it blooms. The leaves are mostly held close to ground level in a tight cluster and are about 6 inches long.

What makes toothache grass especially noteworthy is its unusual flower stalk and resulting seed head. These are held well above the foliage, sometimes by as much as 3 feet. They are solitary and curve gently backward. The individual flowers are arranged in paired rows and look like small spikes.

Toothache grass is only occasionally offered commercially. Because of its size, it is best used in small masses in a mixed planting of wildflowers and other grasses. Plant it near the front half or you may lose it in the rest

Toothache grass (*Ctenium aromaticum*).

of the vegetation until early summer when it blooms. Toothache grass is not especially tolerant of extended drought, so it also needs to be planted in sites that are moist to wet during the summer months. Give it the right conditions, and you will be enamored of this distinctive grass. It is also the caterpillar food of the rare Arogos skipper butterfly.

Wiregrasses (*Aristida* spp.)

There are 18 different species of wiregrasses in Florida. Many are nearly impossible to distinguish from each other. A few, like the "three-awns," are quite distinctive but not likely to be propagated for home landscapes because their spiky seed heads have hooks that stick to your clothes.

Wiregrasses are everywhere in Florida and often the most dominant, and ecologically most important, plant in the understory. Wiregrasses are short and fine leaved, and they carry fire through many of Florida's major habitat types. All grasses tend to burn quickly and easily, but fires in areas dominated by wiregrass stay low in the understory and out of the crowns of the trees. The relationship between wiregrass and fire is so well tuned that many do not flower and set viable seed if they do not burn during the month of May or June. Some wiregrasses spread by rhizomes.

Wiregrass (*Aristida stricta* var. *beyrichiana*).

Wiregrass (*A. stricta* var. *beyrichiana*) is ubiquitous throughout Florida and been given a number of different Latin names over the years, but it is universally known to native plant gardeners, regardless. It is one of the best grasses for landscaping purposes because it is exceptionally adaptable to growing conditions. This species can be found growing vigorously in well-drained sandhill habitats and in wet prairies and savannas where 6 inches of standing water is the norm during the summer rainy season. It occurs in the alkaline soils of the Florida Keys as well as in the highly acidic ones of North Florida's pitcher plant savannas. It is also extremely well behaved. Wiregrass does not produce rhizomes that spread it around the landscape. Over time, it will creep outward from the central growing point, but it does not get much wider than 12–18 inches and no taller than that unless it flowers. And, if you don't burn it, your wiregrass will not seed and spread.

All of this makes it the ideal background grass for a mixed grass and wildflower planting. Wiregrass will allow wildflowers of all sizes a place to fit into and will protect the soil surface from the effects of too much sun while allowing the showier species to stand out. Use wiregrass in scattered clumps throughout a mixed planting area or use it as an alternative to traditional lawn grass, much the way that Western gardeners have adopted buffalo grass (*Buchloe dactyloides*) in no-mow yards. Thankfully, wiregrass is available from a great number of native nurseries. Plant it no closer than 12 inches apart and give it plenty of water to establish it.

7

Wildflowers

Acanthus Family—Acanthaceae

Though the family name is not well known to anyone but plant taxonomists, it contains some very popular wildflowers for home landscapes.
Most have tubular flowers, leaves that are simple, and seed capsules that
burst open when ripe, sending the seeds a foot or more away. Three separate genera in Florida have species that make fine additions to the home
landscape.

Cooley's Waterwillow (*Justicia cooleyi*)

Cooley's waterwillow is the only native member of this genus likely to be
used in a typical landscape setting. Though other members have showy
lavender pink flowers, they require moist to wet soils and are rarely, if
ever, available from commercial sources. The non-native green shrimp
plant (*J. brandegeana*) is the larval food plant for the iridescent green
malachite butterfly of South Florida but is weedy and not a good choice
for cultivation.

Cooley's waterwillow is rare in nature, found only in a three-county
area of Florida near Brooksville. In this region, it occurs in forest gaps and
disturbed edges in moist calcareous soils. It is quite adaptable, however, in
the home landscape, and I have found it easy to maintain. I do not know
how far its landscape range might be extended, but I suspect it could be
used throughout the northern two-thirds of Florida given the right growing conditions.

Cooley's waterwillow is deciduous and dies back to the ground each

Cooley's waterwillow (*Justicia cooleyi*).

winter if temperatures drop below freezing. By early summer, it reaches its mature height of about 8 inches and a diameter of about 12 inches. The leaves are elliptical, and each plant becomes a rather rounded mass of bright green foliage. Flowering occurs for several months in late summer and fall across the crown of each plant. The tiny deep pink flowers are produced in abundance and are quite striking. This is a wonderful wildflower for a partly shaded understory area. Use it near the front and near trails so it can be fully admired. Over time, it will spread by seed. Do not let it dry out completely if you want it to thrive, and give it filtered light or just a few hours of direct sunlight each day. This species is only occasionally offered for sale by commercial sources.

Wild Petunia (*Ruellia caroliniensis*)

Wild petunia is the only member of this genus widely propagated for home landscapes. It is extremely adaptable and tolerates shade to full sun, and moist to extremely droughty soils. As such, it can be used nearly anywhere statewide except in areas that receive direct salt spray. Wild petunia is a deciduous perennial that dies back to the ground each winter. It emerges in early spring and eventually reaches a height of about 12 inches. Blooming occurs from spring through late fall. Butterflies love these flowers, and malachite butterfly caterpillars may occasionally use it as a food source. Normally, plants have only a few flowers open at any one time and they stay open only for a day, but the blooms continue in succession for months. The flowers look somewhat like the common garden petunia (though they are not related) and vary in color from very pale lavender to a much deeper shade of purple. I like to use this wildflower at the sunny edges of woodland plantings and in the front half of sunny mixed wildflower beds.

In more shade, the plants are weaker and bloom less often. Wild petunia is notorious for spreading rapidly throughout the landscape and will fill in most open areas in short time by seeding itself, but this is not an aggressive plant, and the extras can be easily thinned if desired.

Wild petunia (*Ruellia caroliniensis*).

Twinflower (*Dyschoriste oblongifolia*)

Twinflower is so named because it produces two flowers at a time that open across from each other on the main stem. These light purple blooms are most abundant in late spring and early summer, but flowering may be sporadic in other months when temperatures are not too cold. Individual stems rarely have more than a pair of flowers open at any one time, but because this plant forms colonies, they can be quite striking during the blooming season. Butterflies are drawn to the open flowers, and the common buckeye makes occasional use of it as a caterpillar food plant. This is an evergreen perennial ground cover that spreads throughout the landscape by underground runners. Thin wiry aboveground stems arise every few inches, but rarely stand taller than 8 inches.

Twinflower will thrive in most landscape settings statewide. It performs best when given full sun and well-drained soils, but it tolerates some shade and will survive periodic saturated soils. Use it as a ground cover to fill in open areas near walkways or allow it to mix in with other wildflowers in a mixed setting. Although it suckers and spreads freely, it

Twinflower (*Dyschoriste oblongifolia*).

does not outcompete larger species and will occupy only areas that are open. Twinflower is widely propagated by commercial sources.

Amaryllis Family—Amaryllidaceae

Members of this family share many characteristics with the lilies. Both families tend to have trumpet-shaped flowers and straplike leaves that arise from an underground bulb. Several native members of the amaryllis family are widely used in planted landscapes.

Swamp Lily (*Crinum americanum*)

Swamp lily is found throughout Florida in a variety of wetland sites. It has moderate salt tolerance and performs well in all situations where soils are wet to seasonally flooded. Native swamp lilies are a much better behaved, more diminutive version of the Asian swamp lily (*C. asiaticum*) that is so frequently used now in Florida landscapes. Many large straplike leaves develop in a whorl around the main bulb in late winter and eventually reach a length of several feet on mature specimens. It is evergreen in South Florida but freezes back to the soil surface elsewhere.

Although the lush foliage makes an attractive statement in the landscape, it's the flowers that really make this wildflower special. Swamp lily

Swamp lily (*Crinum americanum*).

blooms in late spring and early summer. Stout flower stalks, 2–3 feet tall, arise from the center of the foliage and contain multiple buds. These buds open about the same time, and the flowers last for many days, making a wonderful show. Each flower is bright white with long curving petals and purplish red reproductive structures. They are slightly fragrant and attract the attention of a great many insects. They are pollinated, however, by sphinx moths. The pollinated flowers produce large rounded seed capsules that become heavy enough when ripe to pull the capsule down flush with the wet soil around the parent plant. Over time, these seeds germinate and large colonies of swamp lily result.

Swamp lily is best used at the edges of ponds and other wet soil habitats. It does not mind being inundated by shallow standing water for long periods of time, but can adapt to drier sites if not allowed to dry out for long periods. Give it at least a half day of sun or it will not bloom well.

Spider Lilies (*Hymenocallis* spp.)

Spider lilies are similar to swamp lily, but differ in several significant ways. For one, their large straplike leaves tend to be more erect and more lateral to each other, not whorled around the central bulb. Second, their large white flowers have a papery central disk somewhat like that of a daffodil, and the 6 petals that surround it are thin and spiderlike. There are 11 species of spider lilies native to Florida, including a few very rare endemics.

Fragrant spider lily (*Hymenocallis latifolia*).

Most are nearly impossible to distinguish from each other unless you are a trained taxonomist, and all grow under pretty much the same conditions. Most are deciduous, but the one most commonly grown and sold commercially, fragrant spider lily (*H. latifolia*), is evergreen.

Fragrant spider lily is common to saltwater and freshwater wetlands and moist pinelands throughout much of the Florida peninsula and can be used statewide. Fragrant spider lily is a robust plant. In moist locations, its leaves reach about 2 feet tall, but in drier sites the leaves rarely stand more than 12 inches. Flowering can occur any time from spring to fall, and individual plants may bloom for several months. As with the swamp lily, multiple buds are formed on each flower stalk, and several to many flowers may be open at any one time. As the common name suggests, these are slightly fragrant.

Fragrant spider lily is adaptable and can be used in many landscape settings with good results. Although it prefers moist to wet soils, it will do well in typically sandy soils once established. It also blooms well in most situations except deep shade. Use spider lily in masses as an accent in the landscape or in smaller clusters in mixed plantings. Good companion plants for wet sites include swamp lily, yellow canna (*Canna flaccida*), iris

(*Iris* spp.), spoonflower (*Peltandra virginica*), and any of the native hibiscus (*Hibiscus* spp.). If you live within the northern half of Florida, cardinal flower (*Lobelia cardinalis*) would also be a striking companion to this species. If used in drier sites, plant it with meadow beauties (*Rhexia* spp.), marsh pinks (*Sabatia* spp.), any of the medium-sized St. John's-worts (*Hypericum* spp.), and other species common to moist pinelands.

Rain Lilies (*Zephyranthes* spp.)

Rain lilies are widespread in Florida, relatively easy to grow, and absolutely lovely additions to a home landscape. A great number of non-native rain lilies have found their way into Florida landscapes through the nursery trade, but two native species occur here as well. They are very similar to each other and can be distinguished mostly by subtle differences in their flower structure. One, however, is much more widely propagated than the other.

Atamasco Rain Lily (*Z. atamasca*)

Atamasco rain lily occurs over much of Central and North Florida in one of two distinct forms. Variety *treatiae* is the more common form in peninsular Florida and has very thin, stringy leaves that are slightly less than ⅛ inch wide. Variety *atamasca* has leaves nearly twice as wide and is found mostly in North Florida. Both forms have similar growing needs and occur in a variety of open habitats. Though more abundant in seasonally moist sites, Atamasco rain lily can also be abundant in open pastures with more droughty soils. In most years, it remains evergreen during the winter months. The clumps of thin leaves are dense but rarely taller than about 6 inches. As its name suggests, flowering occurs after rain events, mostly in the spring, but sometimes into summer. The response to rain is immediate. Within 24 hours after a heavy rain event, single-budded flower stalks appear within the leaf mass, and the flowers open two days later. They remain open for only a few days before withering, but during this time each leaf mass is adorned with 3–4-inch white to soft pink trumpet-shaped blooms. This scenario is repeated after each rain for weeks.

Atamasco rain lily is exceedingly easy to keep in a landscape. It can be planted in masses near walkways, as small clumps near the front of a mixed wildflower planting, or even in the lawn. Mowing does not harm it,

Atamasco rain lily (*Zephyranthes atamasca* var. *atamasca*).

but care should be taken not to mow after a rain event during the blooming season so flowers can be admired. Plants slowly increase in girth over time as side bulbs are formed and become their own plants. They also increase their population from seed released from the ripe capsules if these are not mowed first.

Simpson's Rain Lily (*Z. simpsonii*)

Simpson's rain lily occurs over much of the Florida peninsula but is uncommon throughout. Its thin leaves are similar to those of the *treatiae* variety of Atamasco rain lily, and its flowers differ only in the length of the pollen-producing anthers relative to the stigma (the end of the female part of the flower upon which the pollen sticks). In Simpson's rain lily, all the reproductive parts, male and female, are the same length, whereas in Atamasco rain lily, the anthers are much shorter

Simpson's rain lily (*Zephyranthes simpsonii*).

than the stigma. All the specimens I have seen are clear white, with very little evidence of pink once they have opened. Use Simpson's rain lily the same way as Atamasco rain lily, if you can find it for sale. It is only very rarely offered by commercial sources.

Arum Family—Araceae

The arum, or aroid, family includes a great many species used extensively as house plants across North America and as landscape plants in Florida. Several, such as the non-native wild taro (*Colocasia esculenta*), arrowhead vine (*Syngonium* spp.), and elephant ears (*Xanthisoma* spp.), are especially invasive and should not be used outdoors anywhere near a natural area. The family also includes a few wonderful wildflowers, well known to many. Arums have a fingerlike flower stalk (the spadix) surrounded by a leafy spathe. Pollinated flowers along this spadix mature into a fleshy berry. Two genera have members likely to be used in the home landscape, but even these have narrow habitat requirements and need special conditions to thrive.

Green Dragon (*Arisaema dracontium*)

Green dragon is an interesting wildflower and tolerant of average soils but rarely sold commercially in Florida. It behaves much the same way in a

Green dragon (*Arisaema dracontium*).

woodland garden setting as its more common relative, jack-in-the-pulpit (*A. triphyllum*), but has leaflets in 7–9 parts instead of 3–5. The flower stalk stands well above the leaves, but the flowers are thin and not very dramatic. Use it in much the same settings as jack-in-the-pulpit if you can find some to grow.

Jack-in-the-pulpit (*Arisaema triphyllum*).

Jack-in-the-Pulpit (*Arisaema triphyllum*)

Jack-in-the-pulpit occurs in much of Florida in fertile moist woodland soils. It requires dappled shade and moist to saturated soils during the summer months, but sunlight in the early spring to bloom well. Because of this, it prefers deciduous forest understories near wetlands. Jack-in-the-pulpit is one of the first wildflowers to go dormant in the fall, dying back to its underground corm until spring. It may lose its leaves even earlier if it does not produce fruit. It emerges in early spring with its broad 3- or 5-lobed leaves tightly curled around the stem. Within a few more days, it unfurls them and stands up to 2 feet tall. The very distinctive flower is produced at ground level and sometimes stands as tall as the main leaf. If the tiny flowers are pollinated, bright red fruits ripen by early fall along the spadix.

Jack-in-the-pulpit is not commonly available from Florida sources, and plants from nurseries north of Florida do not generally perform well here. The dormant bulbs should be planted in the fall or winter and the planting sites marked. Otherwise, you are very likely to forget where they are. This is a fascinating wildflower for shady moist deciduous woodland areas, and it mixes well with a variety of ferns, and with wildflowers such as wild gingers and violets. Use it near walkways and paths, however, to be able to fully appreciate its wonderful flowers in the spring.

Spoonflower (*Peltandra virginica*)

Spoonflower is a wetland wildflower, and its use is restricted to water gardens and the edges of ponds and streams. In such a setting, it can be effectively used statewide and lends interest and beauty to the landscape. This is a deciduous species that dies back below ground during the winter. In early spring, it emerges much the same way as jack-in-the-pulpit, with its leaves coiled around the main stem. By late spring, its 3-lobed leaves stand several feet tall. Flowering occurs at this time. Spoonflower is not especially showy, and its main interest lies in its attractive foliage. The spathe surrounding the flower spike is green and blends in with the foliage. The ripe fruits in late summer are also green or greenish brown. Its close cousin (*P. sagittifolia*) has a white spathe and arrow-shaped foliage. This one is more striking but occurs only in the northern half of the state. Both species are only infrequently available in Florida from commercial growers, but they are worth seeking out. Mix them with other wetland species like iris, yellow canna, and native hibiscus in water less than 12 inches deep and in a setting expansive enough to show them off effectively.

Spoonflower (*Peltandra virginica*).

Aster Family—Asteraceae

Nearly half the species we think of as wildflowers are members of the aster family. The asters are a widespread and diverse family but share characteristics that separate them from other families. Most notable is the way the flowers are structured. Most asters have two distinct types of flowers arranged in a head. Typical asters have an outer row of ray petals surrounding a dense head of disk flowers. The white non-native Shasta daisy (*Chrysanthemum maximum*) serves as a familiar example of this compound flower structure. In the Shasta daisy, the white-petal ray flowers surround the yellow center. Each of these white petals represents an individual flower, and the yellow center comprises a great many individual and tubular disk flowers. All produce nectar, and each is capable of becoming pollinated and producing a seed. Exceptions do occur in this structure. A few, like the dandelion (*Taraxacum officinale*), produce only ray flowers, and a few others, like the rayless sunflower (*Helianthus radula*), have only disk flowers.

Asters are universally valuable as nectar sources for butterflies, bees, and other pollinators because they produce multiple flower heads, each composed of many individual flowers in close proximity of each other. This translates to bountiful nectar with little effort to retrieve it. Asters are

Typical aster family flower, showing the outer ray petals and inner disk flowers. Specifically pictured is the resindot sunflower (*Helianthus resinosus*).

also important to songbirds and small mammals for the fruit they produce. Aster fruit are properly known as achenes, oblong seeds covered in a thin husk or hull. Sunflower seeds are a familiar example of an achene. Achenes may have a feathery plume at one end that aids in their aerial dispersal away from the parent plant or have none (e.g., sunflowers) and simply fall away from the parent plant at maturity.

Recently, the genus *Aster* has been revised taxonomically, and many of its former North American members have been placed in the genus *Symphyotrichum*. The reason for this may seem confusing to those who are not plant taxonomists, but changes are based on new scientific information and on the rigid rules adopted by the International Bureau for Plant Taxonomy and Nomenclature.

Yellow Buttons (*Balduina angustifolia*)

Yellow buttons or honeycombhead is an annual or biennial, common to much of Florida's most well-drained upland habitats. For much of the year, it exists as a rather innocuous cluster of basal leaves. By summer, however, it begins its rapid growth upward and eventually reaches a mature height of up to 4 feet. Although the main stalk is rather thin and somewhat brittle, yellow buttons forms multiple stems near its top, and each of these develops large numbers of flower heads.

Yellow buttons (*Balduina angustifolia*).

Yellow buttons gets its common name from the bright yellow blooms (both the ray and disk flowers) that adorn its crown in late summer and fall. Individual flower heads are up to 2 inches in diameter. Yellow buttons requires excellent drainage and high levels of sunlight to prosper, and it needs bare sand if it is to reseed and become a persistent member of your wildflower planting. Because of its height, plant it near the back of a mixed species bed.

Greeneyes (*Berlandiera* spp.)

Florida is home to two wonderful species of greeneyes. Both are perennials and resident to well-drained sandy and sunny habitats, and both have bright yellow ray petals that surround a green central core. Given the right growing conditions, greeneyes are long lived and extremely tough. They form a deep taproot that gives them exceptional drought tolerance. They also produce large achenes attached by a papery bract. This bract does little to aid the heavy seeds in dispersal, and most of the seeds end up falling close to the parent plant. Over time, greeneyes will spread slowly by seed and fill in open gaps. Both species are commercially available.

Soft greeneyes (*Berlandiera pumila*).

Soft Greeneyes (*B. pumila*)

Soft greeneyes is found throughout the northern counties of the state but can be grown successfully further south into Central Florida. Soft greeneyes is deciduous during the winter and emerges in early spring. After it emerges, it quickly grows upright to a mature height of 18–24 inches. Soft greeneyes tends to have a distinct blooming season during late spring to early summer. The flowers may be 2½ inches across. Especially striking about them is that the disk flowers are bright red while they are open. Soft greeneyes is an excellent addition to the midregion of a mixed wildflower planting. Because it is upright, use it in small clusters of 3–5 plants for greatest impact.

Florida Greeneyes
(*B. subacaulis*)

Florida greeneyes is endemic to Florida and found mostly in the peninsula and eastern Panhandle. It is evergreen and spends the winter as a rosette of basal leaves, close to the ground. Florida greeneyes is also a bit more sprawling than soft greeneyes and tends to be more wide than tall. Mature specimens rarely stand taller than 1 foot. Flowering is most abundant in the late spring, but can occur year-round if winter temperatures do not get too cold. The flowers are a bit smaller in diameter than those of soft greeneyes, and the disk flowers are yellow instead of red. Florida greeneyes works

Florida greeneyes (*Berlandiera subacaulis*).

very well near the front half of a mixed wildflower planting but needs full sun and excellent drainage to perform at its best. It can be used as a mass planting as a border or is effective in small clusters when mixed with other medium-sized wildflowers and short grasses.

Sea Oxeye Daisy (*Borrichia frutescens*)

Sea oxeye daisy is resident in brackish water and coastal habitats throughout most of Florida, but it is extremely adaptable and can be planted in nearly any landscape setting except extremely droughty soils. Its silvery stems stand several feet tall, and these are clothed in thin silvery green foliage. Its bright yellow flowers are produced near the tops of each stem and

Sea oxeye daisy (*Borrichia frutescens*).

are present most months. In southern Florida, it may bloom through the winter. This wildflower makes a striking statement in the landscape, but it is not appropriate in small planting areas because it suckers extensively. Sea oxeye daisy is best used in areas where an expansive planting is desired. This species is commonly available from commercial nurseries.

Chaffheads (*Carphephorus* spp.)

The chaffheads are closely related to the blazing stars and share some of the same wonderful attributes of this widely grown genus. Six species occur in Florida, but only three are commonly available commercially. The chaffheads are deciduous during the winter and spend much of the spring and early summer as rosettes of bright green, almost succulent, leaves. Flowering occurs in fall, and all have extremely showy bright lavender flowers. They make a stunning addition to any landscape setting and are especially attractive to butterflies. Each species, however, has rather specific habitat needs that have to be met for it to prosper. In the right location, they are extremely tough and long lived. In the wrong location, they quickly expire and disappear. Use these species in clusters of no fewer than 3 plants, mixed with other wildflowers and native grasses.

Florida Paintbrush (*C. corymbosus*)

Florida paintbrush is perhaps the state's best butterfly magnet. Patches of blooming Florida paintbrush in the late summer and early fall seem to be perennially covered by butterflies of all kinds, and they stand out strikingly in the landscape. Named for the shape of its broad, flat flower head (i.e., corymbose), Florida paintbrush may stand as tall as 3 feet, and its flower heads may be nearly 6 inches across. This wildflower occurs in

Florida paintbrush (*Carphephorus corymbosus*) with nectaring monarch. Photo by Christina Evans, with permission.

well-drained sandy habitats throughout the peninsula and the eastern half of the Panhandle. Plant it in similar conditions in the home landscape. It will quickly perish if given too much moisture at its roots, but water it deep or it may wilt and not flower sufficiently. Sandy soils that allow water to percolate easily are the best soils for this species.

Vanilla Plant (*C. odoratissimus*)

Vanilla plant is found throughout most of Florida in the understory of mesic pinelands and open meadows. Its name comes from the vanilla-like fragrance of its leaves, especially noticeable when they wilt. In Florida's past, this plant was harvested commercially and the leaves added to pipe tobacco to lend its fragrance. This industry disappeared with the advent of artificial flavorings and now the plant is valuable mostly for its wonderful flowers. The flowers of vanilla plant are much smaller in size than those of the Florida paintbrush and deeper purple in color. Flowering occurs in late summer and early fall. The flower stalks may

Vanilla plant (*Carphephorus odoratissimus*).

stand 4–5 feet tall and make quite a dramatic effect when planted in a mass in large landscapes. Vanilla plant has less drought tolerance than Florida paintbrush and requires a bit of extra moisture during the summer season to prosper.

Deer Tongue (*C. paniculatus*)

Deer tongue is also found throughout much of Florida but occurs primarily in wetter sites than vanilla plant. Named for its club-shaped flower stalk and its long tongue-shaped leaves, deer tongue has flowers similar in size and shape to those of vanilla plant. Blooming occurs later in the fall, often after the other two species are nearly done. The flower stalks are about 3 feet tall. Deer tongue requires more moisture to survive than the other species described here and can tolerate shallow standing water for

Deer tongue (*Carphephorus paniculatus*).

weeks during the summer rainy season. Without additional moisture, it will decline and disappear.

Green-and-Gold (*Chrysogonum virginianum*)

Green-and-gold is a wonderful wildflower for the dappled sunlit edges and openings of a wooded landscape setting, although it can tolerate somewhat higher levels of sunlight if it has to. This wildflower is relatively rare in Florida but quite widespread in states to our north and west and is commonly used as a ground cover. The southern form of green-and-gold, (var. *australe*), hugs the ground and spreads by runners, much like a strawberry. Eventually, it forms colonies, its deep green, slightly

Green-and-gold (*Chrysogonum virginianum*).

toothed oval leaves providing a wonderful contrast to its bright yellow 5-petal flowers. Flowering occurs in spring and lasts for several weeks into early summer. Although green-and-gold is native to only a few counties in North Florida, it can be grown successfully into the central peninsula. Give it good drainage and dappled light. Too much moisture or deep shade will kill it quickly, but if you have filtered sun or morning sun at the edge of a trail or woodland, green-and-gold makes a wonderful addition to the landscape. Alone, it makes a beautiful ground cover for areas sometimes difficult to plant, but it mixes well with other wildflowers, grasses, and ferns of open deciduous forest habitats.

Goldenaster (*Chrysopsis* spp.)

The goldenasters are a diverse group of perennial wildflowers characterized by rounded basal leaves of varying degrees of "wooliness" and bright

The basal leaves of goldenasters (*Chrysopsis* spp.) are normally covered with dense white "hairs," even in species whose upper leaves are shiny, such as this narrowleaf goldenaster (*C. linearifolia*).

yellow daisylike flowers that bloom in the fall. The genus contains some of Florida's rarest species as well as some of our most common roadside weeds. The best species make very interesting additions to a mixed wildflower planting. Though some keep their basal rosette of leaves throughout the winter, all lose the rest of their foliage in winter and begin their upward growth in spring. They are native to well-drained soils and sunny areas, but most are adaptable to typical landscape conditions and extremely drought tolerant. Despite their adaptability and attractive flowers, very few are commonly grown and sold commercially.

Cottony Goldenaster (*C. gossypina*)

Cottony goldenaster is my favorite species in this genus, but almost never sold commercially. It occurs on coastal dunes and on well-drained sands in sandhill and scrub habitat throughout the Panhandle and the northern third of the peninsula. Cottony goldenaster exists as a basal rosette of woolly elliptical leaves for much of the year but produces numerous flower stalks in late summer that are procumbent, stretching out across the open sand for 2–4 feet before terminating in a cluster of flower heads that turns up slightly. Each flower head is nearly 1 inch across. If you have room for the sprawling flower stalks, cottony goldenaster makes a striking addition

Cottony goldenaster (*Chrysopsis gossypina*).

to a coastal or scrub wildflower planting. Give it some space and mix it with any false rosemary (*Conradina* spp.), beach verbena (*Glandularia maritima*), dune sunflower, sea oats, and similar species.

Maryland Goldenaster (*C. mariana*)

Maryland goldenaster is frequently found in well-drained pinelands throughout North Florida and south to the central peninsula. This species is more compact than most other members of this genus and rarely stands taller than 18 inches. It has elliptical bright green foliage and produces large yellow flowers from summer into early fall. Its compact growth form, attractive foliage, and wonderful blooms make it a worthwhile candidate for home landscapes, but it is only rarely offered in Florida. Though native nurseries throughout the eastern half of the United States frequently offer it for sale, such plants are unlikely to thrive in Florida.

Maryland goldenaster (*Chrysopsis mariana*). Photo by Shirley Denton, with permission.

Coastalplain goldenaster (*Chrysopsis scabrella*).

Coastalplain Goldenaster (*C. scabrella*)

Coastalplain goldenaster is the one member of this genus regularly offered commercially. It tends to be a bit lanky in its growth form and may reach 3–4 feet tall at blooming time in early fall. The blooms are similar to those of other species described above but are confined to the crown. Flowering lasts for several weeks in the late summer or fall. This wildflower is common in well-drained soils throughout much of Florida, except for the western Panhandle, and is quite adaptable. Because of its size, coastalplain goldenaster is best used near the back of a mixed wildflower planting where it can blend in with other robust species and be noticed mostly during its extended fall blooming season.

Mistflower (*Conoclinium coelestinum*)

With its powder-blue flowers, mistflower provides an attractive addition to the home landscape. In Florida, it is native to the sunny edges of wetland habitats nearly statewide. In the landscape, it has more drought tolerance than might be expected and can be grown in many landscape settings if it receives some additional moisture during extended periods

Mistflower (*Conoclinium coelestinum*).

of drought and less than full sun. It can tolerate more sun when grown in wetter conditions. Mistflower is a rather sprawling, multistemmed plant. When grown in sunny wet conditions, it often grows fairly erect and may reach nearly 3 feet in height, but in other settings, it often falls over as it gets larger and may require staking to look its best.

What it lacks in form, it makes up for in flowers. Mistflower blooms from late spring through late fall, and the broad flower heads may contain more than 50 individual sky blue flowers. When grown in mass, this display is quite attractive. Mistflower can be quite variable in flower color, size, and growth form. It also tends to spread in the landscape over time because of the large numbers of seeds it produces. Before including this species in your landscape, make sure you start with high-quality plants with the attributes you want.

Tickseeds (*Coreopsis* spp.)

Tickseeds are found throughout Florida in a wide variety of habitats. Their universal presence and bright yellow ray flowers appealed enough to the state legislature to get them adopted as the State Wildflower in 1991. The legislators adopted all 12 species in the genus. Tickseeds vary greatly in growth habit and form. Most have bright yellow ray flowers, but one species has pink: Georgia tickseed (*C. nudata*). Most prefer moist soils and full sun, but a great many are adaptable and suitable to typical landscape settings. Several are widely grown and available commercially for the home landscape.

Lanceleaf tickseed (*Coreopsis lanceolata*).

Lanceleaf Tickseed (*C. lanceolata*)

Lanceleaf tickseed is common to a wide variety of upland and moist-soil sites throughout the northern half of Florida. I sometimes call it "honeymoon coreopsis" as Alexa and I first noticed it growing in profusion during our honeymoon trip through North Florida. We have grown it ever since in our Pinellas County landscape from the few seeds we collected along a roadside due shortly to be mowed. As its name implies, lanceleaf tickseed has long linear leaves, sometimes three-parted, but often not. They form a dense basal rosette that may span more than 12 inches. Blooming occurs in late spring and may occur sporadically into the summer. The flower stalks are 2–3 feet in height, and each flower head may be 2 inches across. Both the ray and disk flowers are bright yellow in color. Lanceleaf tickseed is a short-lived perennial, but it persists well over time through reseeding. Plant this species near the front half of a mixed wildflower bed and do not mulch around it too heavily. Given some bare soil for its seed to fall into, lanceleaf tickseed will remain a beautiful focal point for a great many years.

Common Tickseed (*C. leavenworthii*)

Common tickseed is the species most often called "coreopsis." It is found nearly throughout Florida and is extremely common in nearly every type of open, moist-soil habitat. And, despite its natural affinity for moisture, it is very adaptable and commonly grown in sites significantly more droughty. Common tickseed is a lanky annual that will never win awards for its foliage.

Common tickseed (*Coreopsis leavenworthii*).

After starting out as a basal rosette of rather thin leaves, it rapidly grows up-ward, producing multilobed but small leaves upward on the stem. Common tickseed eventually reaches a mature height of about 2–3 feet and produces bright yellow flowers on the tips of the stems. Flowering can occur dur-ing nearly every month from late spring through fall. Individual flowers are rather small (about 1 inch across) with a dark disk. Common tickseed produces large numbers of seeds and spreads rapidly if conditions are favorable. For this reason, I often restrict its reseeding by deadheading many of them. This is a species that looks best when planted in a mass. Individual plants can be almost unnoticed; a mass of it can be spectacular.

Purple Coneflower (*Echinacea purpurea*)

Purple coneflower is a common component of open prairie and glades communities throughout much of the eastern two-thirds of North Amer-ica, but it is naturally quite rare in Florida and occurs in only two counties along the Georgia border. Because of its rarity here, many of the plants offered for sale in Florida originate from sources to our north, and this fact may help explain the difficulty in maintaining this species in the land-scape everywhere except in northernmost Florida. Purple coneflower is

Purple coneflower (*Echinacea purpurea*).

a beautiful wildflower and a wonderful butterfly and wildlife plant. Its rough dark green leaves appear each spring and are arrow shaped and form a dense rosette just above the soil surface. The flower stalk begins development in late spring, and flowering in Florida typically occurs in summer. Although flower stalks may reach 4–5 feet tall in the Midwestern prairies where I was born, they are often shorter in Florida and rarely exceed 3 feet. Flower heads are normally smaller, too, often only several inches across.

Purple coneflower is distinctive nonetheless. The bright pink-lavender ray petals surround a spiky central disk of orange-colored disk flowers. Individual plants often produce many flower stems, and individual flower heads can persist for weeks before fading. Purple coneflower seeds are eagerly eaten by seed-eating birds.

In areas south of our first few tiers of counties, treat this species as a short-lived perennial or even an annual. Collect or purchase seed each year, and keep it going by sowing seed in good potting soil in the fall and transplanting the seedlings back into your planting bed in late winter. Despite the work, purple coneflower adds a lot of character to a mixed bed of wildflowers and native grasses. Plant it in small clusters of 3–5 plants each in the middle section of your planting area. It is especially attractive combined with other medium-tall wildflowers, such as yellow coneflower (*Ratibida pinnata*) and butterfly milkweed (*Asclepias tuberosa*) as well as medium-tall grasses such as Elliot's lovegrass and hairawn muhly grass.

Elephant's Foot (*Elephantopus elatus*)

Although this genus contains several similar-looking species, only this one is likely to be propagated and made available to the home gardener. Elephant's foot gets its common name from the shape of its large basal

Elephant's foot (*Elephantopus elatus*).

leaves, though I believe it takes some imagination to see the "elephant's foot" in them. These leaves are 4–6 inches long and form a dense rosette at ground level. In most of Florida, these leaves persist through the winter. Flower stalks are produced in early summer and may reach 3–4 feet tall. The individual flowers have light lavender to almost pink ray flowers and tiny white disk flowers. Although they are small, individual flower heads may contain several dozen open flowers at any one time. Elephant's foot tends to wander in a garden setting, spreading slowly from its basal rosette from areas where it is first planted and establishing new plants from seed. Although this is not one of Florida's showiest wildflowers, it has a certain charm and can be attractive if planted in clusters in settings that are somewhat expansive. Elephant's foot can tolerate partial shade as well as full sun and is adaptable to moist and dry soils. Use it in a mixed wildflower planting near the middle of the bed and cluster it in groupings of at least 5 plants per cluster.

Thoroughworts (*Eupatorium* spp.)

Florida has a total of 16 species of thoroughworts, and they occur in nearly every type of habitat across the state. A few are rare, but most are common components of open wet to dry habitats. The extremely common weed,

Most thoroughworts (*Eupatorium* spp.) are quite similar to each other and differ slightly in leaf shape and shape of the flower heads. Most are nearly interchangeable in the wildflower garden. This is semaphore thoroughwort (*E. mikanioides*), common to the southern half of Florida in moist open habitats.

dog fennel (*E. capillifolium*), is a member of this genus and found nearly everywhere in Florida where soil is disturbed. All species are deciduous perennials, and most have rather broad flat heads of small white flowers. A few have pink to light purple blooms. Many species are difficult for the average person to identify and only a few are commonly cultivated and available to the home gardener. All can be interesting additions to the landscape if planted in scattered clumps of multiple plants in areas expansive enough to accommodate them. I do not recommend most of them, however, in small garden settings as they tend not to be very showy close up.

Joe-Pye Weed (*E. fistulosum*)

Joe-pye weed is a wonderful butterfly nectar plant and a commonly recommended addition to butterfly gardens across most of eastern North America. In Florida, it is native only to the northern half of the state and does not perform well too far south of its native range. Despite its ability to attract butterflies, joe-pye weed is a difficult choice for most landscape settings. It requires moist soils to perform well, becomes extremely tall, and suckers extensively. Joe-pye weed grows rapidly in the spring from its overwintering basal leaves and reaches a mature height of 6–9 feet by late summer. Once planted, it quickly forms large dense colonies and dominates the landscape. Therefore, joe-pye weed is best used in areas where the moist soils are clearly confined by drier uplands. Given the right location, it can be stunning. Its large masses of deep pink flowers provide a focal point that can't help but turn heads. Use it at the edges of ponds and marshes

Joe-pye weed (*Eupatorium fistulosum*).

where a natural look is desired. A good companion plant for this setting would be Elliott's aster (*Symphyotrichum elliottii*).

Mohr's Thoroughwort (*E. mohrii*)

Mohr's thoroughwort is resident to pineland habitats throughout most of Florida and adaptable to typical home landscape settings. Because of its adaptability, it is often grown commercially, but it is not particularly striking alone in the landscape. The elliptical foliage is rather nondescript but serves to identify it from other closely related members of this genus. It reaches its mature height of about 3 feet by late summer and produces flat heads of bright white flowers. Although not especially showy, Mohr's thoroughwort adds valuable diversity to a mixed planting of native grasses and wildflowers. Plant it in small groupings, no closer than 3 feet apart, in the central portion of the bed and add it into expansive naturalistic

Mohr's thoroughwort
(*Eupatorium mohrii*).

plantings. Mohr's thoroughwort suckers in the garden, but not aggressively. It also may spread by seeding.

Blanket Flower (*Gaillardia pulchella*)

Blanket flower is one of the most easily recognized and widely used wildflowers in Florida. In nature, it is most common on beach dunes, where it occurs with species such as dune sunflower, beach verbena, and blue porterweed (*Stachytarpheta jamaicensis*). It is extremely adaptable, however, and will thrive in nearly any setting statewide where the soils are reasonably well drained and where it receives full sun.

Blanket flower acts like an annual in most garden settings, regardless of climate. Individual plants grow quickly to their mature size (18–24 inches tall and 12–18 inches across), bloom profusely for several months, and then die. At this time, they should be allowed enough time to scatter their mature seeds. Even though the dead flowers look unkempt, deadheading these plants too early will prevent them from reproducing, and your population will rapidly decline over time. If you scatter the seeds, or let nature do it for you, new seedlings will appear as soon as the rains return in late spring or early summer.

Use this wildflower in mixed plantings with other species that share its growing requirements. It will crowd out smaller diminutive species, and it won't perform well if planted among species that shade it. Blanket flower will ramble throughout a garden once planted, so be prepared to thin the seedlings if they appear in locations where they are not wanted. I have found blanket flower in my backyard when every plant in my landscape was in my front yard the year before. The brightly colored outer petals (the ray flowers) come in a vari-

Blanket flower (*Gaillardia pulchella*) with nectaring gulf fritillary.

ety of shades, colors, and forms. This diversity adds to its charm and will be most noticeable if you let your plants reseed naturally.

Garberia (*Garberia heterophylla*)

Garberia is a woody shrub native to the excessively well-drained sands of Florida's scrub communities. It is endemic to Florida, listed as a threatened species, and naturally occurs only within the central portion of the peninsula, but, despite its natural rarity, garberia can be grown throughout much of Florida if given the right soil and sunlight conditions. Garberia produces a brittle woody stem that eventually reaches 3–4 feet tall. It also produces multiple branches, creating an irregular shape and a broad, rounded crown. Its leaves are evergreen, rounded, and blue-green in color. Garberia is unlikely to be planted as a foliage plant except by those looking for something unusual. What makes it exceptional are its flowers.

Garberia (*Garberia heterophylla*).

In the fall, the crown of a well-grown garberia is covered with light lavender-pink blooms, making the annual wait worthwhile. Few wildflowers attract more butterflies than garberia, though it also appeals to bees and other pollinators.

Its major drawback in the home garden is its great sensitivity to growing conditions. I have killed a great many individuals in my life by planting them in locations without the necessary drainage. Garberia requires pure sand to prosper and good light levels to grow and bloom properly. It will forgive partial shade, but not saturated soils. Plant them no closer than 3 feet apart and near the back of a mixed wildflower planting. Do not crowd them with other species. Good tall companion plants include yellow buttons, palafoxias (*Palafoxia* spp.), and many of the blazing stars. Garberia is routinely propagated by commercial native plant nurseries.

Sunflowers (*Helianthus* spp.)

It makes sense that in a land as sunny as Florida, we would have a large number of sunflowers in our native flora. Florida is home to 16 species, and several commonly grown non-natives including Jerusalem artichoke

(*H. tuberosus*) and annual sunflower (*H. annuus*), the source of commercial sunflower seeds. For the most part, sunflowers are deciduous perennials that thrive in open sunny locations. Many become quite tall and common to moist soil habitats, but there are notable exceptions that make wonderful additions to drier sites. Nearly all spread throughout the landscape by underground suckers and eventually form dense colonies in areas where their habitat needs are met. Most sunflowers have broad yellow-petal flowers and make very showy additions to the landscape. Only a few, however, are generally available through commercial sources for the home landscape. It is hoped that more will be grown in the future.

Narrowleaf Sunflower (*H. angustifolius*)

Narrowleaf sunflower is extremely common throughout the northern two-thirds of Florida and can be grown even further south if added to a landscape with the proper growing conditions. This species prefers the moist soils found at the edges of open wetlands and ditches, but it can also be found in upland areas. Although it is adaptable to drier sites, it will fail if kept too dry for too long—especially during the heat of summer. This is one of our tallest species and grows rapidly each summer to its mature height of 6 feet or more. Flowering occurs in late summer and early fall. The flower heads are composed of yellow ray petals surrounding a dark central disk. As this plant suckers aggressively in moist soil, it will eventually colonize large areas. This can be a problem in the wrong location, but spectacular at the edges of ponds or

Narrowleaf sunflower (*Helianthus angustifolius*).

in swales where it can be confined by adjacent uplands. Do not use this plant in small landscape settings as it is simply too large.

Dune or Beach Sunflower (*H. debilis*)

Dune or beach sunflower is the most widely grown native sunflower in Florida and available from a wide variety of commercial growers. Native to coastal dunes along the east coast of Florida to around Titusville and the west coast north to Pinellas County, it can be grown outside this range if given well-drained soils and plenty of sun. The only conditions that will kill it are shade, soils that remain wet, or excessively cold temperatures. Temperatures in the mid-20s F may damage the above-ground foliage, but it will resprout unless exposed to prolonged cold below that. In better conditions, it may bloom year-round and spread outward from the main stem to form a large plant many feet across. The west coast form (*H. debilis* subsp. *debilis*) tends to stand taller (about 1–2 feet) than the east coast form (*H. debilis* subsp. *vestitus*), which is quite prostrate. Use this species to cover open sandy areas in full sun, and be prepared to prune it occasionally to maintain it where it is wanted. It may also spread by seed. Dune sunflower makes a showy border wildflower if used alone, but can

Dune sunflower (*Helianthus debilis*).

be added to mixed coastal plantings. Use it with blanket flower, beach verbena, and any of the coastal morning glories (*Ipomoea* spp.) and combine it with sea oats and bitter panic grass if you are fortunate enough to require a coastal dune planting.

Florida Sunflower (*H. floridanus*)

Florida sunflower is quite similar to narrowleaf sunflower, described above. The leaves are wider, and the flowers differ in that the central disk flowers are often yellow instead of dark purplish red. Florida sunflower occurs naturally only within the northeastern peninsula and should not be attempted in South Florida. Otherwise, it has similar growth habits to those of narrowleaf sunflower and similar growing needs. Florida sunflower is only rarely offered for sale by commercial growers.

Florida sunflower (*Helianthus floridanus*). Photo by Shirley Denton, with permission.

Rayless Sunflower (*H. radula*)

Rayless sunflower is the most unusual member of this genus in Florida. As its common name suggests, the typical yellow ray petals are absent or greatly reduced, and all that remains is the central disk. While these purplish tubular flowers attract a wide assortment of butterflies and other pollinators, they are not showy. The aesthetics of this plant lie in its strangeness and its foliage. Rayless sunflower inhabits open pinelands and fields and prefers soils that are seasonally moist. It is quite adaptable, though, to typical landscape settings and does not require supplemental watering except in periods of extreme prolonged drought.

The broad, deep green, rounded hairy leaves hug the ground, and the plants form extensive colonies over time. Blooming occurs in the

late summer and early fall and persists for many weeks. The flower stalks stand 1–2 feet above the basal leaves, and each plant may produce several. Use this plant in a mixed wildflower setting with species with showier blooms, such as the chaffheads and blazing stars. In a mixed setting, its unusual flowers and attractive foliage add a unique element to the overall landscape, and the butterflies it attracts make its inclusion worthwhile.

Rayless sunflower (*Helianthus radula*).

Resindot Sunflower (*H. resinosus*)

Resindot sunflower is one of our few native sunflowers resident in deep sandy inland habitats. As such, it can be used in settings where most other native sunflowers fail. It occurs naturally in only three central Panhandle counties but is common in states immediately north of us. Resindot sunflower gets its name from the many glands that dot the upper surfaces of its leaves. The broad deep green leaves are rough to the touch, and the tiny hairs that cover their surface and the surface of the stems are visible on close examination. This is a robust species that may reach 6 feet tall or more by late summer. Numerous side stems are produced, and the ends of all the branches produce multiple flower buds. The fully opened flower heads may be 3 inches across. Both the ray and disk flowers are bright yellow.

Because of its size, use this species near the back of a mixed wildflower planting or in the interior of a more-extensive landscape. It is adaptable to most landscape settings, but needs good drainage and high sunlight for best performance. Although it is naturally rare in Florida, we have grown it for years in several Pinellas County landscapes, and I believe it can be used in most parts of the state if given the conditions it prefers. Resindot sunflower will sucker but not as aggressively as most and usually only near the parent plant. Few commercial sources currently exist for it, but this may change as the demand for more drought-tolerant wildflowers increases.

Resindot sunflower (*Helianthus resinosus*).

Woodland Sunflower (*H. strumosus*)

Woodland sunflower is another tall sunflower resident to North Florida. Like the resindot sunflower, however, it can be successfully grown well south of its range if given the proper growing conditions. As its name suggests, woodland sunflower occurs in open woods and at the edges of shady woodlands. It performs best when not planted in full sun and given soil that is somewhat moist. It has quite a bit of drought tolerance when given filtered or part sun, but it will succumb quickly if summer rains are spotty and extra moisture is not supplied. Woodland sunflower is a lanky plant with a thin stem that often bends over under the weight of the developing flower heads. It reaches 6 feet tall or more by its late summer blooming season and flowers for many weeks. The flower heads are nearly 3 inches across, and the bright yellow ray petals are more pointed than those of most other species. Given the right conditions, woodland sunflower suckers extensively in the landscape and over a year or two

may produce hundreds of individual stems. Too much shade or sun (or droughty soils) will limit its spread, but it is difficult to control elsewhere. Woodland sunflower is often available from commercial growers in Florida.

Woodland sunflower
(*Helianthus strumosus*).

Blazing Stars or Gayfeathers (*Liatris* spp.)

I have an extreme fondness for blazing stars. I incorporate them into every wildflower garden I plant and grow as many species as I can. Their tall spires of rich lavender flowers are my favorite signal that fall is here, and the huge numbers of butterflies they attract keep me fascinated as I survey my garden each fall. Florida has more blazing star species than any state or province in North America (17) and more endemic species (4). They occur in nearly every habitat and growing condition, and they vary from being extremely common to exceedingly rare. Blazing stars are deciduous. Most spend the winter underground as a corm, but a few remain as basal rosettes of grasslike leaves. They send up their flower stalks in summer. Young plants are likely to produce only one, but the corms of older plants eventually get quite large and produce multiple stems. Blooming occurs once the stalk is fully mature, and the buds at the top open first. Relatively few of our many blazing stars are commonly available from commercial sources. I have included these and a few others below.

This mixed patch of blazing stars (*Liatris* spp.) near Brooksville, Hernando County, is a magnet for pollinating insects. The dominant species is elegant blazing star (*L. elegans*).

Chapman's Blazing Star (*L. chapmanii*)

Chapman's blazing star is one of many restricted to sites with deep, well-drained sands and plenty of sun. It occurs across Florida but is extremely sensitive to habitat conditions. Chapman's blazing star produces a rather stout flower stalk, and the leaves follow it upward well past the lower buds. The length of the flower stalks varies; heights of 2–4 feet are most common. Blooming begins in September, a month earlier than most. Because of the plant's stout nature, the flower stalks are not as prone to falling over as a few other species. Chapman's blazing star is a wonderful addition to a mixed wildflower planting, but it needs nearly perfect drainage to survive. Soils that remain too wet or compacted will cause the corms to rot.

Chapman's blazing star (*Liatris chapmanii*).

Elegant Blazing Star (*L. elegans*)

Elegant blazing star is unique among Florida species as its flowers are actually white. The pinkish or light lavender color is caused by the bracts that surround the flower heads. Elegant blazing star occurs naturally only within the northern half of Florida in well-drained sandy habitats. It has a bit more tolerance of soil moisture than Chapman's blazing star, but they often occur together in nature. Elegant blazing star eventually reaches a mature height of 3–4 feet. The flower stalks are thick and have an overall "fuzzy" appearance. Blooming occurs in

Elegant blazing star (*Liatris elegans*).

October. This is a rather fussy species and performs well only when given sandy soils with excellent drainage and full sun. I have grown it successfully in Pinellas County, but it is not a good choice for South Florida landscapes. Its flower stalks also have a tendency to tip over and may require staking to keep them upright. This tendency is reduced if the plants are not grown in soil too fertile or conditions too shady.

Garber's Blazing Star (*L. garberi*)

Garber's blazing star is a tropical blazing star, found only in the southern half of the Florida peninsula and in the pinelands of the Bahamas. Because of this, it is the best choice for South Florida landscapes in areas that have less than perfect drainage. It is a very adaptable species and can be grown into North Central Florida and in a variety of growing conditions. Garber's blazing star is one of just a few species that can survive periodic/seasonal inundation by water and short-term drought. The flower stalks are shorter than most other species, rarely standing taller than 3 feet and often less. Blooming begins in September. Because of its more diminutive nature, plant this species in clusters of at least 5 and scatter them throughout the front half of a mixed wildflower planting. This species is only rarely offered, but it is well worth seeking out, especially by gardeners in the southern half of Florida.

Garber's blazing star (*Liatris garberi*).

Graceful blazing star (*Liatris gracilis*).

Graceful Blazing Star (*L. gracilis*)

Graceful blazing star is one of the most widely distributed and adaptable blazing stars in Florida and a wonderful candidate for most landscape settings. Graceful blazing star occurs in well-drained soils throughout Florida, but it will tolerate short periods of saturation. Flower stalks reach a mature height of 4–5 feet, and flowering occurs in October and early November. The flower buds are held well away from the main stem by tiny stalks called pedicles. This gives the whole flowering stalk a rather bushy appearance, though the individual flowers are actually quite small. Graceful blazing star is one of the easiest members of this genus to maintain in the landscape and can be grown statewide in soils of varying drainage. It will not tolerate excessive moisture, however. Because of the plant's structure, the flowering stalks are often prone to falling over and may require staking to keep them fully upright. This species reseeds easily in most garden settings and is likely to increase its numbers over time, if allowed to. Thankfully, this is one of the most widely available blazing stars from commercial growers and relatively easy to find.

Clusterleaf Blazing Star (*L. laevigata*; syn. *L. tenuifolia* var. *quadriflora*)

Clusterleaf blazing star is subject to a bit of taxonomic debate. Most Florida taxonomists consider it to be a variety of the more widely distributed scrub blazing star (*L. tenuifolia*) described below, but it has very distinct characteristics, and I have sided with those who consider it a separate species. Clusterleaf blazing star is distributed throughout Florida but confined to areas with deep, excessively well-drained sands. In those areas, it is rather common and a beautiful addition to the natural landscape. Unlike scrub blazing star, clusterleaf blazing star produces a thick rosette of basal leaves that are nearly ¼ inch wide and sometimes evergreen. In my gardens in Pinellas County, where I grow it and scrub blazing star side by side, it tends to bloom a few weeks earlier (early October), and the flower buds are a bit larger and held more outward from the flower stalk. This species makes a wonderful addition to a mixed wildflower planting, but only

Clusterleaf blazing star (*Liatris laevigata*).

in sunny locations with deep sands. It is often available from commercial sources, but most do not distinguish it from scrub blazing star and may actually have both species mixed together in the same growing area. Make sure you get the species you expect.

Dense Blazing Star (*L. spicata*)

Dense blazing star is the only species common to wetland edges and open habitats that sometimes stay flooded for weeks at a time. It is very adaptable, however, and does well in most typical home landscape settings, tol-

erating more drought than might be expected. Dense blazing star occurs statewide except in the Keys and is common to a great many natural landscapes. It is a robust, showy species and often stands 5 feet tall or more by blooming time. Relatively large flower buds are held tightly to the main stalk. The flowers open in October, and blooming is typically over by early November. Despite the plant's height at maturity, the stalks do not commonly fall over and they require staking only occasionally. Plant this species in clusters of at least 5 and use it near the back of a mixed wildflower planting. Like graceful blazing star, it reseeds itself well in most garden settings and will increase its numbers over time. A very closely related species, described only for the south-central west coast of Florida, savanna blazing star (*L. savannensis*), is sometimes sold as dense blazing star. It can be told apart from dense blazing star by the tiny teeth on the margins of the bracts that lie just below the flower buds and by noticeable hairs on the lower half of the leaf margins. This species is native to pineland habitats and more tolerant of droughty soils, and it should be grown commercially for gardeners in the southern half of the state.

Dense blazing star (*Liatris spicata*).

Scrub blazing star (*Liatris tenuifolia*).

Scrub Blazing Star or Grassleaf Blazing Star (*L. tenuifolia*)

Scrub blazing star is very similar to clusterleaf blazing star, but its leaves are very thin and needlelike and its flower stalk tends to be shorter with smaller flowers held close to the stalk. This species is not one of our showier members, but it is especially useful in extending the blazing star blooming period in the landscape, generally being the last to bloom in early November. This species requires excellent drainage and high sunlight to perform well, but it makes a good addition to a wildflower landscape composed of species with similar requirements. Mix it with Chapman's, elegant, and clusterleaf blazing stars as well as with silkgrasses (*Pityopsis* spp.), scrub buckwheat (*Eriogonum* spp.), eastern silver aster (*Symphyotrichum concolor*) and others, and place it near the front half of the planting area or it will get lost among its more robust neighbors.

Salt-and-Pepper (*Melanthera nivea*)

Salt-and-pepper occurs statewide in a variety of habitats, from moist to well drained. In many situations, it appears weedy and seems an unlikely candidate for the home landscape. Specimens grown in low light levels or in rich soils can reach 3–4 feet in height, with woody stems and rather coarse leaves. In high light and lower nutrient soils, it remains shorter and denser, characteristics that generally make it more attractive in the

Salt-and-pepper (*Melanthera nivea*). Photo by Roger Hammer, with permission.

landscape. What keeps this wildflower in demand and almost always available from commercial growers is its wonderful blooms. Well-grown salt-and-pepper produces huge numbers of flower heads, and each is composed of many small bright white tubular flowers. Flowering occurs throughout most of the year if freezing weather does not interrupt it. The common name comes from its unusual black anthers (the pollen-producing part of the flower). The contrasting black and white is striking, and the flowers attract a wide assortment of pollinating insects, including butterflies. Salt-and-pepper is a deciduous perennial. Maintain its shape by regular pruning unless you like the natural, somewhat straggly look. Use it near the back of a mixed wildflower planting or in a mass as a border, with each plant spaced about 3 feet apart.

Golden Ragwort (*Packera aurea*; syn. *Senecio aureus*)

Golden ragwort occurs naturally only within a three-county area of the north-central Panhandle in open wetland edges. It is the only perennial

Golden ragwort (*Packera aurea*).

member of this small genus and often keeps its round basal leaves through the winter. Golden ragwort is somewhat "weedy" in nature but makes a very interesting addition to a wetland wildflower planting when grown in cultivation. Its rosette of glossy 8-inch leaves is attractive, especially if planted in clumps. Flowering occurs in spring. The 2–3-foot stalks are multibranched, and all the buds occur at the tips, making for a dense rounded crown of bright yellow blooms. Both the ray and disk flowers are yellow.

Golden ragwort is the only member of this genus that is sold commercially, and it is only occasionally offered. It has some tolerance of drought but needs to be kept moist to wet during the heat of summer. If kept wet, it will tolerate full sun, but it seems to do best if given filtered sun or full sun for half days. It has prospered in my wetland garden planting in Pinellas County for many years and can likely be used throughout much of the peninsula if given the appropriate conditions. Although it has a rather short blooming season, its flowers come on early in the season at a time when many others aren't in bloom, and its attractive foliage provides a counterpoint to less verdant species with which it might be planted.

Palafoxia (*Palafoxia* spp.)

Another robust member of the aster family is palafoxia. Two species in this genus are commonly available from commercial sources, and they share many characteristics. Both occur in well-drained sandy soils and full sun, and both are deciduous multistemmed perennials that become quite tall at maturity, about 4–5 feet by late summer. Blooming occurs in the fall, and large numbers of white to pinkish white flowers adorn the ends of each stem. There are no ray flowers, only disk flowers in each head. The flowers are tubular in shape, and the anthers and stigmas (the reproductive parts of the flower) extend out of the tubes and curl backward. This gives them a very unique appearance.

Palafoxias require large spaces or they can look out of place in the landscape. If given the right conditions, however, they make a very attractive addition to a mixed planting. Use them as screens near the back of the planting area or in the middle of expansive landscapes. Because of their height, they mix well with other tall wildflowers native to open, excessively well-drained sites. Good choices would be resindot sunflower, kidneyleaf rosinweed (*Silphium compositum*), various blazing stars, sky blue salvia (*Salvia azurea*), and eastern silver aster. Good grasses to add to this planting would be lop-sided Indiangrass and splitbeard bluestem.

Feay's Palafoxia (*P. feayi*)

Feay's palafoxia is endemic to Florida. It grows a bit taller than coastalplain palafoxia (*P. integrifolia*), described below, and the overall aspect of the plant is a bit coarser. In this species, the flower heads are smaller and the flowers are decidedly tubular.

Feay's palafoxia
(*Palafoxia feayi*).

Coastalplain Palafoxia (*P. integrifolia*)

Coastalplain palafoxia stands about 1 foot shorter on average (3–4 feet) than its close cousin, and the heads of its flowers are a bit broader and more likely to be pinkish in color. The individual flowers have recurved petals surrounding the tubular center, and this gives them a fuzzier, more dainty appearance. Coastalplain palafoxia occurs in much of Florida except for the western Panhandle and is more adaptable to a typical well-drained garden setting.

Coastalplain palafoxia
(*Palafoxia integrifolia*).

Phoebanthus (*Phoebanthus grandiflorus*)

Two species of phoebanthus are native to Florida. Both are endemic, but only one is likely to be available from commercial sources. The other, thin-leaved phoebanthus (*P. tenuifolius*), is found only in a small area of the Panhandle and is quite similar to its more common cousin. Phoebanthus occurs throughout the peninsula in well-drained sunny locations. It is a deciduous perennial that dies back to the ground in late fall and appears again in early spring. The thin, wirelike stems grow quickly and eventually reach a mature height of about 3–4 feet in early summer. Stiff linear leaves are alternate on the stems and rather tiny and inconspicuous, making this species less aesthetically attractive than many other asters from a foliage perspective. It's the broad yellow flowers, produced for weeks during the early summer, that recommend this wildflower for the home landscape. A single flower, 2–3 inches in diameter, is produced atop each 4-foot stem. The thin bright yellow ray petals and flattened core of yellow disk flowers are somewhat reminiscent of some of our sunflowers, and the two genera

Phoebanthus
(*Phoebanthus
grandiflorus*).

are closely related. Like most sunflowers, phoebanthus suckers profusely underground and eventually produces expansive stands where conditions are to its liking. But, because each stem is so thin and wiry, it does not tend to crowd out other robust species planted with it.

Phoebanthus is only occasionally available from commercial sources, but it is worth seeking out for certain landscape settings. It is not a good choice for small planting beds because it is tall and difficult to contain. Use it in larger landscapes in full sun and sandy soils with excellent drainage, and combine it with other taller wildflowers and native grasses. Few wildflowers bloom as early in the summer as phoebanthus. Because of this, its inclusion can extend the blooming season of a sandhill planting and add a great amount of interest to the landscape.

Narrowleaf Silkgrass or Grass-Leaved Goldenaster (*Pityopsis graminifolia*)

Four species of silkgrasses occur in Florida, but only narrowleaf silkgrass is widely sold in Florida by commercial nurseries. In North Florida, pineland silkgrass (*P. aspera*) is sometimes also sold, though the two may be intermingled and misidentified at the nursery. Narrowleaf silkgrass is an extremely common component of many of Florida's sunny open habitats statewide, and it tolerates a wide range of soil moisture conditions, from xeric sandhills and scrubs to moist prairies and flatwoods. The common

Narrowleaf silkgrass (*Pityopsis graminifolia*). Photo by Christina Evans, with permission.

denominator for its presence is sun, as it will not tolerate too much shade. Narrowleaf silkgrass earns its name from its grasslike leaves covered with silvery silky hairs. The dense hairs give the leaf blades a very distinctive appearance and lend an aesthetic quality that makes this wildflower a wonderful foliage plant. Though it is deciduous, narrowleaf silkgrass is absent for only a short time in the winter. For much of the year, it blends into the true grasses that occur around it, standing 1–2 feet tall. Blooming usually begins in the fall and lasts well into early winter, depending on temperature. Masses of small yellow aster flowers cover the crowns of each plant. Flower size is quite variable; the larger-flowered forms may be 1 inch across and nearly twice as large as others. Narrowleaf silkgrass seems to rebel against open spaces and suckers outward from the parent plant to fill in any gaps around it. It is not aggressive, though, and gives way to large, more robust neighbors. It also produces large numbers of seed and reproduces this way too.

Narrowleaf silkgrass is one of the best wildflowers to mix with other species, regardless of soil conditions. It can form the foundation for other taller wildflowers and adds color when few others are still doing so in early winter. Give it open sunny conditions and it is likely to persist forever. Narrowleaf silkgrass is a favorite forage plant for rabbits, and they will keep it in check if present. If you have rabbits, you may need to protect your plantings to get them established. After that, it is unlikely that their foraging will harm them.

Yellow Coneflower (*Ratibida pinnata*)

Yellow coneflower is a common component of the tallgrass prairies of the Midwest and much of the eastern half of North America, but in Florida it occurs naturally only in limestone glades in Liberty and Gadsden

Yellow coneflower
(*Ratibida pinnata*).

counties, on our border with Georgia. Thankfully, this wonderful wild-flower is adaptable to a wide variety of open upland habitats and can be effectively used in landscapes throughout much of North and Central Florida. Plant it in sunny locations with well-drained soils and ample moisture during the growing season. It has good drought tolerance but will expire if exposed to prolonged periods with no rainfall unless watered occasionally and deeply.

Yellow coneflower is a deciduous perennial that becomes dormant for several months during the winter. In warmer climates, well out of its natural range, it may maintain a rosette of basal leaves, but normally even these yellow and wither as winter progresses. The foliage of this plant is quite attractive and consists of a rosette of 6–12-inch multitoothed bright green leaves. By late spring, the solitary flower stalk begins to become noticeable and is fully mature by summer. At this time, it will stand 1½–3 feet tall. Each stalk contains as many as 6 flower buds, and each blooms over a period of several weeks. The blooms of yellow coneflower comprise numerous long drooping yellow ray petals, surrounding an elongated central grayish disk. The flowers are butterfly favorites. Established plants may form side shoots, and each will produce a flower stalk.

Yellow coneflower is widely used in wildflower gardens across eastern North America and is often available from native plant growers in Florida. Despite its natural rarity in Florida, I have grown it for a great many years in my landscape in Pinellas with good success—though individual plants tend to expire after two or three growing seasons. Use it in clumps of at least 5 plants and mix them into the middle section of a wildflower planting. It may need extra water during the typically droughty months of April and May but is extremely drought tolerant once established.

Black-Eyed Susans (*Rudbeckia* spp.)

This is a wonderful wildflower genus and contains some of the best species for home landscapes. Although many of us associate this genus with the common black-eyed susan (*R. hirta*) and its many cultivated forms, like the gloriosa daisy, Florida is home to nine distinct species that occur in a very wide diversity of habitat types. Most are available from commercial sources. Some black-eyed susans are annuals, and a few others are best considered biennials or very short-lived perennials. Only a few live longer than two years, but most persist in a landscape through reseeding if they are in the proper growing conditions. This requires the home gardener to not mulch these plants too heavily and to allow some bare soil for the seed to fall into. Some of the best species are described below. Many of them have "coneflower" as part of their common name as they share some of the same characteristics as the yellow coneflower described above.

Black-Eyed Susans (*R. hirta*)

Black-eyed susan is found statewide in a great diversity of conditions. For the most part, it is an upland species with good drought tolerance, but it will not persist in extremes of soil moisture, droughty or wet. In Florida, black-eyed susan is best considered a biennial or very short-lived perennial that may bloom for more than one season, but certainly not more than two. Florida varieties differ greatly from those to our north. Ours are lankier, have smaller and fewer leaves, and have much smaller flowers. Because of this, it may be tempting to plant stock from elsewhere, but they will not persist over time and may not even last a season. Black-eyed susan grows rapidly from seed and may begin flowering by early summer; flowering generally lasts until first frost. Over time, this species tends to make its way into most parts of the landscape through reseeding. I make sure I always have black-eyed susans in my home landscapes. I love their

simplicity and their willingness to bloom for most of the year. Plant them in the middle portion of a mixed wildflower bed and mulch lightly.

Black-eyed susan (*Rudbeckia hirta*).

Cutleaf Coneflower (*R. laciniata*)

Cutleaf coneflower is one of my favorite wildflowers. Like the yellow coneflower, it has beautiful sharply lobed foliage during much of the year and produces numerous large yellow flowers for about a month in late summer and early fall. These blooms have long striking yellow ray petals and an elongated disk of greenish yellow disk flowers. The flowers are held 2–4 feet above the basal leaves, and multiple blooms occur on each one.

Cutleaf coneflower is reported from only five counties in North Florida and occurs only in seasonally moist habitats with plenty of sun. It is a bit more adaptable in the home landscape, though. I have grown it now for many years in Pinellas County, and it has persisted well in a site with a bit of extra moisture during the driest months. I have also planted it in locations where it receives some protection from the midday sun. This makes a fantastic mass planting near a walkway or border. It also works well in a mixed planting of species with similar growing requirements, such

Cutleaf coneflower (*Rudbeckia laciniata*).

as obedient plant (*Physostegia virginiana*) and various moisture-loving asters. Cutleaf coneflower is not widely grown in the nursery trade, but should not be too difficult to locate.

Softhair Coneflower (*R. mollis*)

Softhair coneflower is one of our few truly drought-tolerant black-eyed susans and a wonderful species for areas that receive full sun. Native to most of North Florida, it occurs in sandhills and open woods in soils with good drainage. Softhair coneflower is an annual or biennial. It may bloom the first year from seed but often remains as a basal rosette of spatulate leaves until blooming during the second year. As its name implies, soft-hair coneflower has foliage covered by soft "hairs" that make it feel and look a bit velvety. This foliage will persist through winter. By late spring to very early summer, the flower stalk emerges from the center of the ro-sette and eventually reaches a height of 3–4 feet. The stalk produces many side branches, and flower buds are produced in large numbers on each. Blooming occurs in midsummer. A softhair coneflower in full bloom is spectacular. Each robust plant may have as many as 30 flower heads open at a time. The flowers are very similar to the common black-eyed susan, but the heads are larger and the central disk is flat. Overall, the flowers are as wide as 2½ inches.

Softhair coneflower makes an interesting addition to a mixed wildflower planting in locations large enough to accommodate its size. Place it near the back of a planting and mix it there with some of the more robust sandhill blazing stars, palafoxia, yellow buttons, and the like. This species is very hardy in most landscape conditions, but it cannot tolerate too much shade or poor drainage. Because it can persist only through reseeding, do not mulch it heavily. I have kept this species in my Pinellas County landscape for many years, and it has expanded outside its original planting area, producing large numbers of seedlings. Many of these do not appear until the sec-

Softhair coneflower (*Rudbeckia mollis*).

ond year, so don't give up if it seems as though you may have lost it from your landscape. Softhair coneflower is sometimes available from commercial sources in Florida.

Shiny Coneflower (*R. nitida*)

Shiny coneflower is a naturally rare species listed by the state as an endangered species. Found in scattered locations in North and Central Florida, it is most abundant in wetlands near and around the St. Johns River. But despite its natural rarity, shiny coneflower is reasonably adapted to the home landscape in most of Florida as long as its need for moist soils can be met. This species is a long-lived perennial. Unlike most other members of this genus in Florida, shiny coneflower produces a large rosette of basal leaves that are quite attractive. The 18-inch, oval, glossy green leaves are semierect and evergreen in my landscape in Pinellas County. The 3-foot flower stalks are produced, several per plant, in spring, and the flowers

Shiny coneflower
(*Rudbeckia nitida*).

open by early summer. Shiny coneflower produces large flower heads, up to 2 inches across. The bright yellow ray petals are thin and droop away from the dark, pointed central disk. Blooming occurs over several weeks, and sometimes a short second flowering occurs in fall.

Shiny coneflower has some tolerance of drought, but it will persist and thrive only when provided soils that are periodically wet—especially during the typical rainy season in summer. It also requires good levels of sunlight. Plant it with other robust wetland wildflowers at the edge of a pond or within a swale or use it in mass in a part of the landscape that receives additional moisture. Shiny coneflower is only rarely available from commercial nurseries in Florida, but it is worth seeking out if you have the conditions it needs. Once you have a few, they are easy to propagate from seed.

Brown-Eyed Susan (*R. triloba*)

Brown-eyed susan is rather rare in Florida and has been documented in only a few counties in the central Panhandle. It is native to open fields, roadsides, and open woods where it receives ample sunlight and soils with good drainage. Brown-eyed susan is an annual or biennial. Most plants in my Pinellas County landscape produce flowers from the seedlings that germinate each spring, and all of my plants die by early winter. As its Latin name implies, the leaves often have 3 lobes. Almost everything about this species is diminutive: the leaves are only about 2 inches long, and the basal rosette is only about 6 inches in diameter. By summer, the flower stalk becomes evident, and it eventually reaches 2–4 feet in height. It is

Brown-eyed susan (*Rudbeckia triloba*).

multibranched and numerous flower buds are produced. Although the flowers themselves are only ⅔ inch in diameter, a well-grown plant may have many dozen in bloom at any time, and this is quite attractive. Brown-eyed susan is a miniature version of the common black-eyed susan in terms of flower structure and color.

Brown-eyed susan should be planted in a mass for best effect and mixed with other species that won't overwhelm it near the front half of a planting area. Do not mulch it heavily, or it won't be able to reseed itself. Provide it ample sunshine in North Florida, but partial sun further north for best results. It also requires soils with good drainage that do not dry out completely. This is a drought-tolerant wildflower, but it needs a bit of additional water during periods of extreme drought. Few commercial sources currently propagate it at this time, but it can be found with a bit of searching. For the right setting, the effort will be amply rewarded.

Rosinweeds (*Silphium* spp.)

Many of our most attractive wildflowers have common names that include the word "weed" that seem to denigrate their real character. Such is the case with this genus. Rosinweeds are robust wildflowers with attractive foliage and bright showy blooms. In many locations within North America, they play a major visual role in the landscape and are used extensively in restoration and prairie re-creation projects. They are perennials with deep taproots, capable of withstanding periods of drought, and with rosettes of large, leathery, often rough leaves. The bright yellow flowers are held on stout stalks that often tower well above the neighboring foliage, and these are magnets for butterflies and other pollinators.

Florida is home to two species of native rosinweeds, and both make exceptional additions to the wildflower landscape. Because they are tall, use them at the back or interior portions of the landscape. I believe they look best when planted in small clusters of 3–5 plants and in settings expansive enough to make them not seem too much out of place. Both species are available commercially and are described below.

Starry Rosinweed (*S. Asteriscus*)

Starry rosinweed is widely available from commercial growers and extremely adaptable in the home landscape. Although it is most abundant in seasonally moist open habitats throughout much of Florida, it has a great deal of drought tolerance and can be used most anywhere except exceedingly well-drained sands. Starry rosinweed has large oval leaves that persist through the winter if conditions are not too cold. Flowering can occur during most months from late spring to late fall but is most common in summer. The flower stalks reach a mature height of 3–4 feet, and the flowers are composed of round yellow ray petals surrounding a flat greenish yellow disk.

Starry rosinweed
(*Silphium asteriscus*).

Kidneyleaf rosinweed (*Silphium compositum*) with nectaring variegated fritillary. Photo by the author.

Kidneyleaf Rosinweed (*S. compositum*)

Kidneyleaf rosinweed is native to well-drained sands and open sunny habitats common to the sandhills and open fields of North and North Central Florida. As such, it has more drought tolerance than starry rosinweed and is the better choice for landscapes in very sandy areas. It also has the more attractive foliage. Its leaves may be as long as 18 inches and they are deeply lobed. Few of Florida's wildflowers make more of a statement in the garden with their foliage. The leaves, however, are deciduous and disappear by early winter to return once more by February. The flowers of kidneyleaf rosinweed are very similar to those of its close relative, but they are a bit smaller and the disk flowers are reddish while they are open. The flower stalks are taller, up to 6 feet. This species is less commonly available from commercial sources.

Goldenrods (*Solidago* spp.)

If it weren't for the falsehoods spread about them being the cause of fall respiratory illnesses, goldenrods would likely be far more widely used in home landscapes. The truth be told, it is the pollen of ragweeds (*Artemisia* spp.) that is responsible for such things as hay fever, but because both genera bloom at the same time and often in the same locations, goldenrods

Goldenrods (*Solidago* spp.) come in a wide variety of sizes and shapes but nearly always have small yellow flowers in late summer and fall that attract pollinators in large numbers. Contrary to what many still believe, they do not contribute to hay fever.

have erroneously been given half the blame. Goldenrods are perennial, often deciduous wildflowers that produce large numbers of tiny yellow flowers in the late summer and fall. Twenty distinct species are native to Florida, but most are difficult to distinguish from each other without a degree in plant taxonomy. They occur in every habitat throughout the state, and most species are tough and adaptable. Their flowers provide wonderful fall color and attract the attention of a great many pollinators, including butterflies.

In the garden, goldenrods have positive and negative attributes. They mix well with a large number of other wildflowers and grasses and can be used effectively with species such as blazing stars, goldenaster, palafoxia, ironweed (*Vernonia* spp.), and the like, but many species sucker extensively from underground runners once established, and these can be difficult to control. In a naturalistic planting, this is not a problem; the excess plants can be easily pulled and planted elsewhere. In a more formal planting, however, goldenrods can be a nuisance. Most are not sold commercially. The ones that are typically available are described below.

Pinebarren Goldenrod (*S. fistulosa*)

Pinebarren goldenrod is common statewide in a wide variety of habitats. It tolerates moist to wet soils as well as most upland settings that are not too droughty. This is a robust species that produces a stout stem that reaches 6 feet tall by late summer. The flower heads are arranged in an irregular panicle. This species suckers aggressively and often produces dense stands that exclude other species. It is best used in expansive landscape settings or as a screen. It is very difficult to maintain otherwise.

Pinebarren goldenrod (*Solidago fistulosa*)

Sweet goldenrod (*Solidago odora*).

Sweet Goldenrod (*S. odora*)

Sweet goldenrod is a bit more diminutive than some and better behaved than most. It occurs statewide in well-drained upland habitats, such as sandhills and open woodlands. Sweet goldenrod often stands less than 3 feet tall at maturity, and the stem is thin and often prone to bending over slightly. The flower heads are arranged a bit more symmetrically than those of pinebarren goldenrod, but are also open panicles. This species suckers, but does so less aggressively. For this reason, it is one of the easiest species in this genus to maintain in a typical landscape planting. Only the variety *odora* has the fragrant foliage from which this species gets its Latin and common names. If you live in South Florida and wish to use this species, variety *chapmanii* is a better choice.

Seaside Goldenrod (*S. sempervirens*)

Seaside goldenrod occurs statewide in coastal dunes and open disturbed fields on sandy soils. It is our most robust species, producing extremely stout stems that often exceed 6 feet in height. As its Latin names implies, it is also evergreen. Large straplike basal leaves remain year-round and make this species relatively easy to identify during all months. Seaside goldenrod produces thick wand-shaped flower heads during the late summer, and these bloom well into late fall. This species can be breathtaking along the coast in late fall, with thousands of migrating monarch butterflies clinging to its flower heads, but its large size and tendency to spread are limitations that should be considered in all but the most expansive landscape settings.

Seaside goldenrod
(*Solidago sempervirens*).

Wand Goldenrod (*S. stricta*)

Wand goldenrod occurs statewide in moist to average soil habitats and is adaptable to the conditions found in most landscape settings. During most of the year, it blends into the surrounding vegetation and goes largely unnoticed. Its basal leaves are thin, and its 3–4-foot main stem is skinny and mostly leafless. It becomes quite evident, however, in the fall as it blooms. The flower heads are arranged somewhat like those of blazing stars: linearly at the top of a central stalk. Wand goldenrod produces long underground rhizomes and suckers well away from the parent plant, but because of its diminutive size, it is easy to thin and contain to those areas where it is most wanted.

Wand goldenrod
(*Solidago stricta*).

Stoke's aster (*Stokesia laevis*)

Stoke's aster is rare in Florida but commonly sought for home landscaping. Many commercial varieties are marketed in garden catalogues, and most gardeners have some experience with it. In nature, Stoke's aster occurs in moist open habitats along roadsides, pine savannas, and pitcher plant (*Sarracenia* spp.) bogs. It tolerates some shade, but prefers open sunny locations. In the garden, it has good tolerance of typical landscape conditions and requires additional water only during periods of extended drought. Although it is native to only a few counties in northernmost Florida, it can be used effectively well south as long as it gets a bit of protection from the full brunt of the summer sun. Its basal leaves, arranged in a dense cluster, stand about 8 inches tall and remain evergreen during

Stoke's aster (*Stokesia laevis*). Photo by Shirley Denton, with permission.

most winters. Flowering occurs in summer, generally after the onset of the rainy season until early fall. The blooms are what have made this plant so popular. Each head is held about 24 inches above the ground and is nearly 2½ inches across. The outer ray petals are broad and deeply toothed, and both the ray and disk flowers are lavender pink to light blue in color. The large heads of showy flowers are unique in form and color and especially attractive to butterflies as a nectar source.

Stoke's aster is best planted in a mass and used near the front of the landscape bed. The plants are especially attractive when used near walkways and in conjunction with other butterfly nectar and larval food plants. Although this species is available in a wide assortment of garden catalogues and in a variety of colors, use specimens that originate from Florida stock for best results. Stoke's aster sometimes spreads by seed but is generally well behaved in a landscape. It can be easily propagated from seed collected after blooming is completed or by dividing large clumps once the plants are well established.

Asters (*Symphyotrichum* spp.)

Until rather recently, a great many species in the aster family were lumped together as members of genus *Aster*, but, alas, this fairly simple arrangement has been recently revised by plant taxonomists. Some "asters" were

Most former members of the *Aster* genus have been moved taxonomically to *Symphyotri-chum*. A few unique species, such as flaxleaf aster (*Ionactis linariifolia*) and whitetop aster (*Sericocarpus tortifolius*) have been moved to different genera. *Left:* Flaxleaf aster (*Ionactis linariifolia*). *Right:* Whitetop aster (*Sericocarpus tortifolius*).

removed and put into new genera that now contain only a few species. Good examples are the beautiful flaxleaf aster (*Ionactis linariifolius*) and the interesting and widespread whitetop aster (*Sericocarpus tortifolius*). Most, however, were moved to a genus name with a somewhat difficult spelling: *Symphyotrichum*. A total of 27 species are recognized to be native in Florida.

Asters are long-lived perennials with typical heads of daisylike flowers. Most have a great many ray flowers in shades of blue to white surrounding a center of yellow or white disk flowers. Asters occur throughout Florida in nearly every habitat and growing condition. Most sucker extensively from underground rhizomes and form colonies, and most flower in the fall and early winter, near the end of the growing season. Because of this, asters are one of our most recognizable signals of the passing of fall to winter, even in locations without good fall color in shade trees.

Despite the large number of species and widespread distribution, few native asters have been routinely propagated and grown commercially for the home landscape in Florida. This is regrettable, because so many have attributes that make them valuable members of a mixed wildflower planting: hardiness, beauty, and wildlife value. The small but beautiful pearl crescent butterfly uses many members of this genus as caterpillar food plants. I have included a few species in the descriptions below that I believe have exceptional potential but are only rarely offered. The rest are species relatively easy to locate from a commercial nursery.

Scaleleaf or Whipcord Aster (*S. adnatum*)

Scaleleaf aster is found statewide in open pinelands and fields. It prefers sites with a bit of extra moisture, but it is drought tolerant once established and can survive long periods of drought as well as almost any other wildflower in Florida. Scaleleaf aster will not win any beauty contests for its foliage, but part of its charm is in its "weirdness." It emerges each spring and immediately begins producing multiple thin stems clothed in tiny leaves that look like scales. By late spring, each plant may have more than a dozen of these stringy stems, venturing off in all directions for several feet, sometimes lying close to the ground instead of growing erect. By fall, this strange-looking plant begins producing large numbers of flower buds near the ends of the stems, and by late fall, the plant is covered in

Scaleleaf aster (*Symphyotrichum adnatum*) with nectaring green metallic bee.

tiny crystalline blue flowers. Often, these are the very last blooms in my garden, and they will continue to bloom through frost and freezing temperatures until February. This species was once impossible to find from commercial sources, but a few have recently begun offering it. It is hoped this trend will continue. This species does not aggressively sucker and spreads only slowly in a landscape once established.

Climbing Aster (*S. carolinianum*)

Climbing aster is perhaps the most widely grown and propagated aster in Florida—for good reason. Although it is common statewide to riverbanks and other freshwater wetland habitats, it is adaptable and will thrive in most traditional landscape settings except in areas adjacent to saltwater. Climbing aster is semiwoody and grows much like traditional vines. If not pruned, its many stems may reach more than 8 feet in length. In nature, these long stems weave their way through the adjacent vegetation. In a home landscape, it does best if grown on a fence or trellis. It can also be kept along the edges of decks if regularly pruned to keep it in an almost shrublike state. Climbing aster produces some of the most exquisite flowers in the genus. Flowering is heavy if the plants receive sufficient sunlight. Each flower head is more than 1 inch in diameter, and the ray petals

Climbing aster (*Symphyotrichum carolinianum*).

vary between pale pink and a rich violet blue. The disk flowers are bright yellow. Few wildflowers are more fragrant, and it is easy to detect its presence in the wild from a distance; thus the flowers are pollinator magnets. Flowers are produced in late fall to early winter. Cut the spent foliage back in late winter, after it is finished blooming, to keep it tidy.

Chapman's Aster (S. chapmanii)

Chapman's aster is found in the open moist savannas and marsh edges of North Florida, though it has also been reported from St. Lucie County on the southwest coast. I have grown it in my Pinellas County landscape for several years and believe it can be grown in much of Florida if provided the right conditions. Chapman's aster is deciduous during the winter months and produces very little foliage in the spring. Its basal rosette of thin leaves remains almost hidden in the adjacent foliage for much of the spring and early summer. By July, the thin flower stalks become evident, and they reach their mature height of about 2–3 feet in late August to September. Flowering occurs in early fall. Large flower buds at the tips of the main stems open to produce stunning 1-inch-diameter flowers with cornflower blue ray petals and a yellow disk. From a distance, the flowers appear suspended in air as the stems disappear in the background. Chapman's aster is rarely offered by commercial sources. Use it in moist sunny locations with species requiring similar conditions: tickseed (*Coreopsis*

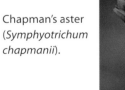

Chapman's aster
(*Symphyotrichum chapmanii*).

spp.), glades lobelia (*Lobelia glandulosa*), toothache grass, etc., and plant it in clumps of at least 5 plants per grouping. Although this aster has some drought tolerance, it does not persist if kept too dry. I have not found it to sucker, but older plants eventually produce multiple leads and flower stems.

Eastern Silver Aster (*S. concolor*)

Eastern silver aster occurs statewide in well-drained sandy uplands. This is a very drought-tolerant species but adaptable to most landscape settings except areas that are poorly drained. Its common name is derived from its wonderful silvery green foliage, a result of the many silky hairs that clothe its leaves and stems. Each spring, mature plants produce as many as a dozen stems, and each may reach a length of 4–5 feet. If left to reach this size, these stems will fall over (if not supported by stakes or adjacent plants) and wind their way through the vegetation before turning up-

ward in fall prior to flowering. If pruned a bit in early summer, the stems will stay shorter and more upright. Early summer pruning will not reduce blooming.

Eastern silver aster produces exquisite flowers in one of the loveliest hues in nature. They are cornflower blue, more than 1 inch in diameter, and produced in profusion at the ends of the stems. This aster suckers, but not aggressively. Over time, it will spread throughout the landscape and form colonies. Use this species in scattered clumps throughout the back half of the planting bed. Give it plenty of sun and soil not too rich or moist. Eastern silver aster is only occasionally

Eastern silver aster (*Symphyotrichum concolor*).

offered by commercial nurseries, but it is well worth the time to search it out.

Rice Button Aster (*S. dumosum*)

Rice button aster occurs statewide in a wide variety of forms which has caused taxonomists fits in the past. Most, simply now agree to lump them all together as one species. In most forms, this species occurs as a thin-stemmed, and multi-branched specimen that rarely stands taller than 2–3 feet. The leaves are small and linear. Rice button aster suckers extensively from its creeping woody rhizome and it produces its thin stems at regular intervals as it extends itself underground. Over time, areas become well populated by this wildflower, but it rarely produces dense stands because of the way it grows. Flowering occurs mostly in the fall, but spring flushes can sometimes occur as well. Each flower head is rather small (about ½–¾ inch across), but each stem produces large numbers. The ray petals come in shades of white, pink, and light lavender while the disk flowers are brownish yellow. Because of its adaptability and ease of propagation, rice button aster is frequently offered by commercial sources. It can be a wonderful addition to a mixed wildflower/native grass landscape, but it may have to be thinned regularly to keep it in check—especially in sites where the soils have dependable moisture and good fertility.

Rice button aster (*Symphyotrichum dumosum*).

Elliott's Aster (*S. elliottii*)

Elliott's aster is native nearly statewide and occurs in areas of high soil moisture and sufficient sunlight. This is a robust deciduous species with a stout central stem that reaches a height of 4–5 feet by its fall blooming season. Large, shiny green oval leaves extend well up the stem and along the many side branches near the top. Flowering occurs across the whole crown of this species, and the flowers are mildly fragrant. The ray petals are pinkish lavender to white and the central disk is bright yellow. Elliott's aster suckers

Elliott's aster (*Symphyotrichum elliottii*).

aggressively in moist soil habitats and eventually forms rather dense colonies. This habit makes for spectacular displays along roadside ditches, along pond edges, and in other naturalistic plantings, but it is a problem in more formal landscapes. Although suckers are easy to thin, it is a task that must be done throughout the growing season to ensure that neighboring species in the landscape will have room to thrive as well. Elliott's aster is nearly always available from a few commercial sources and should not be difficult to find.

Georgia Aster (*S. georgianum*)

Georgia aster is extremely rare in Florida, found only in a small portion of Leon County, near Tallahassee. It is almost as rare in Georgia, where it is considered a threatened species. Throughout its limited natural range, Georgia aster occurs in the edges and openings of deciduous upland

Georgia aster (*Symphyotrichum georgianum*).

forests and in cleared areas such as power line rights-of-way. Georgia aster is a very robust species and easy to notice in a landscape. Dense clusters of basal leaves appear in the spring. Each leaf may be as much as 6 inches long, more than 1 inch wide, and rough to the touch. Often the undersides are purplish in color. The flower stalks are produced in summer and reach a mature height of 4–5 feet in fall. Few wildflowers can match the rich blue-purple color of Georgia aster in bloom. Large numbers of 2-inch flower heads adorn the ends of the multiple stems and last for weeks. Each flower is composed of the blue-purple spidery ray petals surrounding a reddish central disk, and, unique to this species, the anthers are white. Despite its rarity, Georgia aster is being propagated by several commercial nurseries in Florida and is available to the home gardener. I have grown it for several years as far south as Pinellas County and believe it can be used in much of North and Central Florida. Georgia aster suckers, but not aggressively. Plant it in sunny to partly sunny locations in well-drained soil. Because of its size, plant it in the back of a small bed as a screen or in the middle of a more expansive planting.

Walter's Aster (*S. walteri*)

Walter's aster is somewhat similar to scaleleaf aster but occurs naturally only in the northern third of Florida in well-drained upland locations. Each spring, it forms a rosette of arrow-shaped leaves, and by summer begins growing upward. The main stem produces large numbers of side stems, and eventually a mature specimen may stand 4–5 feet tall with a wide crown. The leaves on these stems and branches are much reduced in

Walter's aster (*Symphyotrichum walteri*).

size, but unlike those of scaleleaf aster, they bend backward. By fall, the crown of a well-grown Walter's aster is covered in small flowers. The ray petals are normally light lavender in color while the disk is bright yellow. Walter's aster is only rarely available to the home gardener but worth the effort. Use it as an accent plant, spaced at wide intervals and near the back of the planting area. It does best in full sun and in well-drained soils and can be used well into Central Florida.

Crownbeards (*Verbesina* spp.)

Crownbeards are a genus of rather tall, lanky, and "weedy" perennial semiwoody wildflowers. Many are common to semishady locations in moist soil habitats, but a few occur in well-drained uplands. All of our seven native species produce yellow flowers, except frostweed (*V. virginica*), which has white ray and disk flowers. None are readily available commercially except for frostweed.

Frostweed, or winged stem as it is sometimes called, occurs statewide in a variety of uplands. It can be found in moist soil within light gaps in a forest and in disturbed open fields. As such, it is extremely adaptable to the wide range of conditions that might be present in home landscapes. Frostweed emerges quickly in early spring and may reach a mature height of more than 6 feet at maturity in fall. The succulent stems have distinct

Frostweed (*Verbesina virginica*).

"wings" along their length, and the large coarse lanceolate leaves occur all the way up the length of the stem. For much of the year, frostweed looks "weedy," but in late fall it is transformed, when its crown becomes enveloped in white blooms. For the most part, each flower head comprises 4–5 ray petals and many small disk flowers. The blooms are often alive with pollinators, especially butterflies of all sizes and species. I believe this wildflower is best used in small clusters at the edge of a woodland or in a gap in the canopy of a woodland landscape and not as a focal point of a more open setting.

Ironweeds (*Vernonia* spp.)

Florida has six native species of ironweeds. All are found in relatively open habitats and characterized by open panicles of deep lavender flowers in the late summer months. Most ironweeds are deciduous, producing many wiry stems and suckering profusely in good growing conditions. All make wonderful additions to a mixed wildflower planting, but only two are regularly offered.

Common Ironweed (*V. angustifolia*)

Common ironweed occurs throughout the northern two-thirds of Florida in the understory of pine flatwoods and in open woods and fields. Its Latin name is derived from its narrow leaves. After emerging in spring, it grows quickly to a height of about 4 feet. The flower heads are rather small, but large numbers are produced across the tops of the many branches. Common ironweed is drought tolerant and adaptable, but responds poorly to

Common ironweed (*Vernonia angustifolia*).

extended periods of drought. Given sufficient moisture during the heat of midsummer, it will sucker and form extensive colonies. These colonies, however, rarely prevent other species from coexisting with it. This wildflower is frequently grown commercially. Plant it in open mixed wildflower settings in the back of small beds or in the middle of more-expansive plantings. It mixes well with other tall wildflowers, such as blazing stars, eastern silver aster, palafoxia, and sunflowers, and grasses such as lop-sided Indiangrass and splitbeard bluestem.

Blodgett's Ironweed (*V. blodgettii*)

Blodgett's ironweed is a subtropical wildflower found only in the lower third of the Florida peninsula and the Bahamas. It is most frequently found in moist to wet pinelands and open savannas, often in soils where limestone is at or near the surface. It is adaptable, however, and can withstand some drought once established. This is a wonderful wildflower for South Florida landscapes. Its wiry stems arise in the spring and grow to a mature height of 1–2 feet. The evergreen, irregular-shaped glossy leaves occur opposite each other on the stem, and each plant produces several stems. Unlike other Florida ironweeds, Blodgett's ironweed does not produce a distinct basal clump of leaves.

Flowering occurs mostly in the summer and often over several months. The open panicles of rich purple flowers are quite striking and attract a wide variety of butterflies and other pollinators. Use Blodgett's ironweed near the front half of a mixed wildflower planting so it can be more easily seen and admired. It can be combined with other low to medium-tall wildflowers such as red salvia, common tickseed, and skullcap (*Scutellaria integrifolia*). This species is only rarely offered commercially, but it is hoped this will change as it is an attractive wildflower for South Florida gardens and deserves much wider use in the home landscape.

Blodgett's ironweed (*Vernonia blodgettii*) with nectaring gulf fritillary.

Giant Ironweed (*V. gigantea*)

Giant ironweed is a large robust species common to most of Florida except the extreme southern peninsula. Although deciduous during the winter, giant ironweed reaches a mature height of 6 feet or more by summer when blooming is initiated. The leaves are rough and wide, and slightly toothed at the margins. The flowers are exceptionally beautiful with their deep purple color, and butterflies swarm to them. Giant ironweed can be grown in open areas in North Florida, but does best with less sun further south and a bit of extra moisture. Use this species at the edge of more shady areas where it will receive sun for only half the day, or put it in the filtered

Giant ironweed
(*Vernonia gigantea*).

light produced by a canopy of naturally spaced pines (*Pinus* spp.). If provided the right growing conditions, giant ironweed will sucker aggressively and spread throughout the landscape, limited by reaching areas of
too much sun or droughty soils. Giant ironweed is commonly propagated
and widely available to the home gardener.

Bellflower Family—Campanulaceae

This family contains some wonderful wildflowers common to states north
of Florida, but few species well adapted to our gardens here. The common
but weedy Venus' looking-glass (*Triodanis perfoliata*) has attractive but
small deep blue flowers and can be found throughout much of Florida
in roadsides and other disturbed sites, sometimes as a lawn "weed." The
true bellflowers (*Campanula* spp.) are represented by three species in
Florida, but only American bellflower (*C. americana*) is a likely candidate

for landscape purposes in northernmost Florida. None of the bellflowers are currently commercially propagated in Florida. Only the lobelias (*Lobelia* spp.) are commonly propagated and made available for the home landscape. Several of these are spectacular, whereas a few others are so diminutive as to be of interest only to connoisseurs.

Cardinal Flower (*Lobelia cardinalis*)

Cardinal flower is well known to most wildflower enthusiasts, and its flowers are the most brilliant scarlet red of any species in North America. In Florida, its natural range extends only as far south as the central peninsula, but it can be successfully grown south of this limit if care is given to providing the conditions it requires. Cardinal flower is mostly deciduous but usually overwinters as a flat basal rosette of succulent leaves. In

spring, this mass of leaves begins to grow vigorously and eventually reaches a diameter of about 6 inches. It remains in this state until early summer; the glossy leaves with reddish edges make an attractive landscape accent. A stout flowering stalk begins to elongate from the center of this rosette and eventually reaches its full height by summer. In well-grown specimens, flower stalks may reach 4–5 feet, rarely taller. Flowering occurs from July to September. The large, showy blooms open at the top of the stalk first. Each flower has an exceptionally large lower lip and a deep throat that contains nectar of particular interest to hummingbirds and butterflies. The timing of flowering coincides with the slow migration south of Florida's native ruby-throated hummingbird, and it is one of the very best wildflowers for those interested in creating a hummingbird garden.

Cardinal flower is not an easy wildflower in much of Florida. It is susceptible to a wide assortment of pests and herbivores   Cardinal flower (*Lobelia cardinalis*).

that seek to keep it from reaching its blooming potential, and it quickly declines if not kept wet enough or if mulched too deeply in winter. After years of attempting to grow this beautiful wildflower successfully in my landscape, I have found that much of the secret lies in keeping it in shallow water instead of moist soil. I now keep my plants in large pots and place them an inch below the surface of my pond. In this condition, they are out of reach of most insect pests and mammalian herbivores. Plants grown this way can also be kept in more sun, and blooming is more robust. If you grow them directly in soil, plant them in filtered sun or in areas that receive direct sunlight for only a few hours per day, and give them saturated organic soils. Cardinal flower will slowly propagate itself by producing "pups" (small plantlets) off the sides of the main rosette. After many years, these colonies can be substantial. Plants also produce seedlings from the abundant seed crop each fall. In addition, numerous plants can be produced simply by cutting the flower stalk after seed is harvested and laying it in shallow water or on saturated soil.

Glades Lobelia (*Lobelia glandulosa*)

Glades lobelia is far less known to Florida gardeners than cardinal flower, but has its own charm and makes a very worthy addition to a home landscape. Glades lobelia occurs statewide in seasonally wet pinelands and in the edges of open wetlands. It can be easily grown in moist soil areas and tolerates occasional drought a bit better than its close relative. It overwinters as a rosette of straplike leaves and blooms in late summer. The flower stalk rarely stands taller than 3 feet and is thin and prone to dropping over with the weight of the flowers. The blooms themselves are light lavender in color with a definite white eye-spot. They attract the attention of butterflies and other pollinators. Glades lobelia is only occasionally available from commercial sources. Do not attempt this plant if you cannot keep it moist, especially during the heat of summer.

Glades lobelia (*Lobelia glandulosa*).

Buckwheat Family—Polygonaceae

Many members of this family are common weeds in fields and disturbed sites, but a few are wonderful wildflowers that can hold their own in a landscape setting. All produce achenes for fruit, hard seeds surrounded by papery bracts. No members of this family are widely propagated commercially, but a few are occasionally available. The species described below have very good landscape value and are worth adding to a wildflower garden.

Scrub Buckwheat (*Eriogonum tomentosum*)

Scrub buckwheat occurs throughout the northern two-thirds of Florida in well-drained sandy and sunny locations. It is largely deciduous during the winter and evident only by its spent flower stalk from the previous fall. In spring, an irregular rosette of straplike basal leaves is produced. The upper surface of each leaf is a dull gray green in color while the underside is covered by a dense mat of white feltlike hairs. Flower stalks are produced in summer and reach a mature height of 2–3 feet by midfall when blooming is initiated. Scrub buckwheat produces a broad head of white flowers that may be 6 inches or more across. In full bloom, this plant is very attractive.

Scrub buckwheat (*Eriogonum tomentosum*).

Scrub buckwheat prefers full sun and excellent drainage and cannot tolerate dense soils or too much moisture around its roots. Use it in a mixed wildflower/native grass planting with wiregrass, and wildflowers such as blazing stars, narrowleaf silkgrass, kidneyleaf rosinweed, sky blue salvia, and eastern silver aster. Though very infrequently sold commercially, it is easily propagated from seed.

October Flower (*Polygonella polygama*)

October flower is common to well-drained sunny locations throughout much of Florida. It is deciduous and emerges each spring as an irregular rosette of small oval leaves. Eventually, it produces a stiff, thin set of stems that reach 2–3 feet in height. Flowering occurs in the fall, hence its common name. Each bloom is tiny and bright white, but the crowns of each plant are covered in wispy panicles of these flowers, and the image it creates is quite attractive. October flower is a species that looks its best when used in association with other showier wildflowers. Plant it in small groupings as accents in the middle portion of a planting and surround it with other sandhill and scrub species such as scrub and Chapman's blazing star, narrowleaf silkgrass, scrub buckwheat, and the like. I have not found this species to be especially long lived in the garden, and it disappears quickly if kept too wet during the summer months. Give it lots of sun and deep sandy soils.

October flower (*Polygonella polygama*).

Large-flowered jointweed (*Polygonella robusta*).

Large-Flowered Jointweed (*Polygonella robusta*)

This species is one of Alexa's favorite wildflowers, so we always try to keep some of it in our home landscape. Like October flower, it is native to well-drained sandy habitats throughout much of Florida, and it requires plenty of sunlight to perform well. It is a deciduous wildflower that produces large numbers of thin linear leaves at the soil surface in spring. For much of the summer, the plant assumes a rather nondescript form, but it quickly sends up many wiry spikes with tightly closed flower buds in early fall. By October, these buds burst open and cover the tops of the plant with white and pink flowers. Over the next few days, these flowers turn rosier and eventually become rusty brown before finishing up the show. Large-flowered jointweed flowers attract small native bees, but few butterflies. This wildflower is easy to grow but requires well-drained sands and full sun. I have not found individuals to be long lived, but over the years of its life, it will expand into a clump several feet across and provide exceptional color each fall. It is easy to propagate from seed. Collect it with permission of the landowner, a few from any one plant, in early winter when the seed heads are deep brown and dry.

Buttercup Family—Ranunculaceae

A great many species in this family are popular wildflowers to our north: anemones (*Anemone* spp.), delphiniums (*Delphinium* spp.), hepaticas (*Hepatica* spp.), meadow-rues (*Thalictrum* spp.), and buttercups (*Ranunculus* spp.). Most have very limited ranges in North Florida and are not easily grown outside this range. Because of this, they are not widely propagated here and are rarely offered by commercial nurseries. Only two genera have more widespread use in Florida wildflower gardens.

Columbine (*Aquilegia canadensis*)

Columbine occurs throughout much of eastern North America, but in Florida it is quite rare and naturally occurs in only a few locations in North Florida in deciduous woodlands with limestone near the soil surface. In the garden, however, it is adaptable to parts of the state well south of its natural range if given its required growing conditions. Columbine is a very short-lived perennial that survives over time by producing large seed crops and numerous seedlings. Do not expect this beautiful wildflower to persist if you mulch it too heavily or if you are not prepared to collect some seed each year and grow it in flats. It is deciduous. The distinctive

Columbine (*Aquilegia canadensis*).

compound leaves appear in early spring, and the 2–3-foot flower stalk is quickly produced. Flowering occurs in late spring. The yellow and orange 5-parted flowers hang upside down atop the stems, with several open at any one time. Large quantities of nectar are produced inside the 5 "horns" of each bloom, and this nectar attracts hummingbirds. Without this bird in your garden, seed production is greatly reduced. I have had the most success in my Pinellas County landscape growing this plant near the foundation of my home on the west side and beneath the foliage of short deciduous woody plants. Here, it gets a soil more alkaline than elsewhere in my landscape and direct sunlight for only brief periods each day during the summer and fall. I also find that I have to give it extra water during periods of drought or it will die back to the ground. Despite its natural rarity in Florida, it is offered for sale by a number of Florida commercial sources. Do not attempt this species, however, using stock from outside the state.

Clematis (*Clematis* spp.)

Clematis are extremely popular garden flowers and occur in a wide assortment of colors and textures. Our native species, however, are far more subdued and only infrequently offered to the home gardener, but despite their more understated aesthetic, several have qualities that should make them more widely grown. All have bell-shaped flowers with the tips of the sepals curving backward from the fused lower portion. These flowers are little more than 1 inch long, in various shades of purple and rosy lavender, but they are sometimes produced in profusion. All our native clematis are herbaceous vines with twining tendrils, except for one that is upright. All of them also require a bit of extra moisture to thrive.

Pine Hyacinth (*C. baldwinii*)

Pine hyacinth occurs in moist pinelands and open fields throughout the Florida peninsula. Though it does not occur naturally in the Panhandle, it would likely prosper if given the needed growing conditions. Unlike other members of this genus in Florida, pine hyacinth is an upright herbaceous species. It dies back to the ground in winter and emerges in the spring as several thin upright stems with linear opposite leaves in widely variable shapes. These stems rarely exceed 1 foot in length and usually remain erect if grown in sufficient sun. By late spring, the wiry flower stalks emerge and reach a height of about 2 feet. Each has one flower bud, but individual plants produce several over the course of the extended flowering season. Just prior to blooming, the bud curls under, and the open flowers are upside down. The "bell" portion at the top is light lavender in color while the reflexed tips are white.

Pine hyacinth requires extra moisture to maintain its foliage and flower. It may go dormant during periods of drought and then reemerge and flower once the rains return. Extended drought will kill it. Plant this species near the front of a mixed wildflower planting with other

Pine hyacinth (*Clematis baldwinii*).

short species such as twinflower and wild petunia. It is only infrequently offered by commercial nurseries, but can be grown from seed. Seed is sometimes difficult to germinate and may take many months to break its dormancy.

Swamp Leather Flower (*C. crispa*)

Like most members of this genus, swamp leather flower is a deciduous vine. It occurs naturally throughout much of Florida, except the extreme southern counties, in wet forested habitats where it gets filtered sun or direct sun for only short periods. Because of this, it requires conditions in the landscape that are not always easy to provide, but if you have a wet or moist soil location that is not too sunny, swamp leather flower can provide an attractive and interesting accent in the landscape. It emerges quickly in the spring and begins to ramble up and through the adjacent vegetation. Individual stems will reach 6 feet or more in length before flowering is initiated in late spring or early summer. The shape of the flowers is typical of other Florida species, and the flowers are lavender to rosy purple in color. The flowering season generally lasts for several months. Because of the vining nature of this species, it grows best if given a small trellis to grown on. If used in a natural setting, place it near woody wetland

Swamp leather flower (*Clematis crispa*).

species, such as most of the St. John's-worts (*Hypericum* spp.), and let them climb up through the foliage. Swamp leather flower is only rarely offered commercially.

Canna Family—Cannaceae

Only one canna is native to Florida, yellow canna (*Canna flaccida*). This species occurs statewide in a variety of wetland habitats. Although it can survive somewhat drier conditions, it does not thrive unless planted in sites that remain moist to wet throughout the year and have 6–12 inches of standing water during the summer. Its 3–4-foot pleated leaves remain evergreen when temperatures stay above freezing, but are deciduous elsewhere. Flowering occurs in late spring through summer. The flower heads are held about 12–18 inches above the basal leaves. Each flower remains fully open only during the morning hours, but individual plants produce flowers successively for several weeks. The large frilly petals are a pure canary yellow and quite showy. They are mostly pollinated by bees, though the leaves are used by the canna skipper as a larval food.

Yellow canna spreads rapidly by means of its woody underground rhizome and eventually forms large stands in areas with ideal habitat. Such areas are breathtaking when the plant is in bloom, but its growth habit makes it difficult to maintain in a small landscape space. This is an excellent landscape choice for the edge of a pond in water no deeper than 12 inches. Mix it with other medium-tall wetland wildflowers such as Dixie

Yellow canna (*Canna flaccida*).

or blue flag iris (*Iris hexagona* and *I. virginica*, respectively) and most of the native hibiscus.

Carrot Family—Apiaceae

While some of our most popular herbs are in the carrot family (e.g., fennel, dill, and parsley) along with the carrot itself, few of the many native wildflowers in this family are used in the home landscape. A few are rather weedy, but others have attributes that make them excellent additions. Most carrot family members produce umbels (loose open clusters of tiny flowers) of white flowers that are quite attractive. Their foliage is often highly aromatic and rich in essential oils, and the individual leaves are finely dissected and "feathery." Most produce a woody tap root, and many work well as part of a butterfly garden as they serve as the larval food plant for the beautiful eastern black swallowtail. Queen Anne's lace (*Daucus carota*), the wild form of the common garden carrot, is not native, but introduced from Eurasia. The native species best suited to home landscapes are described below. Both are fairly widely grown by commercial native plant nurseries.

Button Snakeroots (*Eryngium* spp.)

These species are sometimes referred to as "eryngos" and include a wide variety of deciduous herbs from creeping ground covers to tall erect species. They are the exceptions in the family when it comes to flower

Many button snakeroots (*Eryngium* spp.), like this fragrant button snakeroot (*E. aromaticum*), are small and inconspicuous. A few are also food plants for the caterpillars of eastern black swallowtail butterflies, and all are characterized by flower heads in a spiny ball.

structure. The button snakeroots produce rounded heads of flowers subtended by spiny bracts. The flowers themselves are either white or powder blue, depending on the species. Few snakeroots seem to be eaten by eastern black swallowtail caterpillars, and most, therefore, are not useful in a butterfly garden. The exceptions are two species not currently propagated commercially: the extremely rare wedge-leaved button snakeroot (*E. cuneifolium*) of the southern Lake Wales Ridge and the common, but rather inconspicuous, fragrant button snakeroot (*E. aromaticum*) native to dry pinelands throughout much of Florida.

Marsh Rattlesnake Master (*E. aquaticum*)

This species occurs throughout the northern two-thirds of Florida in seasonally wet habitats, such as the edges of marshes and ponds. In the spring, it produces thin rounded grasslike leaves with tiny teeth that eventually stand about 12 inches tall. In late spring, multiple flower stalks emerge from the leaf mass, and they reach up to 5 feet tall by midsummer. By this time, most to all of the basal leaves have disappeared, and all the foliage is confined to the stem. The flowers are powder blue in color and produced in large numbers. These attract butterflies and a wide variety of bees. Marsh rattlesnake master requires wet to moist soil to persist and blooms much better if given a location that receives ample sunlight. Use

Marsh rattlesnake master (*Eryngium aquaticum*) with nectaring green metallic bee.

this species at the edge of a pond or other water feature where it won't be inundated by more than 1 inch of water for long periods. This is a spectacular wildflower that adds a great deal of interest to the landscape, but do not attempt it if you cannot keep it wet.

Rattlesnake Master (*E. yuccifolium*)

Rattlesnake master is native to moist pinelands and savannas across all of Florida. Its Latin name refers to its foliage, which looks similar to the leaves of yucca (*Yucca* spp.): needle-like and spiny along the margins. Rattlesnake master prefers moist soil, but it will adapt to drier locations once well established. Do not expect it to persist, however, during extreme drought during the heat of summer if you are not prepared to give it some supplemental watering. This species often persists through the winter with its basal leaves intact when temperatures do not go below the mid-20s F. From the center of this whorled leaf mass, a single, multibranched flower stalk emerges in summer and eventually stands 2–3 feet tall. The flowers

Rattlesnake master (*Eryngium yuccifolium*).

are white, but are so small within the spiny flower head as to appear green-ish. Rattlesnake master is not the most beautiful wildflower in Florida, but it adds a very interesting accent to a mixed native grass/wildflower planting. Use it in small clumps of 5–7 plants each, planted on 1-foot centers, and mix it with species that prefer average to seasonally moist soil, such as wiregrass, dense blazing star, narrowleaf silkgrass, and common ironweed. Over time, it will form small colonies around the original plant.

Water Dropwort (*Oxypolis filiformis*)

Water dropwort is a wetland native that occurs throughout Florida. Though it prefers evenly wet conditions at the upper edges of marshes and ponds, it will also perform well in moist soils that occasionally dry if they get ample moisture during the heat of summer. As its Latin name implies, water drop-wort has long thin "filiform" leaves. These are several feet long and some-what succulent, and they often droop over. The flower stalk is produced in early summer and stands 4–6 feet tall by the late summer–early fall blooming season. The round umbels of white flowers occur on the top of the main stalk as well as the ends of the many side branches and are quite showy. At this time, water dropwort is a magnet for eastern black swal-lowtails looking for plants on which to lay their eggs. I have grown water dropwort for many years in my cre-ated wetland. Use it near the center of such plantings and mix it with various St. John's-worts, marsh rat-tlesnake master, golden ragwort, and similar species. This plant is only oc-casionally grown commercially but is easy to propagate from seed once you have a few.

Water dropwort (*Oxypolis filiformis*). Photo by Christina Evans, with permission.

Catchfly Family—Caryophyllaceae

The catchflies or campions (*Silene* spp.) include some of the most spectacular wildflowers in North America, but all the more beautiful species are exceedingly rare in Florida and difficult to keep in most landscape settings. Catchflies are deciduous herbaceous perennials that produce a rosette of simple basal leaves in the spring. All our species occur in limited ranges in open deciduous woods where they get filtered sun in the summer months and a bit of extra moisture and soil fertility. They do not tolerate high sun and extreme temperatures here, so growing them in the landscape requires finding the correct microclimate. I have grown four of our best catchflies in my Pinellas County landscape, far outside their natural ranges, but I do so by keeping them in large pots in good potting soil with ample drainage and regular watering. They would all likely die at my latitude if I planted them directly in my landscape. Many wildflowers, such as the catchflies, can be kept for years in such settings, either in single-species plantings or mixed with others. Pots can be moved to take advantage of changing seasonal light conditions, and it is easier to maintain their correct watering needs. Landscape pots can also lend a more artistic element to the landscape if used appropriately.

Fringed Campion (*S. catesbaei*; syn. *S. polypetala*)

Fringed campion is a low-growing species that rarely stands more than 6 inches tall, but it spreads over an area about 1 foot wide. It produces large numbers of amazing light pink flowers in the late spring. The tips of the 5 petals are fringed, and each flower is more than 2 inches across. Despite its great natural rarity, this plant is available from a few commercial sources. If you can find it, make sure you do not give this species too much sunlight during the summer months.

Fringed campion (*Silene catesbaei*).

Royal Catchfly (*S. regia*)

Royal catchfly is the "king" of the catchflies and one of the showiest wildflowers anywhere. It is the tallest of the three species described here and may reach a height of 3 feet by early summer. The flower stalks have many side branches, and flower buds are produced on the ends of each. The blooms are brilliant scarlet red with the typical 5-parted petals of the genus. They are hummingbird pollinated but also attract the attention of butterflies such as the cloudless sulphur. Flowering can occur over a wide period from summer to fall but is generally confined to a one-month period from July to August.

Royal catchfly (*Silene regia*).

Firepink (*S. virginica*)

Our other red catchfly spends most months as a basal rosette of oval leaves. In the late spring, it produces multiple flower stalks that stand 12–18 inches tall. Each of these produces multiple carmine red flowers for which it gets its common name. The petals are deeply notched at the tips, and this further distinguishes it from royal catchfly. I have had less success with this species than with other catchflies, but the reason may have more to do with the source of the plants I've tried than with the

Firepink (*Silene virginica*).

species itself. While fringed and royal campions are being propagated within Florida, I know of no commercial source in the state for firepink. It is hoped that someone will make this beautiful wildflower more available to Florida gardeners.

Dutchman's-Pipe Family—Aristolochiaceae

This mostly tropical family includes a great many non-native species grown extensively in Florida for their large showy blooms and use in butterfly gardens. Most non-native Dutchman's-pipes are suitable larval plants for the gold rim or polydamas swallowtail, but very few are suitable for the pipevine swallowtail. Several native Dutchman's-pipes occur in Florida, but only one is regularly cultivated.

Woolly Dutchman's-Pipe (*Aristolochia tomentosa*)

Woolly Dutchman's pipe is the most widely propagated native member of this genus and the most robust. Other native species are inconspicuous vining ground covers and not grown commercially at this time. Woolly

Dutchman's-pipe is native to the understory of deciduous floodplain forests in North Florida. It can be grown further south into Central Florida in more typical landscape settings, but its habitat needs must be reasonably met. Do not attempt to grow this deciduous vine in full sun or in total shade, and do not plant it in well-drained soils or droughty conditions. Give it above-average soil fertility and filtered light during the summer months and higher light during the spring.

Woolly Dutchman's-pipe (*Aristolochia tomentosa*). Photo by Gil Nelson, with permission.

Woolly Dutchman's-pipe is a weak-stemmed herbaceous or slightly woody vine that extends in all directions for 10 feet or more. The rounded leaves are slightly woolly and clothe the stems in abundance. Small, rather nondescript yellowish pipe-shaped flowers occur between March and May. This wildflower is mostly of interest to butterfly gardeners. Woolly Dutchman's-pipe is only rarely offered by Florida nurseries and is listed as a state-endangered species because of its natural rarity here.

Wild Ginger (*Asarum arifolium*; syn. *Hexastylis arifolia*)

Wild ginger is also known as "little brown jugs" because of its tiny but uniquely shaped flowers. Its common name is derived from the fact that its leaves and roots produce a high concentration of aromatic oils with the scent of ginger. This is an understory ground cover found naturally only in northernmost Florida. It prefers the slightly richer soils these forests provide and filtered sun during the summer months, but it can be grown well south of its natural range. Wild ginger is not likely to be grown for its tiny urn-shaped brown flowers, but for its attractive foliage. It is a slowly creeping ground cover that produces heart-shaped variegated leaves every ½ to 1 inch. These leaves stand several inches above the ground. Over time, this makes a wonderful accent in a shady forested planting. Plant several at intervals of about 3 feet. Good companion plants are violets,

Wild ginger (*Asarum arifolium*).

trillium (*Trillium* spp.), jack-in-the-pulpit, and similar spring-blooming wildflowers. Include ferns, such as Christmas and southern lady fern, and ebony spleenwort. Wild ginger is rarely grown commercially but can be found with a bit of perseverance.

Gentian Family—Gentianaceae

The gentians are well known to many as dye plants, but they include a great many species in various genera, from trees and shrubs to herbaceous wildflowers. The flowers are often star shaped, with their petals and sepals fused. The stamens (the male portion of the flower) are attached to the inside of the petals. None of Florida's true gentians (*Gentiana* spp.) are commonly available from commercial sources, and most are uncommon in nature. I do not cover them here as none are easy candidates for the home landscape. In this family, only the marsh pinks (also known as rose gentians) are common enough in Florida to be seriously considered for roles in a home landscape setting.

Marsh Pinks or Rose Gentians (*Sabatia* spp.)

The various marsh pinks are widely distributed throughout Florida in wet savannas, marshes, and moist pockets within pinelands. None are truly upland species with significant tolerance of droughty soils, but the white-flowered shortleaf marsh pink (*S. brevifolia*) is common in pine flatwoods throughout Florida and has reasonable tolerance of typical landscape conditions if not allowed to dry out too much during the heat of summer. Of the 12 species native to Florida, 4 have white petals and the remaining 8 are pink. Most have 5 petals, but a few have 10 or more. Many are rather difficult to distinguish from each other without close examination, and none are currently propagated commercially in Florida on any regular basis. Because members of this species are annuals, they are difficult to maintain in a landscape unless conditions are right for them to reseed effectively.

The marsh pinks can be especially showy additions to a mixed wild-flower planting at the edges of moist areas, such as ponds and marshes. If planted in a mass, they produce large numbers of flowers from early summer to fall. They are not particularly interesting from a foliage stand-point, however, and most stand 1–2 feet tall at maturity. The best choices

Bartram's marsh pink (*Sabatia decandra*).

Large-flower marsh pink (*Sabatia grandiflora*).

statewide are shortleaf marsh pink, which rarely stands taller than 18 inches; large-flower marsh pink (*S. grandiflora*), which has wonderful pink 5-petaled flowers and stands several feet tall; and Bartram's marsh pink (*S. decandra*; syn. *S. bartramii*), which stands 3 feet tall at maturity and has extremely showy 10-petaled flowers. In North Florida, a particularly attractive choice would be angular marsh pink (*S. angularis*).

Heliotrope Family—Boraginaceae

The heliotrope family includes a few common herbs, such as borage (*Borago officinalis*), and several showy native woody species such as geiger tree (*Cordia sebestena*) and the strongbarks (*Bourreria* spp.). Most have distinctly hairy leaves. Of the herbaceous species, only the heliotropes (*Heliotropium* spp.) are widely grown in the home landscape. Heliotropes have tiny tubular flowers arranged on curved fingerlike flower heads. Flower heads occur at the ends of each of the many stems, and flowering occurs during most months except winter. The tubular flowers are especially attractive to butterflies, bees, and other pollinators and are thus effective additions to butterfly gardens. The three species most commonly available from commercial sources are described below.

Scorpion's Tail (*H. angiospermum*)

Scorpion's tail is frequently found throughout the southern half of Florida in semishady locations and in open disturbed sites. In the northern portion of its range where winter freezes are likely, it acts like an annual; further south, it is a short-lived perennial. Treated as an annual, it could be planted statewide, well north of its natural range. As a perennial, it

Scorpion's tail (*Heliotropium angiosperum*).

requires temperatures that do not get too far below the mid-20s F. Scorpion's tail grows rapidly to a mature height of 2–3 feet. It is often somewhat wider than tall. The leaves are arrow shaped and rough, with deep-set veins. Very tiny white flowers are produced in abundance from late spring through late fall. Each produces large numbers of seeds that allow this wildflower to persist, and often spread, in the landscape. Scorpion's tail has all the characteristics of a "weed," especially the ability to spread quickly into disturbed sites, but it can be quite attractive in the landscape when given a little attention and kept pruned a bit to maintain its shape.

Seaside Heliotrope (*H. curassavicum*)

Seaside heliotrope occurs in coastal areas throughout most of North America, but is not commonly available from Florida nurseries as it is in other states. This is an annual wildflower of coastal dunes and adapted to high salt spray and extreme conditions. Its succulent silvery foliage lies prostrate on the sandy soil, and eventually each of its many stems reaches a length of about 12 inches. Very tiny heads of bright white flowers occur on the ends of each branch, and blooming can occur during most months if temperatures are not too cold. The flowers are not especially showy. The real landscape value of this species is its distinctive foliage.

Seaside heliotrope (*Heliotropium curassavicum*). Photo by Roger Hammer, with permission.

Seaside heliotrope is a good addition to a coastal planting and is most effectively used in a mass near the front of a planting or near paths and walkways. It does not need to be used in coastal settings, but it requires high light and sandy soil if it is to thrive.

Pineland Heliotrope (*H. polyphyllum*)

Pineland heliotrope is the most widely used member of this family in Florida landscapes. Though native to moist pinelands and brackish water edges throughout much of peninsular Florida, it is extremely adaptable to growing conditions and can be used virtually anywhere. It is sensitive to cold, however, and all the aboveground portions will turn black when temperatures reach freezing. This affects

Pineland heliotrope (*Heliotropium polyphyllum*) with nectaring wasp.

its aesthetic qualities but does not kill it, and it will reemerge stronger than ever once warmer conditions return. Two forms that differ significantly from each other are considered the same species by current taxonomy. The white-flowered form is generally quite prostrate and rarely stands taller than about 8 inches. The yellow-flowered form grows more upright and normally stands 12–18 inches tall. Both forms have narrow lance-shaped evergreen foliage and develop stout woody stems over time. The branches extend outward in all directions and root periodically where they touch bare soil. Especially long taproots develop and are virtually impossible to pull out of the ground. The deep roots also make this plant extremely drought tolerant. Over time, it forms a dense ground cover 3–4 feet across that shades out nearly everything beneath it.

Pineland heliotrope is stunning in bloom and flowers nearly year-round if not frozen back. In North Florida, blooming is confined to late summer and fall. Use this plant as a ground cover for sunny locations where other plants are difficult to grow. Keep it pruned to confine it. Because it is cold sensitive, it is not a good choice for areas that regularly freeze, and because it is so aggressive, it is best not mixed with other wildflowers that might be overwhelmed by it.

Hibiscus Family—Malvaceae

Asian and African hibiscus (*Hibiscus* spp.) are common to Florida landscapes. They have been hybridized extensively, and a wide range of flower colors and forms have been developed. What too few Floridians realize is that there are a number of wonderful native species as well. The hibiscus or mallow family is composed of woody to semiwoody perennials with saucer-shaped blooms consisting of 5 fused petals. Most of Florida's most spectacular species are deciduous and die completely back to the ground in early winter, and most are native to wet-soil habitats and often grow in shallow water during the summer months. The family also includes the ubiquitous Caesarweed (*Urena lobata*), which colonizes nearly every upland disturbed site in peninsular Florida. Caesarweed could be nature's model for Velcro; its many spiny seeds stick to everything brushing against it. Therefore, it is not a good landscape choice. Most of our best selections are within the *Hibiscus* genus, though there are a few exceptions.

Woodland Poppy Mallow (*Callirhoe papaver*)

Woodland poppy mallow is a rather rare herbaceous wildflower in Florida with a limited natural range in the northern sections of the state. Despite this, it is adaptable in home landscapes and can be grown to South Central Florida. Woodland poppy mallow occurs in open woodlands with ample sunlight and average well-drained soil. It overwinters as a small rosette

Woodland poppy mallow (*Callirhoe papaver*).

of basal leaves or is completely deciduous, but in spring it sends out wiry stems that extend in all directions along the ground. They reach a mature length of several feet. Small, deeply lobed leaves clothe the stems. What makes poppy mallow such an attractive landscape plant are its wonderful blooms. Flowering occurs in late spring to early summer, and numerous flowers are produced over 2–4 weeks. Each is about 2 inches across and composed of 5 magenta petals surrounding a white column of fused reproductive parts.

Poppy mallow is extremely drought tolerant, once established, as it produces a thick woody taproot that extends several feet into the ground. I have grown it successfully in Pinellas County in locations that receive half-day sun and a bit of supplemental water in extended periods of drought. Use this species as a ground cover in alkaline to average soils, but space individual plants at least 1 foot apart. Mix it with other low-growing wildflowers, such as twinflower and wild petunia, near the front of a planting bed or next to pathways and trails. This species is often available in limited numbers from commercial sources and can be further propagated from seed collected from your own plants. Woodland poppy mallow is sometimes fed on by the caterpillars of the common checkered skipper butterfly.

Pineland Hibiscus (*H. aculeatus*)

Pineland hibiscus occurs throughout North Florida in wet pinelands, open savannas, and roadsides. Although it prefers wet to moist soils, it

Pineland hibiscus
(*Hibiscus aculeatus*).

is more drought tolerant than most other native hibiscus and will persist in average soils as long as it is given a bit of extra moisture during the hot months of summer and filtered sun during midday. This is a rather "untidy" species as it tends to be multistemmed and grows somewhat prostrate across the ground. Stems are rarely taller than 2 feet, but may extend 4–5 feet in all directions from the main trunk. Its Latin name refers to the prickly hairs that cover most parts of the plant and make it rough to the touch. Flowering occurs during the summer after periods of rain and may last for several months. The creamy white flowers have a distinctive maroon throat and are 2–3 inches in diameter. Each is fully open only during the morning hours for one day and closes by afternoon.

Pineland hibiscus makes an interesting accent when used in expansive landscape settings. I believe it looks best when planted in small clusters of 3–5 plants and mixed with taller wildflowers and native grasses, all adapted to seasonally wet soils and full sun. If you wish to use it in locations that are less wet, plant it in half sun and be prepared to water it occasionally during periods of drought. Pineland hibiscus is infrequently available from commercial nurseries.

Scarlet Hibiscus (*H. coccineus*)

Scarlet hibiscus occurs nearly statewide and produces one of the most brilliant red blooms of any wildflower in Florida. Its use, however, is best in sites with extremely wet soils or shallow standing water. In my experience in Central Florida, it eventually fades and dies when planted in soils that do not remain moist. I am told that it is more adaptable in North Florida. Scarlet hibiscus emerges in the spring and quickly develops a stout semiwoody stem that reaches a mature height of 5–9 feet by summer, depending on growing conditions. Its large deeply divided leaves look like marijuana, and I have heard stories over the years of folks whose plants were reported to local law enforcement by concerned neighbors. When the plants come into bloom in midsummer, however, this resemblance is completely lost. Each flower is flat, nearly 8 inches across, and has 5 scarlet red petals. These attract hummingbirds as well as butterflies and other insect pollinators. Over time, scarlet hibiscus produces multiple stalks from its main base, and each blooms profusely for several months.

Use this wonderful wild-flower at the edges of ponds or other permanently wet sites. It can handle brackish conditions as well as fresh and can be kept for years in pots set in water features no deeper than 12–18 inches. If grown in pots, be prepared to divide your plants every two or three years or they will outgrow them. Scarlet hibiscus is the most widely propagated native hibiscus in Florida.

Scarlet hibiscus
(*Hibiscus coccineus*).

Swamp Hibiscus (*H. grandiflorus*)

Swamp hibiscus is very similar in habit and growing requirements to scarlet hibiscus, and the two can be mixed in a planting to great effect. Unlike scarlet hibiscus, its leaves are silvery green in color because of the many whitish hairs that cover their surface. They are also arrowhead shaped, with coarse teeth along the leaf margins. Swamp hibiscus blooms in late summer; its flowers

Swamp hibiscus (*Hibiscus grandiflorus*).

are a soft pink with a deeper rose throat. It can be grown statewide and tolerates fresh and brackish water. Swamp hibiscus is regularly propagated by commercial nurseries and usually easy to locate.

Rose Mallow (*H. moscheutos*)

This hibiscus is rarely offered by commercial nurseries in Florida, but it is a wonderful species and well deserving of a place in the landscape. In many respects, its growth form and requirements are similar to those of scarlet and swamp hibiscus, but it rarely stands taller than 6 feet at maturity and is often shorter. Its leaves are arrow shaped, but without coarse teeth along the margins. The undersides are grayish in color, resulting from a feltlike mat of hairs that cover them. Rose mallow blooms in summer. The large 6–8-inch-diameter flowers are composed of ivory white petals and a blood red throat. These are stunning, especially when seen in a mass.

Rose mallow requires wet soils to prosper and can be planted in brackish to freshwater conditions. Its natural range only extends into North Central Florida, and it should not be attempted too far south in the peninsula. Plant it in small clusters at the edges of ponds and other permanently flooded sites with shorter wetland wildflowers and grasses. Rose mallow is only infrequently offered by commercial nurseries in Florida.

Rose mallow
(*Hibiscus
moscheutos*).

Saltmarsh Mallow (*Kosteletzkya virginica*)

Saltmarsh mallow is a rather weak multibranched herbaceous species common to salt- and freshwater marshes throughout Florida. Its thin stems are prone to bending over as the plant reaches its mature height of 6–8 feet, and its leaves are narrow and somewhat triangular in shape. Despite this less-than-showy description of its growth form, saltmarsh mallow can make a dramatic statement in certain home landscapes because of its wonderful blooms; the 5 petals are a rich pink in color and they surround a yellow fused column of reproductive parts. Flowering occurs mostly in summer and lasts for several months. Although saltmarsh mallow has a bit more drought tolerance than most of its close relatives described above, it performs best when provided wet to seasonally moist soils. In somewhat drier conditions, it can thrive if planted in filtered sun or in sites protected from midday sun, but do not attempt it in locations that dry out during the heat of summer. Saltmarsh mallow is often available from commercial sources in Florida.

Saltmarsh mallow (*Kosteletzkya virginica*).

Indian Pink Family—Loganiaceae

This is a small family poorly represented in Florida, but it contains two important wildflowers extensively used in home landscapes. The family includes a great many members that are highly poisonous if ingested, including the tree that produces strychnine and herbaceous plants that produce curare. No member of this family, including those described below, should be used around young children who may chew or consume the foliage.

Carolina yellow jessamine (*Gelsemium sempervirens*).

Carolina Yellow Jessamine (*Gelsemium sempervirens*)

This evergreen vine is common to the northern two-thirds of Florida. It occurs in a wide variety of habitats, from semishady woodlands to sunny open fields, and is adaptable to nearly every home landscape condition except high salts. Its stems are thin and woody, and it twines its way throughout the landscape, rambling up and over adjacent trees and shrubs and sometimes forming an impenetrable ground cover. Like most vines, it also produces suckers and spreads underground to wide areas of the landscape if left unchecked by regular pruning. But despite its somewhat aggressive nature, Carolina yellow jessamine is a beautiful addition to the home landscape if contained on a trellis or fence. Its canary yellow trumpet-shaped flowers are produced in profusion in early spring, and the blooming season can last for several weeks. The flowers are highly fragrant as well, and a garden full of these blooms smells magnificent and serves to attract a wealth of pollinators, including hummingbirds if they are passing through. Be judicious in inhaling the fragrance deeply or in enclosed areas.

Use Carolina yellow jessamine to cover fences and trellises, or allow it to grow up into the canopy of larger shade trees. If you do the latter, however, you will miss much of the fragrance and color of the blooms. Do not use it as a ground cover if you wish to mix it with other species or need to walk across it. The tangle of its stems makes it difficult for one to navigate.

Indian Pink (*Spigelia marilandica*)

This is a wonderful wildflower for the understory of deciduous woodlands with filtered sunlight in the summer and reasonably rich but well-drained soils. It is native throughout North Florida, but difficult to grow too far south into the peninsula. If provided the conditions it requires, however, it is an absolutely stunning addition to the home landscape. Indian pink is deciduous and makes its appearance in early spring before the canopy trees have leafed out. Soon, the main stems reach their mature height of 1–2 feet and the flower buds form atop them in small clusters. The leaves are oval in shape and opposite each other up the stems. The blooms are what make this species such an outstanding wildflower. The carmine red petals are fused nearly to the tip and then divide into a 5-pointed star, revealing the bright yellow inside.

Over time, Indian pinks slowly spread and form patches in the

Indian pink (*Spigelia marilandica*).

forest understory. When this occurs, the carpet of rich green foliage and bright red and yellow flowers adds a great deal of interest to the forest floor. Use Indian pinks beneath deciduous trees from North Central Florida northward throughout the Panhandle. Mix them with other spring-blooming forest wildflowers such as violets (*Viola* spp.), wild ginger, green dragon, and green-and-gold. Add any of the medium to smaller ferns for texture. Indian pinks should be planted in clusters of at least 3–5 and spaced no closer than 12–18 inches apart. Because of its great beauty, Indian pink is widely propagated and available from commercial nurseries for the home landscape.

Iris Family—Iridaceae

Many of Florida's native irises are diminutive and likely to be mistaken for something else. The true irises (*Iris* spp.) are rather typical of the family, but the blue-eyed grasses (*Sisyrinchium* spp.) and ixias look a good

Bartram's ixia (*Nemastylis floridana*).   Celestial lily (*Calydorea caelestina*).

deal less like the garden irises with which we may have grown up in our gardens. All irises in Florida prefer moist to wet soils and rather sunny conditions. Many have stout woody rhizomes beneath the soil surface that slowly elongate over time to produce new plants, though a few have bulbs or corms. The ixias include two spectacular but quite rare wildflowers, Bartram's ixia (*Nemastylis floridana*) and celestial lily (*Calydorea caelestina*). Both of these are sometimes available, but they require very specialized conditions to prosper. I have grown them in my Pinellas County landscape for years using pots with good success, but they cannot be planted in most landscape settings and live. If you add them in pots, use good potting soil, place the pot in a partial to mostly sunny area, and keep the soil evenly moist to wet, especially during the summer. Although the flowers of these two irises are breathtaking, each remains open for only a few hours during one day before closing: celestial lily in the late afternoon in the fall and Bartram's ixia during the early morning in the spring and summer. Flowers are produced successively over several weeks. The species I describe below are more widely available and a bit easier to grow in the landscape.

Dixie or Prairie Iris (*Iris hexagona*)

Dixie iris occurs nearly statewide in pond edges, marshes, and forested wetlands. Although it can grow in partial sun, it will become leggy in

such conditions and pro-
duce few flowers. This is a
robust plant that will retain
its leaves through winter if
conditions are not too cold.
Mature specimens normally
stand 2–3 feet tall and eventually spread throughout the
landscape by means of their
underground rhizomes. As
its Latin name implies, its
main stem assumes a zigzag
form. The flower buds occur
in the axils of each bend near
the top of the stem, and the
leaves extend above the last
flower. Blooming occurs in
spring and lasts for several
weeks. The flowers come in
a variety of shades of blue
(sometimes white), and are
held on stout flower stalks
that rise 6–12 inches above the basal leaves.

Dixie iris (*Iris hexagona*). Photo by Gil Nelson, with permission.

Use Dixie iris in wetland or pond plantings, areas that remain wet and may be seasonally flooded by 6–12 inches of water. Do not attempt this plant if you cannot keep it sufficiently wet, especially during the heat of summer. It is also difficult to keep in pots because its woody rhizomes continually expand. Mix this wildflower with native yellow canna, cardi-nal flower, and any of the native hibiscus. Dixie iris spreads aggressively, so it is not an ideal plant for small landscape settings.

Blue Flag Iris (*Iris virginica*)

Blue flag is very similar to Dixie iris except for small differences in flower structure and growth form. The stem does not have a zigzag pattern, and the flowers rise above the tips of the foliage. This native iris is found throughout the northern half of Florida and is best used in all but the

Blue flag iris (*Iris virginica*).

southernmost counties. Use this iris as described above in lieu of Dixie iris as they are virtually interchangeable. Both blue flag and Dixie iris are widely propagated and available to homeowners from commercial nurseries.

Blue-Eyed Grass (*Sisyrinchium angustifolium*)

This diminutive iris occurs throughout Florida in a wide variety of moist soil habitats. Although there are several species of blue-eyed grasses in Florida, only this one is widely propagated and available to homeowners for the home landscape. For much of the year, it exists as a clump of evergreen grasslike leaves standing about 6 inches tall. In spring, it produces large numbers of flower stalks from inside these clumps, and masses of 5-petal flowers are present for weeks until early summer. In nature, the flowers are generally sky blue in color, but other color forms are available in the nursery trade, including violet, purple, and white.

Blue-eyed grass makes an excellent ground cover for moist sites at the edges of ponds and water features and along walkways. It spreads rapidly in these conditions by producing new plants from underground rhizomes. Blue-eyed grass eventually forms a beautiful green carpet in all months

Blue-eyed grass (*Sisyrinchium angustifolium*).

and a showy mass of color when flowering. Though it prefers moist soils in sunny locations, blue-eyed grass is exceptionally drought tolerant and tolerant of partial shade. In these situations, however, it will not spread as extensively or bloom as abundantly. Blue-eyed grass is widely propagated and easy to locate from commercial nurseries.

Scrub Blue-Eyed Grass (*Sisyrinchium xerophyllum*)

This drought-tolerant species is only rarely offered by commercial sources, but it is an excellent choice for deep sandy soils and full sun, sites where other blue-eyed grasses would perish. Scrub blue-eyed grass occurs nearly statewide. In most respects, it looks like a robust version of blue-eyed grass. Its grasslike evergreen basal leaves stand about 8–12 inches tall. Flowering occurs in late summer to fall, and the flower stalks stand about 4–6 inches above the foliage. The color of its blooms is rarely as rich a blue as blue-eyed grass, and they are not produced as profusely; however, clumps of scrub blue-eyed grass provide a very attractive element to a mixed bed of wildflowers in xeric growing conditions.

This species is very slow to spread outward from the main clump. Use it in small masses of at least 3–5 plants and space them about 12 inches apart in the front half of the planting bed. Good companion plants include many of the buckwheats, scrub mints, scrub St. John's-wort (*Hypericum*

tenuifolium), and narrowleaf silkgrass. Presently, scrub blue-eyed grass is rarely propagated by commercial nurseries and may be difficult to find.

Scrub blue-eyed grass (*Sisyrinchium xerophyllum*).

Legume Family—Fabaceae

The legumes are a large and diverse group of plants that contain many of our most important food and forage crops as well as some of our showiest trees and shrubs. Legumes are generally fast growing and important in improving soil fertility. Nodules on their roots are capable of capturing atmospheric nitrogen and transferring it to the soil. All members produce beanlike fruit that split longitudinally, exposing many hard seeds. These seeds are very nutritious to wildlife, but some are poisonous to humans. The foliage is also nutritious and frequently browsed by gopher tortoises, rabbits, deer, and other wildlife. Many species of butterflies use legumes as food for their caterpillars.

Leadplants (*Amorpha* spp.)

Leadplants are deciduous woody shrubs that produce fingerlike racemes of brightly colored flowers at the tips of their branches. These flowers are important nectar sources for butterflies, bees, and other insect pollinators. The foliage is also attractive, consisting of lush feathery compound leaves along the length of each stem. Two species are considered native to

Florida, and each is adaptable and easy to grow in the home landscape. Caterpillars of southern dogface sulphur and silver-spotted skipper butterflies feed on both species.

False Indigo or Leadplant (*A. fruticosa*)

False indigo is normally a tall, narrow-crowned, multistemmed shrub, capable of reaching more than 10 feet tall at maturity. It is found throughout Florida, typically at the edges of stream banks and openings within forested wetlands. It has a high tolerance of seasonal flooding and can withstand several inches of standing water for months at a time. In the homes landscape, however, it adapts extremely well to average soil and withstands long periods of drought once established. The specimens I have planted in my home landscape have never required supplemental

False indigo (*Amorpha fruticosa*).

watering, even during times when seemingly more drought-tolerant species were wilting. False indigo blooms sporadically throughout the growing season, but peaks during the late spring to early summer. The flowers are a deep indigo blue, and this color contrasts beautifully with the bright orange anthers that extend from inside each flower tube. False indigo may become a bit lanky over time and responds well to periodic pruning to keep it in better form. Keeping it a bit shorter also keeps the blooms at a height where they can be more easily admired.

Dwarf Indigo (*A. herbacea*)

This species occurs throughout Florida in well-drained sunny locations. It is exceedingly drought tolerant and a wonderful choice for large planting

Dwarf indigo
(*Amorpha herbacea*).

spaces with deep sand and plenty of sun. It rarely stands more than 2–3 feet tall but grows outward and is often much wider than tall. The foliage is a beautiful grayish green and forms a nice contrast to the foliage of adjacent plants in the garden. The flowers are not as showy as those of false indigo. Normally, they are a creamy white, but the yellow-orange anthers and the purplish brown of the unopened buds provide additional interest. Flowering occurs in summer.

Because this plant takes up a lot of room in the landscape, it is not a good choice for small spaces. If you have a more expansive location in good sunlight and well-drained soil, mix it with other tall wildflowers such as kidneyleaf rosinweed, blazing stars, eastern silver aster, and sky blue salvia, as well as grasses such as lop-sided Indiangrass. Dwarf indigo is only rarely offered commercially, so it may take some looking to locate it. It is quite easy to grow from seed collected in the fall.

Wild Indigo (*Baptisia* spp.)

The wild indigos are in a genus that includes eight species of native deciduous herbaceous wildflowers with showy pealike blossoms. Some are exceedingly rare and a few are endemic. All are restricted to the northern half of Florida, and very few are adaptable enough to thrive very far south down the peninsula. These are mostly spring blooming, and flower colors range from white and yellow to blue. Most are rounded and shrubby, reaching a mature height each spring of 2–3 feet. Most also occur in well-drained sunny locations, though a few inhabit moist soil habitats.

Although the wild indigos are attractive and interesting, only wild white indigo (B. alba) is grown commercially, and even this species is often difficult to locate.

Wild white indigo occurs in a variety of habitats throughout the northern third of Florida, including open pinelands, riverbanks, and edges of deciduous forests. It emerges in early spring and grows quickly to a height of about 2 feet. Most often, it is wider than tall, and the many small branches are densely covered in 3-parted bluish green leaves. Multiple flower stalks are produced in March to early April, and these stand about 12–18 inches above the foliage. Relatively large showy bright white blooms crown the tops of the plant for several weeks. This species is

Wild white indigo (*Baptisia alba*).

the reputed caterpillar food plant of a rare skipper known only from the Panhandle: the wild indigo duskywing.

Wild white indigo makes an extremely interesting accent to a mixed wildflower planting bed. Give it at least a half day of sun and average drainage, scatter isolated plants throughout the back half of the bed, and do not crowd it. I have grown wild white indigo in my Pinellas County landscape, but it has not persisted over time, and I do not recommend it for landscapes in the southern half of the peninsula.

Partridge Pea (*Chamaecrista fasciculata*)

Partridge pea is the only member of this genus likely to be planted in a home landscape. Most others are weedy with small yellow or whitish yellow flowers. All partridge peas are annuals or short-lived perennials, and they persist in disturbed habitats by producing large numbers of seeds. The seedlings grow rapidly to maturity and flower sometime from late summer to early winter. The 5 petals are a rich yellow color and quite showy against the finely dissected compound leaves and reddish stems. Partridge pea normally does not stand taller than 2 feet and may be as wide as tall. During its late summer to fall blooming season, it also attracts the attention of several butterfly caterpillars that use it as a food plant: little and cloudless sulphurs, gray hairstreak, and ceraunus blue. These same butterflies often ignore partridge pea at other times. The seeds are eaten by a variety of songbirds, and its foliage is browsed by rabbits, deer, and other wildlife. Although partridge pea is extremely adaptable

Partridge pea (*Chamaecrista fasciculata*).

and has wildlife value, it has a tendency to spread rapidly wherever it finds an opening. If you decide to use it, be prepared to thin the excess seedlings each spring so it doesn't take over. This wildflower is a better choice for expansive areas landscaped in a more natural approach than for small ordered areas. Partridge pea is routinely propagated by commercial native plant nurseries.

Prairie Clovers (*Dalea* spp.)

Florida has four native prairie clovers, and three are excellent candidates for the landscape. They are deciduous perennials that produce deep woody taproots and finely dissected compound leaves. Tiny but showy flowers occur on rounded or cylindrical heads at the ends of their numerous stems. None are widely propagated. If you attempt to grow them from seed, germination is vastly improved if you stratify the seed by putting them in a cup, pouring boiling water over them, and letting it cool before sowing. These are beautiful wildflowers and deserve more attention. None of our native species are commonly propagated by commercial nurseries. Prairie clovers are used as food by the caterpillars of southern dogface sulphur butterflies.

Pink Prairie Clover (*D. carnea*)

This species is sometimes referred to as whitetassels, as two of its three distinct varieties have white flowers instead of pink. Variety *carnea* is found throughout peninsular Florida and is most common in pine flatwoods that are seasonally moist. It has soft pink flowers and grows somewhat close to the ground, producing large numbers of wiry red stems that rarely stand taller than 18 inches. It has 7–9 leaflets per leaf. Variety *albida* occurs in well-drained sandhills throughout the northern third of Florida. It grows more erect than the other varieties and often stands 2 feet tall, with

Pink prairie clover (*Dalea carnea*).

5 leaflets per leaf. Variety *gracilis* occurs only in the central and western Panhandle and tends to grow as a vining ground cover in dry to moist pinelands. All varieties of pink prairie clover are attractive in bloom and mix well with other wildflowers in a typical landscape setting. Plant more than one individual in the front half of the planting bed, spacing them no closer than 3 feet apart, and combine them with other short to medium-tall wildflowers and native grasses such as wiregrass. Pink prairie clover is the most adaptable species in this genus.

Feay's or Scrub Prairie Clover (*D. feayi*)

Feay's prairie clover occurs in deep sandy soils throughout much of peninsular Florida. It is erect and reaches a mature height of about 2 feet by its fall blooming season. The leaves are light green in color and very finely dissected. Mature plants have a decidedly rounded appearance. In the fall, a great many round flower heads are produced across the crown of each plant, and these flowers are a beautiful rose pink in color.

Feay's prairie clover (*Dalea feayi*).

Feay's prairie clover is extremely sensitive to growing conditions and will perish quickly if kept too wet or not given exceptionally good drainage. Do not attempt this species if you cannot meet these requirements or give it full sun. Feay's prairie clover is not a long-lived perennial and rarely spreads in the home landscape. If you can meet its rigid growing requirements, it is a wonderful wildflower to mix with other species. Use it in the middle portion of the planting area and combine it with October flower, scrub St. John's-wort (*Hypericum tenuifolium*), greeneyes, and various scrub mints.

Summer Farewell (D. pinnata)

Summer farewell is a lanky 2–4-foot-tall perennial wildflower with thin red woody stems and finely dissected foliage. It occurs nearly statewide in well-drained sunny locations. Although less showy than other Florida prairie clovers, it has a singular charm all its own. As its common name suggests, it blooms in the late fall. By October, it begins to form its flower buds, and these occur in abundance at the ends of all the branches. The flower buds are bright red in color and quite attractive. Tiny white flowers appear in late October to November, and these are followed by the ripening seeds. Each seed is attached to a silvery "fuzzy" appendage that crowds the outside of the spent flower bud. I like this stage the best; the silvery seed heads remain for much of the winter.

Summer farewell is adaptable to most typical landscape sites, but it requires good drainage or its taproot will rot. It also needs high levels of sunlight to bloom properly. Because it is rather tall and lanky, plant it in clusters of at least 3 and place it in the back half of the planting bed. It looks best in expansive planting areas and mixed with wildflowers such as narrowleaf silkgrass, blazing star, Florida paintbrush, and any of the asters adapted to dry sites.

Summer farewell (*Dalea pinnata*).

Lupines (*Lupinus* spp.)

I include a brief discussion of lupines only because they are such beloved wildflowers in other parts of the country. From New England to the Rocky Mountains and south, perennial or sundial lupine (*L. perennis*) is a staple of the wildflower garden, and across most of Texas, the bluebonnet (*L. texensis*) is revered as the state flower. That is not the case in Florida. Perennial lupine occurs in well-drained sandy sites throughout the Panhandle, but it is not routinely propagated in Florida, and stock from further north is not likely to survive well here. Perennial lupine stands about 2½ feet tall at maturity and is often wider than tall. The flowers are shades of rose to blue or nearly white. If you reside in the Panhandle and live on a site with deep sandy soil, this would be a species to consider, but look for plants originating from the Deep South, not from New England or Colorado.

Other Florida lupines are even more difficult to grow in a landscape setting and are beyond the skill of most experienced gardeners. That is regrettable as we have some truly beautiful native species. All our lupines are very short-lived perennials that tend to expire at about 3 years of age. From my experience, lupines are small seedlings during the first year, bloom lightly during the second, and flower heavily in the third. Third-year plants produce copious numbers of small hard seeds. These remain viable for many years and often sprout following major disturbances, such as fire or shallow tilling. I have grown all of Florida's lupine species in my Pinellas County landscape, but I have never quite figured out how to repeat my limited successes with any surety. Lupines all grow in extremely well-drained sterile sands in full sun. In the wild, their roots become inoculated by specific rhizobial bacteria and form nodules that enable them to survive the poor soils in which they occur. I have used lupine inoculant on seedlings I have germinated at home but have not yet found this to make a difference in their survival. The vast majority of my seedlings eventually perish about the time they are in their 4–6-leaf stage. If you are fortunate enough to have lupines already growing on your property, be thankful; do not be afraid to disturb them occasionally, and do not let a lot of vegetation encroach on them. They require very open and sunny conditions to survive. Otherwise, these are a group not likely to make their way into garden centers any time soon.

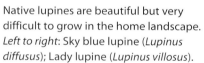

Native lupines are beautiful but very difficult to grow in the home landscape. *Left to right*: Sky blue lupine (*Lupinus diffusus*); Lady lupine (*Lupinus villosus*).

Sunshine Mimosa (*Mimosa strigillosa*)

Sunshine mimosa has become a very popular native ground cover throughout much of Florida because it is extremely tough and attractive. Its very deep woody roots give it great drought tolerance, and it can thrive in nearly any well-drained soil except areas that receive high levels of salt spray or saltwater inundation. In nature, sunshine mimosa is a weedy species that rapidly colonizes open and disturbed ground. In the landscape,

Sunshine mimosa (*Mimosa strigillosa*).

it tends to do much the same, making it a savior to those with expanses of open space to fill or a nuisance to those wanting to mix it with other wildflowers and confine it. I have found that it stays somewhat contained if I shade it with taller native grasses and wildflowers, but I still have to keep it pruned so that it does not escape into spots I want to keep it away from.

Sunshine mimosa is a sprawling ground cover that generally stays less than 2 inches tall. It roots periodically where its stems make contact with the ground and quickly branches out from each of these points. The foliage is dainty and attractive, but it's the beautiful pink "powderpuff" flowers that give it its main charm. These stand 2–3 inches above the ground and are produced in abundance during the spring and summer months. The flowers are mostly of interest to bees, though butterflies will occasionally use them as well. Caterpillars of the little sulfur butterfly make occasional use of this plant as food. Use this species as a ground cover to replace turfgrass, but take care to confine it by putting obstacles such as concrete sidewalks and driveways in its way, or areas of deep shade. Without such obstacles, it may well venture into your neighbor's property.

American Wisteria (*Wisteria frutescens*)

American wisteria is a deciduous woody vine native to wetland habitats in the northern half of Florida. It produces a stout woody trunk and many branches that extend more than 10 feet in all directions. It is much less aggressive and robust than Chinese wisteria (*W. sinensis*), but it can still be

American wisteria
(*Wisteria frutescens*).

difficult to contain. Though a wetland plant, it will thrive in most typical landscape conditions if provided a bit of supplemental watering during extended periods of drought. Alexa and I have kept ours in our front yard for nearly a decade and it has done well despite poor soils and full sun. American wisteria needs the support of a fence or trellis or it will ramble everywhere and its flowers be largely hidden in the adjacent foliage. On a trellis or fence, it will twine its way up and around the supporting structure and eventually form a mass of woody stems. Do not prune American wisteria before it blooms, as the flowers are produced on last year's growth. Masses of lilac-colored blossoms occur from late spring to early summer. American wisteria is one of a great many species reportedly eaten by caterpillars of the long-tailed skipper butterfly.

As this is a woody vine, it needs sufficient room to ramble or it will look out of place and require constant pruning, and because it is deciduous, it loses much of its aesthetic appeal for about 4 months during the winter. But if you have a place for it, American wisteria is a beautiful and useful vine worthy of inclusion in the home landscape. Do not try to mix it with other vines, however, as it will overpower them.

Lily Family—Liliaceae

Florida has many native lilies, but most are rare and difficult to grow and maintain in the home landscape because they require very specific growing conditions that are hard to duplicate. Though most native lilies should be attempted only by experienced gardeners, success is rewarded by their spectacular flowers. These "difficult" members often require moist rich soils, and I have had the best luck growing them in landscape pots where I can carefully control soil, moisture, fertility, and sunlight. Lilies grow from bulbs, and new plants often arise as side bulbs produced from the main one. They have linear straplike leaves, and most species are deciduous. Not all lilies produce the funnel-shaped flowers we often associate with this family.

Lilies (*Lilium* spp.)

True lilies have always been favorites of home gardeners. Their brightly colored flowers are produced for extended periods during the growing season, and they often spread slowly to form wonderful masses of strap-like leaves and color. Florida has four species of native lilies, and all are rare and extremely habitat specific. Turk's-cap lily (*L. superbum*) has been recorded occasionally from a few North Florida counties, but is common to our north. Michaux's or Carolina lily (*L. michauxii*) occurs only in a three-county area in northernmost Florida in rich deciduous woods, and panhandle lily (*L. iridollae*) is a rare wetland lily of the western Panhandle.

All are occasionally of-
fered for sale but require
special care to thrive. The
commonly planted non-
native day lily (*Hemero-
callis fulva*) is not a "lily,"
but an amaryllis.

All four of Florida's native lilies (*Lilium* spp.) are rare and largely unavailable for the home landscape. This panhandle lily (*L. iridollae*) is found only in a few western Panhandle counties.

Pine or Catesby's Lily (*L. catesbaei*)

The pine lily occurs throughout most of Florida, but only in open pine-lands, prairies, and savannas that tend to stay wet during the summer rainy season. If kept too dry, it may not produce leaves during the year and its bulbs will remain dormant until better conditions arrive. Blooming occurs only during years when conditions are ideal: moist and sunny, and often following a fire. Pine lilies flower in late summer to early November. Each plant produces only one bloom, but it is magnificent. The flowers stand several feet above the ground and are bright orange to brick red (sometimes yellow) with darker spots near the base, almost 4 inches across, and held upright. The flowers remain open for about a week before fading and are especially attractive to swallowtail butterflies.

Pine lilies are difficult to propagate as the seedlings are susceptible to fungal diseases and take several years to mature to a blooming-sized adult. Even the side bulbs take several years to reach maturity. For this reason, it is rarely grown by commercial nurseries and may be difficult to find. Do not attempt this plant if you cannot give it moist to wet conditions during the summer and plenty of sunshine. Plant it in small clusters of 3–5 plants, spaced about 1 foot apart. Mix pine lilies with other wildflowers native to moist savannas and flatwoods and with wiregrass or pinewoods dropseed.

Pine lily (*Lilium catesbaei*).

Meadow Beauty Family—Melastomataceae

The meadow beauties (*Rhexia* spp.) are herbaceous perennials native to sunny, moist-soil habitats. They are deciduous and disappear during the

The meadow beauties (*Rhexia* spp.) are a widespread genus found statewide mostly in marshes and moist open savannas. Most species are pink and similar to this Nash's meadow beauty (*R. nashii*).

winter months, but return in early spring. Most have very thin stiff stems and widely spaced linear leaves. At maturity, they reach 12–18 inches in height. What they lack in terms of foliage appeal is compensated by their brightly colored flowers. All the meadow beauties have 4 oval petals that encircle the center like a pinwheel. At the center are the bright yellow reproductive structures. Blooming occurs over a protracted period from spring to fall, and in many species several flowers may be open at any one time per stem. Once the flowers are pollinated, urn-shaped seed capsules result, and these are carried on the stems well into winter.

Meadow beauties are only rarely offered commercially and are difficult to grow unless planted in sites with suitable moisture, especially during the heat of summer, but when these conditions are met, they will sucker and form colonies. None are aggressive and they will not become dominant in a mixed wildflower setting. Most produce deep rose pink blooms. The best of these for much of Florida are tall meadow beauty (*R. alifanus*), pale meadow beauty (*R. mariana*), and Nash's meadow beauty (*R. nashii*). A beautiful yellow-petal species, yellow meadow beauty (*R. lutea*) can be grown in the northern third of the state.

Milkweed Family—Apocynaceae

The milkweeds (or dogbanes) are a group of plants that usually produce a milky, latex-like sap, evident when the leaves and stems are cut or bruised. Many are toxic (hence one of the common names given the family), but some have been used extensively in medicines. The group includes some of our most popular non-native ornamentals: oleander (*Nerium oleander*), periwinkle (*Vinca* spp.), Natal plum (*Carissa* spp.), frangipani (*Plumeria* spp.), confederate jasmine (*Trachelospermum jasminoides*), and mandevilla (*Mandevilla* spp.). It also includes some very popular wildflowers. The most adaptable species for the home landscape are discussed below.

Blue Star (*Amsonia ciliata*)

Blue star is found throughout much of the northern two-thirds of Florida in sites with well-drained sandy soils and full sun. It is a long-lived deciduous perennial that dies back to the ground each winter. In the spring, it makes its appearance as a whorl of soft needle-like leaves. Within a relatively short time, it reaches its mature height of about 18 inches. The thin straight stem is covered by simple leaves that are about 2 inches long and ½ inch wide. These leaves go all the way up the stem to the flower head. Blue star blooms in late spring. Numerous sky blue to whitish blue flowers are borne in a dense panicle that makes this species quite showy.

Blue star is adaptable to the home landscape if planted in soils with excellent drainage and provided ample sunlight. Do not try to use it in locations where it will get shaded by taller neighbors or where water might stand,

Blue star (*Amsonia ciliata*).

even for short periods. This wildflower is rather diminutive and does not stand out when not in bloom. For this reason, plant it in clusters of at least 5 and use it near walkways or the front of a mixed wildflower planting. Blue star does not sucker or spread in the garden.

Eastern Blue Star (*Amsonia tabernaemontana*)

Eastern blue star has much the same wonderful color as its close relative, but it is native to moist soils and the partial shade found in deciduous forest floors. In Florida, eastern blue star is found naturally only in North Florida, but it can be grown well into Central Florida if given the right growing conditions. This deciduous perennial wildflower stands about 3 feet tall by late spring. The main stem is rather thin and tends to bend over a bit with the weight of the flowers. The leaves are similar in length to those of blue star but are lance shaped instead of linear. The light blue to almost white flowers are borne at the top of the stems in a loose panicle. They are quite

Eastern blue star (*Amsonia tabernaemontana*).

handsome, but a bit smaller and less showy than those of blue star.

This is a wonderful addition to a semishaded woodland planting but performs best in deciduous settings where it can receive ample sunlight as it emerges in the spring. Although it prefers moist soils, it will tolerate average conditions once established. Mix this species with violets, Indian pink, wild ginger, jack-in-the-pulpit, and other wildflowers with similar habitat requirements, as well as ferns such as Christmas and southern lady fern, and ebony spleenwort. Both species of native blue stars are only occasionally offered commercially, but they are worth the effort to track down.

True Milkweeds (*Asclepias* spp.)

Milkweeds are well known to Florida butterfly gardeners as the food of monarch, queen, and soldier butterfly caterpillars. All our native milkweeds, except butterfly milkweed, produce the white milky sap that provides the caterpillars protection from birds and other vertebrate predators. By ingesting these toxic chemical compounds, the caterpillars become toxic themselves, and vertebrate predators, such as birds, learn to avoid them. Milkweed flowers are complex in structure and pollinated only by bees and butterflies of a size that fits the size of the bloom. When they are pollinated, they produce distinctive pods that split open to release the seeds, each attached to a fluffy "tail." Florida has 21 native milkweeds, but the most commonly planted species, scarlet milkweed (*A. curassavica*), is not native. Very few native milkweeds are grown commercially, and many are difficult to maintain in a home landscape as they are extremely sensitive to growing conditions. I describe what I believe to be the best choices below.

Purple Milkweed (*A. humistrata*)

Purple milkweed is native to the northern two-thirds of Florida and resident to habitats with excessively well-drained sands and full sun. It is a multistemmed deciduous perennial that dies back each fall and emerges in early spring. Purple milkweed is robust, but sprawling, and sends its multiple stems in all directions across the ground. At maturity, these stems may be more than 2 feet long. Its common name comes from the color of its large oval leaves. They

Purple milkweed (*Asclepias humistrata*).

are a purplish green with pink-purple veins throughout. Purple milkweed blooms in early summer at the end of each stem. The flowers are a dull pinkish white and occur in large rounded heads held about 1 foot off the ground.

Purple milkweed is not the most beautiful native species, but its variegated foliage and large flower masses make it an interesting addition to a large planting area. Do not attempt it in small spaces as it will overwhelm them. This is a difficult species to maintain in containers, so it is rarely grown commercially. In the landscape, it will rot quickly if planted in soils that stay too moist. If you have excessively well-drained sands in a sunny location, a bit of space, and an interest in milkweed butterflies, purple milkweed provides a great many benefits to a mixed wildflower planting.

Swamp Rose Milkweed (*A. incarnata*)

Swamp rose milkweed is one of the most beautiful members of this genus and well worth making a place for in the home landscape. Native throughout peninsular Florida, it occurs in moist to wet soil habitats in sunny locations. In the home landscape, it needs similar conditions to thrive, but it can tolerate occasional short-lived drought once established. Swamp rose milkweed emerges in the early spring and eventually reaches

Swamp rose milkweed (*Asclepias incarnata*).

a mature height of about 3–4 feet. The stems are stout and multibranched while the leaves are lance shaped, up to 6 inches long, and abundant along the stems. Blooming occurs in summer. Large rounded heads of rose pink, slightly fragrant flowers adorn the ends of each stem and are showy.

Use this species in small clusters of at least 3–5 each for the best effect and plant it in locations that stay wet in the summer months, the edges of ponds and other water features. In our Pinellas County landscape, we created a wetland where this species has done well. It withers quickly, however, if the soil dries out. This beautiful milkweed is often available from commercial sources as seed or plants. The seed requires cold stratification to germinate in good numbers. Keep it moist, in the refrigerator, for 2–3 months to break its dormancy.

Swamp White Milkweed (*A. perennis*)

This is the "other" swamp milkweed, but quite a different species from *A. incarnata*, described above. As its common name implies, swamp white milkweed occurs in wetland habitats, including semishaded forests. It can survive lower levels of direct sunlight than our other native species, but becomes lankier and flowers less abundantly in these conditions. Swamp white milkweed requires good soil moisture to prosper. It

Swamp white milkweed (*Asclepias perennis*).

has some drought tolerance and is more easily grown than swamp rose milkweed but eventually fails if not provided with plenty of water during the summer months. This is a somewhat diminutive species. At mature height in the late spring, its many stems rarely stand taller than 2 feet. Each is densely covered by lance-shaped bright green leaves approximately 2 inches in length. Swamp white milkweed blooms in the summer. Although it does not produce large flower heads, each is composed of attractive bright white flowers. This species is commonly propagated for home gardeners and is quite hardy if used in locations that stay moist to wet. For best effect, plant it in small clusters of at least 3 and use it near the front of the planting bed.

Butterfly Milkweed (*A. tuberosa*)

Butterfly milkweed is the most widely recognized native milkweed for the home landscape. It occurs across much of North America in a wide variety of habitats, but in Florida is confined to areas of well-drained sandy soils. If planted in poorly drained soil, its underground stem will quickly rot and the plant will die. Florida butterfly milkweed is often a rather gangly plant compared with specimens found in other states. Our specimens are often single stemmed with short multiple branches, but older individuals may produce several stems from their woody base beneath the soil. Butterfly milkweed is deciduous and emerges in early spring, eventually

Butterfly milkweed (*Asclepias tuberosa*).

reaching a mature height of 12–24 inches. The leaves are oval and a rather dull green in color. What make it so spectacular are its blooms. Butterfly milkweed may bloom at any time from late spring to late fall, and individual plants will produce flowers successively throughout this time period. Large rounded umbels of bright orange to brick red or light yellow flowers provide a color accent few other wildflowers can produce.

Plant it in small clusters for the most impact and near the middle of a mixed wildflower planting. Good companion species are narrowleaf silkgrass, blazing stars, eastern silver aster, Florida paintbrush, and other species common to sandhill and scrub. Wiregrass and pinewoods dropseed are good companion grasses. Do not attempt to grow it from seed or stock originating from outside Florida. Out-of-state plants rarely persist. Even native butterfly milkweed is touchy in regard to growing conditions, but if you can provide the well-drained sands it needs, use it in numbers.

Wild Allamanda (*Pentalinon luteum*)

Native wild allamanda is not the same as the non-native allamanda (*Allamanda cathartica*) sold in most garden centers across the southern half of Florida. Both are members of the milkweed family and both produce beautiful trumpet-shaped yellow flowers, but the native species is a sprawling herbaceous vine with stems that may extend more than 12 feet from the center base. Wild allamanda also produces smaller flowers, but very large numbers of them. Flowering occurs from spring through fall on the evergreen stems. In nature, wild allamanda is common to coastal habitats in South Florida. It is extremely tough and can survive high amounts of salt and sun, as well as soils that vary from dry to wet; it does not survive temperatures much below freezing, however. Wild allamanda needs lots of room and good

Wild allamanda (*Pentalinon luteum*).

levels of sunlight in the home landscape. If you have the space, grow it on a trellis or fence. Just don't attempt it in locations where freezing temperatures are common.

Mint Family—Lamiaceae

The mint family is diverse and contains some of my favorite wildflowers. Within this family are some of Florida's rarest species and some of its most common, everything from woody perennials to herbaceous annuals. What they have in common are highly aromatic foliage, square stems, leaves that are opposite each other on the stems, and tubular flowers that have a large lower petal shaped like a lip. These flowers come in a wide variety of colors, and most are predominantly bee pollinated, though butterflies and even hummingbirds frequent some.

Calamints (*Calamintha* spp.)

This group of mints consists of woody perennials adapted to excessively well-drained sands and high sunlight. All but one are state-listed threatened or endangered species and none are common; however, they include some of Florida's most beautiful mints and deserve far more attention in the landscape than they have been given to date. Three of our four native species are sometimes offered for sale commercially and have great landscape potential. The fourth, toothed savory (*C. dentata*), is beautiful also, but too diminutive to attract much attention from all but the most ardent plant connoisseurs. Do not crowd calamints. Plant them no closer than 2 feet apart and allow for open space between them.

Ashe's Savory (*C. ashei*)

Ashe's savory occurs in parts of the central peninsula, in white and yellow sand scrub. It is rarely taller than 12–18 inches but becomes quite round with age and may be more than 2 feet in diameter. Tiny blue-green oval leaves crowd its many stems. Each leaf curls under noticeably and gives off a wintergreen aroma when bruised. With age, Ashe's savory assumes a sort of bonsai aspect that gives it great ornamental value throughout the year. Flowering is most abundant in late spring, though sporadic blooming occurs into fall. The blooms are normally soft pinkish lavender with darker spots on the lower lip, but some forms may be nearly white or deep lavender.

Ashe's savory does not seem to be a long-lived species in nature. Really large woody specimens are rare, and I suspect that few individuals live more than 5–7 years. Do not attempt this species if you cannot provide it with coarse, sharply drained sands and high levels of sunlight. It will quickly die from root rot if these conditions are not met. This species is rarely offered for sale by commercial nurseries.

Ashe's savory
(*Calamintha ashei*).

Red Basil (*C. coccinea*)

Red basil occurs sporadically throughout North and Central Florida, generally in scrub and sandhill habitats. This is an upright species that

Red basil (*Calamintha coccinea*).

eventually develops a rather stout woody trunk and numerous side branches. Specimens can become 3–4 feet tall but begin flowering at a much smaller size. The leaves are shiny green in color and oval shaped, but they tend to align themselves almost parallel to the stems, and this tends to make the many thin branches look a bit scrawny. Though red basil is not the most beautiful foliage plant in this genus, it has spectacular flowers. Large tubular flowers cover the crowns of each plant from late spring through fall. Each bloom is nearly 2 inches long, and the color can vary from light orange or yellow to deep red. They are hummingbird pollinated, though cloudless sulphur butterflies and a few of the swallowtails also visit them.

Red basil can be grown throughout most of Florida, but must be planted in sites with coarse, well-drained sand and high sunlight. I have killed many of these beautiful mints over the years by attempting them in the typical sandy soil I inherited with the house. Do not make that mistake. Even if they are planted in ideal conditions, expect a few plants to perish in the transfer from pot culture to the landscape. Red basil is normally available from a few commercial native nurseries.

Georgia calamint (*Calamintha georgiana*) with honey bee.

Georgia Calamint
(*C. georgiana*)

Georgia calamint is very rare in Florida and occurs naturally in just two counties in the extreme western Panhandle. Nevertheless, it is easy to grow and propagate and can be used well into South Central Florida with reasonable success. This species develops a strong woody central stem with many ascending side braches. Mature specimens reach about 2 feet tall and are attractive foliage plants. The leaves are deep shiny green and elliptical. Unlike other calamints, it is somewhat deciduous in the winter, and the tops of the plants may also die back at this time. New foliage reappears in late winter. The flowers are reminiscent of Ashe's savory, but a bit more lavender and tubular. Flowering occurs mostly during the late fall and continues into December if temperatures stay above freezing.

Georgia calamint is not a long-lived species, but can live for 5–7 years if given good drainage and sunshine. It is not quite as habitat specific as other Florida calamints and can persist in the sandy soils typical of most Florida landscapes. Currently, this mint is being widely propagated in Florida and should not be too difficult to find.

False Rosemaries (*Conradina* spp.)

Like the calamints, the false rosemaries are a small group of woody perennials native to areas with exceedingly well-drained sands and high sunlight. Most are quite rare in nature and many Florida species are endemic, though they can be grown in landscapes well outside their natural ranges. The false rosemaries tend to be larger and more robust than the calamints; some eventually get almost shrublike, with a stout central trunk and many thin woody branches. All have needlelike evergreen leaves that release a strong minty aroma when bruised and beautiful flowers in shades of light lavender and purple. They make superb additions to sunny landscapes with well-drained sandy soils. Give them plenty of room and space them at least 3 feet apart. False rosemaries mix well with other woody mints and with a wide variety of sandhill and scrub wildflowers such as blazing stars, narrowleaf silkgrass, palafoxias, garberia, and the like. All four or five of our species are available commercially, but only three are described below. Etonia false rosemary (*C. etonia*) is very similar to large-flowered false rosemary (*C. grandiflora*) but found naturally only in Putnam County. Short-leaved false rosemary (*C. brevifolia*) has recently been combined with the more widely distributed false rosemary (*C. canescens*) by most taxonomists, though they have distinct differences and quite distinct natural ranges that do not overlap.

False Rosemary (*C. canescens*)

False rosemary is native to coastal scrubs in the western Panhandle while the former *C. brevifolia* is found only in the Lake Wales Ridge in Polk and Highlands counties. It becomes a large upright shrub over time with sprawling brittle branches, standing 3–4 feet tall and at least as wide. The

False rosemary (*Conradina canescens*).

leaves of the Panhandle population tend to be more "hairy" than the Lake Wales Ridge form, but both are "canescent," and this tends to make the foliage look blue green and a bit fuzzy. Flowering occurs sporadically throughout the year (even in winter if temperatures do not remain below freezing for too many days in a row), but it is heaviest during the spring. The flowers are about ¾ inch long and light lavender with a deeper lavender blotch and a number of purple spots on the lower lip. The Panhandle form tends to have richer colored flowers than the Lake Wales Ridge form.

False rosemary is relatively easy to grow compared with many of the other woody scrub mints. It requires excellent drainage to prosper and is susceptible to root fungal diseases if the soil remains too wet for long. It also needs plenty of sun and elbow room. If given the right growing conditions, it may live for decades. Do not be afraid to prune it judiciously if it begins to spread too far. Propagate new plants from these cuttings. It is quite easy and the best way to add to what you have.

Apalachicola False Rosemary (*C. glabra*)

Apalachicola false rosemary is one of Florida's rarest native mints and has been reported only from Liberty County in the central Panhandle and Santa Rosa County in the extreme western Panhandle. It is also one of the most beautiful members of this genus. Apalachicola false rosemary generally grows as a dense mound and does not get as leggy as other species. The leaves are deep green in color. Mature plants rarely stand taller than 2 feet but may be several feet across. Flowering occurs mostly in the fall, though flowers are also produced in spring and summer. The flower shape is similar to that of false rosemary, but the color tends to be much paler lavender. Apalachicola false rosemary requires the same growing conditions as false rosemary; when these are provided, it is a rather easy species to maintain. Specimens I monitored, planted in Pinellas County scrub, thrived for years and declined only when the area became too overgrown and shaded. This species is a state and federal endangered species and only rarely grown by commercial sources.

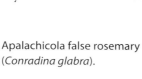

Apalachicola false rosemary (*Conradina glabra*).

Large-Flowered False Rosemary (*C. grandiflora*)

This false rosemary occurs throughout the peninsular east coast of Florida in coastal scrub. As such, it has good tolerance of salt spray but requires

Large-flowered false rosemary (*Conradina grandiflora*).

deep sandy soils and plenty of sun. Large-flowered false rosemary becomes a large woody shrub over time and eventually reaches a height of about 4 feet and a circumference nearly equal to that. Its foliage is shiny and bright green, much like that of Apalachicola false rosemary, but the leaves tend to be a bit shorter and not quite as dense along the stems. Flowering occurs mostly in the spring, though it can occur during any month. Each flower is at least 1 inch long and characterized by elongated lips that droop slightly. The color is light lavender, and the lower lip has dark purple spots. As with other members of this genus, large-flowered false rosemary requires excellent drainage or its roots will rot. This scrub mint is generally available from commercial sources in Florida.

Scrub Balms (*Dicerandra* spp.)

Scrub balms are beautiful but short-lived mints and only rarely propagated for home landscapes. Most are exceedingly rare in nature, found only in excessively well-drained yellow sand scrub. I include them in this book only because they are fascinating additions to a scrub landscape and not that difficult to grow if given full sun and coarse-grained sandy soils. Six species of short-lived perennials and one annual are endemic to Florida. One other annual occurs in a bit wider distribution around Florida. All the perennials are listed as state and federal endangered species and tend to live for only a few years before expiring. Scrub balms tend to grow no taller than 12–18 inches but produce thin branches that grow outward for about the same distance. The leaves are oval, bright green, and highly aromatic. Flowering occurs mostly in the fall. The petals are either pink or white and most are covered in deep red dots.

I have grown all members of this genus at one time or another in my Pinellas County landscape, both in white sand and in yellow, but they cannot be grown together or they will hybridize. The flowers are bee pollinated. Scrub balms persist by producing huge numbers of tiny seeds, and these need to fall on bare sand in sunny locations to germinate successfully. If you can provide these conditions and locate a reputable nursery that has propagated their stock legally, the scrub balms make beautiful additions to a scrub garden. Mix them with other woody scrub mints, blazing stars, silkgrasses, etc., and give them plenty of space so not to be overcrowded.

Florida's scrub balms (*Dicerandra* spp.) are rare in nature and in cultivation. Flowers vary in color from white to pink, and most, like this annual coastalplain scrub balm (*D. linearifolia*), are covered in deep purple markings.

Dotted Horsemint or Spotted Bee Balm (*Monarda punctata*)

Dotted horsemint is one of the most common native mints in Florida. It occurs nearly statewide in a wide variety of upland habitats, is tolerant of salt spray, and will grow nearly anywhere except wetlands. Dotted horsemint is a robust perennial that dies back to the ground in early winter. In the southern half of Florida, it keeps its basal leaves through the winter. Elsewhere, it tends to be fully deciduous and may act more like an annual than a perennial. In late winter to very early spring, it begins to grow rapidly and by late summer stands 4–5 feet tall with multiple woody stems. With its lance-shaped shiny green leaves, dotted horsemint is an attractive foliage plant, but it can almost be too large if used in smaller gardens. If the stems fall over, prune them back a bit in early summer. This will not affect flowering. Flowering occurs for up to four weeks during the fall. The flowers are cream colored with many dots and subtended by large showy lavender bracts. The flowers are arranged in whorls around the tops of the branches. Dotted horsemint is visited by every pollinating insect imaginable. In fact, insects you may have never seen before will make an appearance once this plant flowers, and they will disappear as soon as the season passes. This makes a small patch of dotted horsemint absolutely fascinating to behold during the fall months.

Dotted horsemint should be planted near the back of a planting area or in corners of the landscape where it can grow as a patch by itself. When mixed with other species, it tends to crowd them out over time. Its other negative attribute is its ability to reseed and spread. If left un-

Dotted horsemint (*Monarda punctata*).

checked, dotted horsemint will eventually colonize every bare spot of soil in your landscape. To counter this, cut it back as soon as the flowers begin to wither, and be prepared to pull the seedlings from areas they are not welcome. Otherwise, this is one of the easiest wildflowers to grow in Florida.

Obedient Plant (*Physostegia virginiana*)

Obedient plant is one of four species of *Physostegia* native to Florida, but the only one likely to be sold commercially. It occurs throughout the northern two-thirds of Florida in sunny to partly sunny wet to moist soil habitats and does not perform well in soils that regularly dry out. Obedient plant gets its common name from the fact that you can take its open flowers, push them gently 90 degrees, and they will stay in their new location. In the garden, however, they are not so "obedient." Obedient plant multiples rapidly by underground runners when given moist soil and eventually becomes a dense colony. This ability to multiply can be a wonderful attribute when it is planted at the edge of a pond or stream, but a problem if attempted in a confined space where it needs to mix with other species. Obedient plant produces long linear stems that stand 3–4 feet tall. Blooming occurs in late summer and fall. The deep pink tubular flowers make a spectacular show when grown in a mass. They are pollinated by a wide assortment of insects and by hummingbirds.

Obedient plant
(*Physostegia virginiana*).

False Pennyroyal (*Piloblephis rigida*)

False pennyroyal occurs throughout the Florida peninsula in a wide variety of upland settings. It is very drought tolerant, but it also occurs in the understories of moist pinelands. It has little tolerance for salts, however,

False pennyroyal
(*Piloblephis
rigida*).

and will not persist long in sites that remain too wet. False pennyroyal is a short-lived evergreen perennial. Specimens rarely live more than three years, and it persists in nature by producing large numbers of tiny seeds. Mature specimens are round in shape and about 12 inches tall. The foliage is bright shiny green, dense on its many short branches, needlelike, and especially aromatic, having a fragrance much like that of true pennyroyal. Flowering occurs in spring. Large numbers of rabbit's-foot–shaped flower heads are produced across the crown of the plant, and tiny spotted lavender flowers appear in masses. These are particularly attractive to butterflies and a wide variety of other insect pollinators.

False pennyroyal is a wonderful wildflower for open sunny locations near walkways, paths, and the front of planting beds. Plant it in a mass, with individual plants 12 inches apart. It mixes extremely well with other short wildflowers such as rockrose (*Helianthemum* spp.), morning buttercup (*Piriqueta cistoides* subsp. *caroliniana*), and skullcap (*Scutellaria* spp.). Because it is not long lived, be prepared to replace it every few years. False pennyroyal is easy to propagate from cuttings, but I have never had it self-sow in my gardens with any success.

Salvias (*Salvia* spp.)

Salvias, or sages, are standards in a great many landscapes. There are a huge number of North American species regularly grown and sold commercially for the landscape as well as a great many from South and Central America. Eight species are native to Florida, but only a few are likely to be used in home landscapes. Salvias tend to have brightly colored tubular flowers, but they vary greatly in growth habit. The best species for Florida landscapes are described below.

Sky Blue Salvia (*S. azurea*)

Sky blue salvia occurs in much of Florida in sunny well-drained habitats. It is strictly deciduous and dies back to the ground in late fall. Growth is rapid in spring, and it produces several main stems that reach 4–6 feet in length by late summer. At this stage, it has few basal leaves and the stems are only sparsely clothed in lance-shaped leaves about 1 inch in length. The long stems also tend to lean or fall over; this is especially evident when the plants are grown in too much shade or too rich a soil. Although

Sky blue salvia (*Salvia azurea*).

sky blue salvia is not an especially attractive foliage plant, it is striking when in bloom. In late summer to fall, it produces large numbers of brilliant sky blue flowers. Solitary specimens can get lost in the landscape, but stands of this plant, with their flower stalks waving gently in the fall breeze, make up for any other inadequacies it may have. This is not a plant for small spaces. Plant it in clusters of 3–5 individuals at the back of a sunny well-drained site expansive enough not to make it look out of place. Sky blue salvia is not aggressive in a garden setting and does not spread easily the way most other salvias do. It is also not forgiving of soils that stay too moist.

Red Salvia or Tropical Sage (*S. coccinea*)

Red salvia occurs statewide in a wide variety of upland settings. It can tolerate salt spray and partial shade, but prospers when given full sun and soils with good drainage. Because of this adaptability, it is one of the most widely planted native wildflowers in Florida and one of the easiest to maintain. Red salvia is semitropical in nature. In parts of the state that rarely freeze, it is a short-lived perennial that keeps its basal leaves through the winter and flowers sporadically. Where freezing temperatures are more common, it tends to act more like an annual. Blooming can occur almost anytime, but is most abundant in summer and fall. Mature plants reach 3–4 feet in height, but periodic pruning to keep them about 2–3 feet tall serves to give them a better shape. The abundant flowers are bright scarlet red in color and attract hummingbirds as well as butterflies, bees, and other pollinators. Each flower is about 1 inch long. A variety of other colors are available, including white, salmon, and pink, though these are recessive traits and over time, new plants will mostly be red.

Red salvia is extremely versatile, but it has a tendency to seed heavily and move about the garden. Seedlings need to be thinned each year to keep populations in check, especially in plantings designed to be mixed with other species. In northernmost Florida, this species should persist through annual reseeding. Do not deadhead the spent blooms until winter to ensure that the seeds have been released to the soil beneath.

Red salvia (*Salvia coccinea*).

Lyre-Leaved Sage (*S. lyrata*)

Lyre-leaved sage is also common statewide, but it tends to do best in moist soils in the partially shaded edges of wooded areas, and in moist open savannas and prairies. It is extremely adaptable, however, and can be grown in a wide variety of landscape settings if not given too much sun or drought. Lyre-leaved sage spends much of the year as a basal rosette of oval leaves, each marked by irregular dark purple splotches on the upper surface. Blooming occurs strictly in the spring. Each plant produces a 1–2-foot-tall flower stalk with numerous buds, and each opens to a rich blue flower. Once flowering is over, the stalks quickly mature and die, leaving only the basal

leaves again until next spring. Lyre-leaved sage sometimes produces a second flower stalk in fall, but these buds are cleistogamous, that is, producing seed without ever opening as "flowers."

Use this wildflower as a substitute for turfgrass in semishady areas or in small patches in a mixed wildflower and fern planting that receives sun for half days. It will rapidly spread throughout the landscape when its growing conditions are met but is easy to thin out. Areas of lyre-leaved sage can be mowed throughout the year, if desired, except during the few weeks it is in bloom. It can also withstand some foot traffic if used as an alternative to turfgrass.

Lyre-leaved sage (*Salvia lyrata*) with nectaring honey bee.

Common Skullcap (*Scutellaria integrifolia*)

Common skullcap is far too underused in Florida landscapes, given its many wonderful qualities. The genus *Scutellaria* contains 11 somewhat similar native species, but only common skullcap is generally grown

Common skullcap (*Scutellaria integrifolia*).

commercially and available to home gardens. It is found in a variety of mostly wetland sites throughout Florida, except the most extreme southern counties, but is highly adaptable, tough, and persistent—all attributes that should endear it to gardeners looking for something that requires almost no attention to thrive. Common skullcap dies back to its basal leaves each winter. In spring, it begins to actively grow and eventually reaches a mature height of 12–18 inches. The leaves are somewhat variable in shape. The basal leaves are oval, but leaves heading up the main stem and side branches are more linear. Blooming is most pronounced in the spring. Large numbers of light blue "helmeted" flowers occur at the tops of all the branches. These are pollinated mostly by bees and become a flurry of activity for the several weeks the plants are in bloom. Later, the distinctive papery seed capsules remain for weeks on the spent flower stalks.

Common skullcap spreads throughout the garden by seed and finds its way eventually to nearly every open space available to it. Because of its small size, it does not crowd out its neighbors and its numbers are easy to thin if desired. Use it in the front half of mixed planting beds with other small to medium-sized wildflowers, including twinflower, wild petunia, black-eyed susan, and pink beardtongue (*Penstemon australis*), and mix in a few of the short native grasses such as pinewoods dropseed and wiregrass.

Blue Curls (*Trichostema dichotomum*)

Blue curls is nearly ubiquitous in Florida uplands but especially common in disturbed open fields throughout the state. It is an annual that spreads aggressively by its abundant seed production. Blue curls grows rapidly from seedlings in the late winter and eventually reaches a mature height of about 3 feet in early fall. By then, it is lanky with many side branches and elliptical shiny green leaves. Though a bit weedy looking, it is transformed when in full bloom. Each plant produces hundreds of deep blue flowers with a white, blue-spotted blotch on the lower lip. The stamens are elongated, deep blue, and noticeably curled above the petals, giving it its common name. The large number of uniquely colored and shaped flowers makes a striking appearance, but the flowers fade quickly by early afternoon. New flowers appear each morning for nearly a month.

Blue curls (*Trichostema dichotomum*).

Blue curls is very easy to grow and maintain in most home landscape conditions, except for sites that remain wet for extended periods. It will perform well in nearly every soil type, but it does best when given full sun for at least half the day. Use blue curls in small patches near the back half of a mixed wildflower planting. If you decide to add it, do not mulch your beds heavily or it may not reseed well. Just be prepared to thin out the unwanted seedlings each spring or you will eventually have it everywhere.

Morning Glory Family—Convolvulaceae

Most of us are familiar with morning glories. These herbaceous vines weave their way through fences and trellises, producing brightly colored trumpet-shaped flowers that remain open only during the morning hours. Of the many native morning glories in Florida, most are considered "weeds," and very few are grown commercially and sold for home landscapes. The rather weedy tendencies of most species and their annual nature seemingly outweigh their beautiful blooms in the minds of most, but they can be easily propagated from seed collected from their rounded seed capsules if you wish to add them. Most morning glories bloom for a great many months from late spring to late fall. The few species that are sometimes commercially grown are described below.

Scrub Morning Glory (*Bonamia grandiflora*)

Scrub morning glory is a very rare perennial vine native only to a few open scrub locations in Central Florida. It is infrequently offered commercially but is one of the most beautiful members of the family. Scrub morning glory dies back completely to the ground each winter and resprouts from its woody base in early spring. Multiple leads sprawl across the open sand and eventually reach a length of 6 feet or more. Blooming occurs in late

Scrub morning glory (*Bonamia grandiflora*).

spring and summer. Huge sky blue flowers, 3–4 inches across, are produced singly along the length of the stems for several weeks. They lie sideways on the bare white sand and attract a wide variety of bees and other pollinators.

Scrub morning glory is extremely sensitive to growing conditions. It requires perfect drainage and full sun or it will quickly expire. Do not let it become crowded by nearby plants. It needs open conditions and plenty of "elbow room," so it is not a plant for small landscape spaces. If you can provide these conditions, it is easy to grow. I have kept a small population in my created scrub garden in Pinellas County for a good number of years and suspect it could be grown outside its natural range if care were taken to provide the soil and light conditions it needs.

Beach Morning Glory (*Ipomoea imperati*)

Beach morning glory is a large evergreen sprawling vine native to beach dunes throughout the coastal counties of Florida. It is extremely adaptable and drought tolerant, but prefers full sun and well-drained soils. This is not a plant for small spaces as it produces multiple stems that can reach more than 10 feet in length. On a beach dune, this ability to spread outward and root periodically provides great benefits to beach stabilization, but in a home or commercial landscape it makes it extremely difficult to control. Beach morning glory has thick shiny oval leaves and flowers mostly during summer and fall. The white flowers have a yellow throat and are 2 inches in diameter. Its showy character and its ability to thrive in the most inhospitable sites make it an important wildflower to use in beach restoration projects. It is not recommended for typical landscape settings, however.

Beach morning glory (*Ipomoea imperati*).

Railroad Vine (*Ipomoea pes-caprae*)

Railroad vine has attributes very similar to those of beach morning glory and should be used in much the same way. Once established, it is virtually permanent. The individual runners may exceed 50 feet in length and are covered by large oval, evergreen, cloven-shaped leaves. Numerous 2-inch-diameter magenta-colored flowers occur year-round. These are especially attractive to coastal butterflies as well as to bees and other pollinators. On wide expansive coastal dunes, railroad vine can be an especially attractive wildflower and an important plant for stabilizing sands. Elsewhere, it can be a nuisance.

Railroad vine
(*Ipomoea pes-caprae*).

Blue Jacquemontia (*Jacquemontia pentanthos*)

This South Florida native is not appropriate in landscapes that regularly experience freezing temperatures. It is an evergreen herbaceous vine that twines across the landscape with multiple stems that reach lengths of 6 feet or more. It is most common in moist open prairies and woodlands, but it can tolerate typical landscape settings except extended drought or inundation by either fresh or saltwater. Over time, blue jacquemontia becomes dense and tangled. The ovate leaves overlap each other and shade the ground beneath. For this reason, it is best confined to fences, trellises, and arbors. As a ground cover, it is extremely difficult to maintain. Its

Blue jacquemontia (*Jacquemontia pentanthos*). Photo by Roger Hammer, with permission.

landscape value comes largely from its wonderful blooms. Flowering occurs mostly during the winter and early spring. Large numbers of round ¾-inch-diameter flowers cover the plant during this time and make it extremely showy. The normal flower color is sky blue, but pinkish and white-flowered forms are sometimes offered as well.

Beach Jacquemontia (*Jacquemontia reclinata*)

Beach jacquemontia is primarily a beach dune species. It has a moderate tolerance of saltwater inundation and a high tolerance of spray, and it is best grown in sunny locations where the soils stay evenly moist, but not wet. Beach jacquemontia is native to the southeastern Florida coast and does not perform well in locations that freeze regularly. It is a bit less aggressive and sprawling than blue jacquemontia, and makes a good ground cover on open sandy beach dunes. The many stems reach a mature length of about 6 feet and the small oval leaves are evergreen. Flowering can occur year-round, but peaks from late fall to spring. The blooms are about ¾ inch across and white with 5 pointed petal lobes. Beach jacquemontia is harder to establish than blue jacquemontia and a bit fussier about its growing conditions. Give it plenty of open space and do not let it get too

dry while it is becoming established. Too much water for too long will certainly kill it as well, however. This may be a difficult species to find from commercial nurseries.

Beach jacquemontia (*Jacquemontia reclinata*). Photo by Roger Hammer, with permission.

Passionvine Family—Passifloraceae

The passionvines or maypops are a diverse group of deciduous or evergreen vines common to the New World and often planted for their brightly colored intricate flowers. Passionvines are adept at climbing as they come equipped with tendrils that coil around the stems of neighboring plants, fences, and other structures and help anchor them tightly as they venture off in all directions. A great many non-native passionvines are widely planted in Florida landscapes, both for their beauty and for their value in butterfly gardens. Of these, only the shiny-leaved species are generally used (not the ones with woolly hairs on their leaves) as food by caterpillars of four popular butterflies: the zebra and julia heliconians and the gulf and variegated fritillaries. All our native species are good larval plant choices, but only two are widely propagated. A third, yellow passionvine (*P. lutea*), somewhat resembles the common corky-stem pas-sionvine but is more limited in its use to North and North Central Florida. Here, it makes an interesting addition to the butterfly garden landscape.

Purple Passionvine or Maypop (*P. incarnata*)

This is by far the showiest native passionvine. Its large, lavender flowers can be as much as 4 inches in diameter and are present from late spring to fall. It can be grown statewide, but it is quite particular in its grow-ing requirements. Over the years, I have killed many by not giving them sufficient drainage. Purple passionvine occurs most commonly in open fields and disturbed sandy woodlands and requires sandy, well-drained soils and sunny areas or it will eventually rot. In these conditions, it is an aggressive species, rambling in all directions as much as 10 feet or more from the central root mass and suckering vigorously. New plants may appear more than 10 feet away from the parent, and over time dozens of suckers will be formed.

Use purple passionvine on trellises and fences in open sunny sandy areas and be prepared to thin its suckers if they get too numerous. More often than not, the butterfly caterpillars will do that for you, and you will

Purple passionvine (*Passiflora incarnata*).

need all those suckers to keep the plant going. If you use it as a ground cover, mix it with robust species that can handle its habit of growing over and through them. If your flowers get pollinated (by bees, mostly), pick the fruit when the skins look wilted and yellow in color. The succulent material surrounding the seeds is edible and quite tasty, just not very abundant.

Corky-Stem Passionvine or Winged Maypop (*P. suberosa*)

Corky-stem passionvine is a very inconspicuous species that tends to blend into its surroundings. It is not a species planted for its showy flowers, but for its value in a landscape devoted to butterflies and birds. Named for the corklike "wings" that form along its larger stems, it produces small shiny green oval or 3-lobed leaves that are present year-round except after freezing temperatures. Numerous tiny greenish yellow flowers occur most months, but they can go unnoticed if not looked for. Eventually, pollinated flowers turn into ½-inch-long purple fruit that are eagerly consumed by songbirds.

I like to use this species scattered in my landscape next to shrubs and trees where it can weave and climb through the foliage. In this setting, it is found by butterflies and their caterpillars, but is largely hidden. Corky-stemmed passionvine is very adaptable and can be grown in shady to sunny locations and in moist to droughty soils. It is not especially salt tolerant, but does withstand some salt spray if used near the coast. Plant it in shady locations if you wish it to be visited by the heliconian butterflies and in the sun for the fritillaries.

Corky-stem passionvine (*Passiflora suberosa*).

Phlox Family—Polemoniaceae

This New World family mostly comprises herbaceous flowering plants, distinguished by flowers composed of 5 fused petals with a tubular base. These flowers are often important nectar sources for hummingbirds, butterflies, and certain species of long-tongued moths. The phloxes are widely used in landscapes throughout North America for their ornamental value, but few Florida natives have found a place around our homes and businesses. It is hoped this will change over time and more species will be grown commercially.

Standing Cypress (*Ipomopsis rubra*)

Standing cypress is a biennial, native to areas with well-drained sandy soils and full sun, including coastal dunes, in the northern half of Florida. During much of its short life, it is a rather weedy-looking plant. The first year, it consists only of a basal rosette of finely toothed fernlike leaves. During the second year, it begins a rather rapid ascent, producing a thick herbaceous stalk that eventually reaches a mature height of 3–6 feet. At this stage, the plants resemble small cypress trees. I personally think they look a bit more like the common old-field weed, dog-fennel. Though non-blooming specimens are not especially attractive, they become spectacular in flower. By mid to late summer, standing cypress produces hundreds

Standing cypress (*Ipomopsis rubra*).

of scarlet red tubular flowers along the top third of its main stalk. Each bloom is nearly 2 inches long, and the sheer weight of these flowers often bends the stalks over somewhat. Standing cypress is one of the best wildflowers in Florida for attracting hummingbirds, and the flowers are also frequently visited by cloudless sulphur butterflies.

Standing cypress is not an easy species for the home landscape in Florida. It requires full sun and excellent drainage to survive through the summer months. Given anything less, it will rot. Because it is a biennial, it takes two years to bloom and dies after the seed matures. Commercial nurseries find it difficult to keep it in pots for two years in order to make a sale, and most customers do not want the somewhat weedy-looking plant until it flowers; therefore, it is not grown as extensively as it should be. Plant standing cypress as first-year seedlings in order to make sure they become firmly established in the landscape, and collect the seed after they bloom the next summer in order to propagate it. I have not had much luck maintaining my populations over time by letting the seed fall naturally, so I grow sow them in potting mix and transplant the seedlings. Plant them in clusters of 5–7 near the back of a mixed wildflower planting and give them some support, using any of the taller sandhill grasses nearby. Good choices are lop-sided Indiangrass and some of the bluestems.

Woodland Phlox (*Phlox divaricata*)

Woodland phlox is rather rare in Florida but extremely common throughout eastern North America. As such, it is easy to find commercially. Just make sure that you purchase plants from Florida and not from regions with far different climates and soils. This is a beautiful species and wonderful addition to the landscape if care is taken to provide it what it needs. Woodland phlox performs best in partial shade and under the canopy of deciduous trees where it will get plenty of sun during the winter and early spring. It also does best given organic soils with a bit of extra moisture. Over the winter, it exists as multiple stalks close to the soil surface. In colder parts of the state, it will be fully deciduous. As spring approaches, these stems grow to a height of about 1 foot. Opposite lance-shaped leaves occur along the length of the stem. Blooming occurs in early spring. The flowers, typical to the genus, range in color from almost white to blue and rosy pink and occur in a broad panicle atop each stem.

Despite its restricted natural range in Florida, I have grown this species quite successfully for many years in my Pinellas County landscape and believe it could be grown even further south. Protect it from full sun during the summer, mulch it lightly with leaf litter, and make sure it gets a bit of extra moisture during periods of drought. Woodland phlox is an excellent wildflower for a mixed deciduous woodland understory. Grow it with some of the medium-tall to shorter ferns such as southern lady and Christmas fern or ebony spleenwort and plant it in mass with wildflowers such as violets, Indian pink, wild ginger, and eastern blue star. Over time, woodland

Woodland phlox (*Phlox divaricata*).

phlox will sucker, so leave about 1 foot between each specimen when you are first establishing it.

Downy Phlox (*Phlox pilosa*)

Downy phlox is native to the northern half of Florida and occurs in open sunny areas with deep well-drained sandy soils. It is extremely tough, but delicate looking, a combination that clearly calls for it to be used more in home landscapes. In portions of its range where temperatures do not get below the mid-20s F, downy phlox remains evergreen and can bloom throughout the winter months. Further north, it tends to die back to the ground in winter and emerge again in spring. It produces thin, rather weak stems that rarely grow taller than 1 foot. The flowers occur at the tops of the stems and are most abundant in spring, the colors ranging from white to deep pink and light lavender. Downy

Downy phlox (*Phlox pilosa*).

phlox suckers and eventually produces many stems around the original plant.

I have had great success with this plant in my Pinellas County landscape and it has spread by self-sown seed and suckers. All phlox produce seed capsules that burst open when ripe, sending seeds several feet away. This ensures seedlings will appear in all corners of the garden wherever open soil occurs. Give downy phlox full sun and well-drained sand or it will rapidly decline. Because it is small, plant it in the front of the bed or near trails and walkways. Mulch it sparingly. This species works well with other smaller sandhill wildflowers such as pink beardtongue, twinflower, wild petunia, blue star, and scrub St. John's-wort. In my garden, downy phlox is a favorite forage plant of cottontail rabbits, and they often eat the new stems before they can produce flowers. Alexa reminds me that this is a result of my wildlife gardening approach, but it's a mental stretch I am not always satisfied with. At present, downy phlox is only rarely available from commercial Florida sources. I am hopeful this will soon change.

Pickerelweed Family—Pontederiaceae

This is an extremely small family in Florida, comprising several obscure weedy plants, the highly invasive water-hyacinth (*Eichornia crassipes*), and the common pickerelweed, for which this family is named. These are aquatic plants, useful only in wet and inundated soils.

Pickerelweed (*Pontederia cordata*)

Pickerelweed is extremely common statewide in shallow marshes, ponds, and lake edges. Because of its beauty and adaptability, it is also widely used in wetland restoration projects. In most locations, pickerelweed keeps its heart-shaped basal leaves through the winter. Standing as tall as 3 feet, the shiny green foliage remains attractive year-round. Flowering occurs over many months from spring through fall. The flower stalks are held at least 6 inches above the foliage, and each spike is composed of dozens of showy purple-blue flowers with yellow markings. Butterflies and bees are especially attracted to these blooms and they are nearly always evident, pollinating the open flowers.

Pickerelweed has limited tolerance of drought and can withstand short periodic loss of standing water as long as soils remain moist. It performs best in shallow standing water, no deeper than 18 inches; therefore, it should be used mostly in shallow ponds and water features. Pickerelweed suckers and spreads over time. It can overwhelm more diminutive species, but it holds its own when used with other robust, spreading wetland plants such as native hibiscus, yellow canna, and iris.

Pickerelweed (*Pontederia cordata*) with nectaring Delaware skippers. Photo by Christina Evans, with permission.

Piriqueta Family—Turneraceae

Most members of this family are tropical and semitropical shrubs and herbaceous plants. Many have showy flowers, and a few non-natives are sold commercially for home landscapes. Of our native species, only one is likely to be planted in a home landscape.

Morning Buttercup or Pitted Stripeseed (*Piriqueta cistoides* subsp. *caroliniana*)

Morning buttercup occurs statewide in upland locations. It is quite adaptable to a variety of sun and soil conditions, but prefers average well-drained soils and good levels of sunlight. In such conditions, it produces abundant foliage and blooms profusely. Morning buttercup is a deciduous perennial in much of Florida except the extreme south, where it is evergreen. By early spring, it emerges and produces numerous stems that reach a length of several feet and form a rounded mound of foliage. The leaves are somewhat linear and 1–2 inches long. The flowers are produced at the ends of the stems and plants bloom over several months during the summer. The large 5-petal buttercup flowers are quite showy and pollinated mostly by bees. It is reported as a food plant of gulf fritillary butterfly caterpillars, but I have not seen it used by this species in the years I have kept this plant in my landscape.

Morning buttercup is only rarely offered for sale by commercial sources in Florida. It is extremely adaptable, however, and makes a fine addition to a mixed wildflower planting. Use it in the front portion of the garden and plant it in small clusters of 3–5 individuals. Because this species may slowly sucker and spread over time, plant individuals at least 2 feet apart and mulch lightly between them with pine straw or other similar mulches.

Morning buttercup
(*Piriqueta cistoides*).

Plantain Family—Plantaginaceae

Current taxonomy includes several genera that were once included with the snapdragons (Scrophulariaceae). Under older classification systems, this family comprised mostly the plantains (*Plantago* spp.), plants largely considered lawn and field weeds, but with the relatively recent revisions, several important wildflowers are now included.

Hyssops (*Bacopa* spp.)

The hyssops are wetland species, most common to roadside swales, marsh edges, and other similar habitats throughout much of Florida. They are not appropriate for most landscape settings, but are worth incorporating into areas with seasonally flooded soils because they are attractive ground covers. Two of Florida's three native species are sometimes offered commercially. Water hyssops have succulent leaves and produce long stems that creep across the ground, rooting periodically. They are evergreen in areas that don't experience below-freezing temperatures, but die back otherwise. The flowers are rather small and bell shaped and present mostly during the summer.

Lemon Bacopa (*B. caroliniana*)

Lemon bacopa produces numerous attractive light blue flowers, and its foliage gives off a distinct pleasant lemony fragrance when bruised. It

Lemon bacopa (*Bacopa caroliniana*). Photo by Roger Hammer, with permission.

occurs statewide but is difficult to maintain unless given very wet conditions. Plant this species at the edges of permanently flooded sites, such as pond edges, where it can grow out into water as much as 1–2 inches in depth. It also makes a great specimen for use in a hanging basket, planted in soil that holds moisture well. Do not attempt this species in sites that are not flooded during the summer rainy season.

Water Hyssop (*B. monnieri*)

Water hyssop also occurs statewide, but it has tiny white flowers and its foliage has no scent when bruised. As such, it is more nondescript than lemon bacopa. What makes it worth the investment is its greater adaptability and its use as food by the white peacock butterfly caterpillar. Water hyssop is much easier to maintain in moist soil sites and can tolerate occasional drought for several-week periods as long as it gets rehydrated. While I have lost all my lemon bacopa over several attempts in my Pinellas County landscape, I have been successful with water hyssop, and each season I produce large crops of white peacock butterflies because of it.

Water hyssop (*Bacopa monnieri*).

Beardtongues (*Penstemon* spp.)

Beardtongues are found throughout North America and include a great many species. Most are western, but three are native to Florida. The beardtongues are so named because they have one infertile stamen (the male portion of the flower) inside the lower lip of each flower that looks "hairy" or "fuzzy." Beardtongues are drought-tolerant herbaceous perennials that often keep their elliptical basal leaves through winter. They slowly expand over time and produce multiple growing points within each clump of leaves, each with multiple flower stalks. The leaves tend to turn reddish during the winter. Flower stalks are produced mostly during the summer and fall. Beardtongue flowers are showy and resemble those of the common garden snapdragon. They are at right angles to the stem and may be visited by hummingbirds but are more likely pollinated by bees.

Pink Beardtongue (*P. australis*)

Pink beardtongue is our smallest native beardtongue species and occurs throughout the northern half of Florida in well-drained sandy soils under full and partial sun. It is quite adaptable and can be grown under most common landscape conditions as long as the soils do not remain too wet. The basal leaves rarely exceed 3–4 inches in length. Flowering occurs for an extended period from spring through fall. Multiple flower stalks, about 12–18 inches tall, arise from the foliage, and each produces a succession of light pink tubular flowers, each about 1 inch long.

Pink beardtongue is beautiful but rather diminutive and is best used in a mass near the front of a planting bed or next to trails and walkways. Mix it with other small sandhill wildflowers such as twinflower and wild petunia or with drought-tolerant

Pink beardtongue (*Penstemon australis*).

species such as black-eyed susan. This species is not commonly grown commercially at this time, but is well worth the effort to locate.

Eastern Smooth Beardtongue (*P. laevigatus*)

This species is quite rare in Florida, occurring in only a few counties along the Georgia border. It is native to open woodland edges, generally in well-drained alkaline soils and under relatively high amounts of sunlight. I have found it to be far more adaptable in the home landscape than might be expected and have grown it successfully in my home landscape for many years in average soils. Eastern smooth beardtongue is more robust than pink beardtongue. Its basal leaves are 6–8 inches long, and its flower stalk is typically 2–3 feet tall. Flowering is confined to late spring and early summer. Numerous light pink blooms are produced along each stalk. They are decidedly more open throated than pink beardtongue and a bit larger in size.

Eastern smooth beardtongue (*Penstemon laevigatus*).

Eastern smooth beardtongue is drought tolerant once established, but it should not be used in sites with excessively well-drained sands. Mass it to maximize its effect and use it near the middle section of the bed or as a mass planting along edges and walkways. Although this species is naturally quite rare in Florida, it is easy to propagate and routinely offered for sale commercially. In North Florida, it can be grown in full to part sun, but give it partial sun further south.

White Beardtongue (*P. multiflorus*)

White beardtongue is the largest of our native species and often quite common in well-drained upland habitats throughout the state. Its large elliptical basal leaves may be 6 inches long, and its flower stalk may reach 4 feet tall. As the Latin name suggests, it produces large numbers of white flowers atop each stalk during the summer months. Their shape is somewhat similar to those of eastern smooth beardtongue, but a bit less open throated. The "beard," along the bottom of the lower petal, is black and quite distinct.

This is a robust species that requires well-drained soils to thrive. Do not attempt it in locations where soils retain too much moisture, give it plenty of sun down to its basal leaves, and use it in landscapes that are somewhat expansive. Over time, white beardtongue forms colonies, and these can be quite striking; in small plots, however, it seems out of place. Plant it in small clusters in the back half of the bed and mix it with other robust sandhill species such as many of the blazing stars, sky blue salvia, various asters, and the like. This beardtongue is frequently available from commercial sources in Florida.

White beardtongue (*Penstemon multiflorus*).

Polygala Family—Polygalaceae

Members of this family are diverse, but only the milkworts (also known as candyworts) (*Polygala* spp.) are likely to be encountered. The milkworts are mostly deciduous herbaceous perennials, and the vast majority are common to open wetland habitats. There are exceptions, but most of these are rather small and inconspicuous or extremely rare. Of the 23 species native to Florida, many would make wonderful additions to sites with moist to seasonally wet soil and plenty of sunshine. Some of the best are tall pinebarren milkwort (*P. cymosa*), low pinebarren milkwort (*P. ramosa*), and yellow milkwort (*P. rugelii*), all with large heads of bright yellow flowers, and procession flower (*P. incarnata*) and drumheads (*P. cruciata*) with violet to rose purple blooms. The diminutive orange milkwort (*P. lutea*) and candyroot (*P. nana*), with their orange and lemon yellow flowers, respectively, are good choices too, but need to be used in locations where they can be noticed. All milkworts are best used when massed and added to a mixed planting of short grasses such as wiregrass and toothache grass, and savanna or marsh wildflowers, such as some of the asters and chaffheads, the meadow pinks, and meadow beauties. Currently, none of the milkworts are grown commercially in Florida and may be difficult to find.

The milkworts (*Polygala* spp.) are a varied genus that occur throughout Florida in a wide variety of habitats. None are regularly propagated at this time, however. In clockwise order: Candyroot (*Polygala nana*); Procession flower (*Polygala incarnata*); Drumheads (*Polygala cruciata*).

Rockrose Family—Cistaceae

The rockrose family in Florida includes two very different genera: the unusual but somewhat nondescript pinweeds (*Lechea* spp.) and the brightly colored rockroses (*Helianthemum* spp.). Few members of this family are currently grown commercially, but the rockroses are adaptable and colorful enough to warrant more attention.

Carolina Rockrose (*Helianthemum carolinianum*)

Carolina rockrose occurs in well-drained sunny habitats throughout much of North and Central Florida. It is deciduous and makes its appearance in early spring, producing a flat rosette of 1–2-inch oval leaves. By late spring, it produces a single thin purplish flower stalk which may stand 1 foot tall. The relatively large 5-petal bright yellow flowers are produced from late spring to early summer. These are mostly pollinated by bees. Carolina rockrose is adaptable to most landscape settings, but it requires good drainage and sun to thrive. Because of its small size, plant it in masses and use it near the front of the planting bed or along trails and walkways.

Carolina rockrose (*Helianthemum carolinianum*).

Solitary specimens are not that noticeable, but when planted in a mass it makes an attractive addition to a mixed wildflower setting.

Pinebarren Rockrose (*H. corymbosum*)

This rockrose is my personal favorite. Although it is deciduous in the winter, it forms small tidy mounds of blue-green foliage that add character to the landscape during the rest of the year and dense showy patches of bright yellow flowers from spring to summer. Pinebarren rockrose spreads outward slowly over time and eventually reaches several feet in diameter.

Pinebarren rockrose (*Helianthemum corymbosum*).

As its common name implies, it occurs in well-drained sunny locations but is adaptable and will thrive in normal landscape soils with good drainage. This species occurs throughout Florida. Because individual plants spread outward, plant them no closer than 2 feet apart. I like this species best when mixed with other small wildflowers planted between and used near the front of the planting bed or near walkways.

St. John's-Wort Family—Clusiaceae

St. John's-worts have been well known to herbalists for millennia for the treatment of various ailments, including depression, arthritis, and gastrointestinal problems. The Greeks and Romans documented their use extensively, and they were used across Europe during the Middle Ages to treat all forms of madness. But despite the attention this genus has received for medicinal uses, our native species are only infrequently used as landscape plants. Native St. John's-worts are largely evergreen with attractive foliage, and they bloom most months of the year with showy canary yellow flowers. The flowers are mostly pollinated by bees. Various species occur statewide in every conceivable habitat type, and there are good choices for any landscape setting. Thirty-one distinct species are native to Florida, but only a few are generally commercially available. I have included what I consider the best below.

Sandweed
(*Hypericum fasciculatum*).

Sandweed (*Hypericum fasciculatum*)

Sandweed occurs statewide in sunny, seasonally flooded pinelands, savannas, and marsh edges. It is relatively easy to use in moist to wet-soil areas but is not especially drought tolerant and not a good choice for the typical landscape setting. Well-grown specimens develop thin twisted trunks with attractive reddish brown bark. The dark green needlelike leaves are also especially appealing. Mature specimens eventually reach a height of 3–5 feet with a crown 2–3 feet across. Bright yellow 5-petal flowers occur at the tips of its many branches from early summer through late fall. Given the proper growing conditions, sandweed is certainly one of the most attractive members of this genus, but it is not long lived.

St. Andrew's Cross (*Hypericum hypericoides*)

St. Andrew's cross occurs statewide in wetland and upland habitats. Unlike sandweed, it is adaptable to average growing conditions, and I have grown it for years in our front yard landscape without supplemental irrigation. St. Andrew's cross is an open evergreen woody shrub with a straight main stem and numerous upright side branches. Eventually, it reaches a mature height of nearly 5 feet. The leaves are rather flat, linear in shape, and dull green in color. The 4-petal flowers are a bit paler yellow than most, with the petals arranged more like a capital X than a cross with legs at right angles. While not the showiest member of this genus, St.

Andrew's cross makes an interesting addition to a wildflower garden. Because of its size, it is best used in larger landscapes or as a screen near the back of the garden. Use it as an accent plant, widely scattered in large landscapes, or as a hedge in smaller ones.

St. Andrew's cross
(*Hypericum hypericoides*).

Smoothbark St. John's-Wort
(*Hypericum lissophloeus*)

Smoothbark St. John's-wort is a wetland endangered and endemic species, recorded only in Bay and Washington counties in the west-central Panhandle. Despite its natural rarity, it is being propagated by commercial sources and has fared well for years in my Pinellas County landscape. I suspect it could be grown throughout much of Florida. This is a tall species with needlelike leaves and many thin, limber branches. Mature specimens eventually reach 6–12 feet tall, but growth is

Smoothbark St. John's-wort
(*Hypericum lissophloeus*).

slow. Flowering is confined to the summer and fall; each flower is bright yellow and composed of 5 petals. Smoothbark St. John's-wort is tolerant of occasional periodic drought but will eventually perish if not given mostly moist to wet growing conditions. Because of its height, it is best used as a screen in a small wetland garden or as accents within expansive plantings around a pond or lake.

Myrtle-Leaved St. John's-Wort (*Hypericum myrtifolium*)

This St. John's-wort is sometimes offered commercially and quite attractive. It occurs throughout most of Florida in moist to wet-soil habitats and is not very drought tolerant; therefore, it is not adapted to the average home landscape setting. Mature specimens reach a height of about 3 feet and have a thin main stem and thin branches that often droop. The leaves are oval, rather thick, gray green in color, and clasp the stem. This foliage is especially attractive and gives this plant additional character. Flowering occurs mostly in the spring. The showy 5-petal flowers are bright yellow and larger than those of most other St. John's-worts.

Myrtle-leaved St. John's-wort (*Hypericum myrtifolium*).

Scrub St. John's-Wort (*Hypericum tenuifolium*; syn. *H. reductum*)

This species is the most widely propagated member of this genus in Florida for home landscapes and an excellent choice for open sunny sites with well-drained soil. It occurs nearly statewide and is especially drought

Scrub St. John's-wort (*Hypericum tenuifolium*).

tolerant. Mature specimens rarely grow taller than 2 feet. The strong central stem has reddish bark and many short stems branch off of it. The foliage is evergreen, shiny, deep green in color, and needlelike. Despite its rather short stature, the flowers are large and abundant across the top of the many stems. They have 5 petals and are canary yellow in color. Blooming is initiated in early summer and continues into the fall. This species adapts well to most home landscape conditions, except those that routinely stay too wet. Use it in small clusters of at least 3 individuals, planted at least 1 foot apart in the front half of the planting bed. Because it is evergreen, it mixes well with species that are deciduous during the winter and with short grasses such as wiregrass and pinewoods dropseed.

Four-Petal St. John's-Wort (*Hypericum tetrapetalum*)

Four-petal St. John's-wort is also distributed nearly statewide and occurs in moist to average pinelands. Normally, it is a rather thin erect 3-foot-tall evergreen shrub with sparse side branches. Though its habit is not especially showy, it makes up for this with its interesting foliage and large yellow 4-petal flowers. The foliage is blue green in color and the large oval leaves clasp the stem. The soft-yellow flowers occur from spring through

Four-petal St. John's-wort (*Hypericum tetrapetalum*).

late summer. Four-petal St. John's-wort is reasonably well adapted to most normal landscape settings and can tolerate some drought once established. Use it in mostly sunny locations, or it will get lanky and more prone to bend over. Plant several in small clusters near the middle to back half of the garden and mix it with medium-sized native grasses, such as hairawn muhly, and sturdy wildflowers, such as blazing star and red salvia, to help keep it erect.

Spiderwort Family—Commelinaceae

The spiderworts (*Tradescantia* spp.) and their close relatives the dayflowers (*Commelina* spp.) and roselings (*Callisia* spp.; syn. *Cuthbertia* spp.) are sometimes considered weeds, but many have showy flowers and make excellent additions to the landscape if carefully considered. All species in this family produce succulent leaves and stems that produce a slimy mucus-like sap when broken. The leaves are linear and surround the main stems with a noticeable sheath. Most flower from spring to early winter, but each flower is open only during the morning hours for one day. Flower colors vary between light pink and deep purple even within species. Most spread rapidly in the garden by seed. The dayflowers and roselings are not grown commercially in Florida, though a few have excellent

Common spiderwort
(*Tradescantia ohiensis*).

landscape potential. Only the common spiderwort is widely propagated and frequently used in Florida landscapes.

Common Spiderwort (*T. ohiensis*)

This spiderwort occurs throughout the northern two-thirds of Florida and is common to open disturbed habitats such as fields and roadsides. It is extremely adaptable and thrives in nearly any landscape condition. If grown in too much shade, it will get lanky and not bloom well, but it will tolerate just about anything else. When conditions are mild, it will persist over winter as a clump of lilylike basal leaves. Each leaf is about ½ inch wide and 6 or more inches long. Over time, these clumps expand outward, and mature plants may be almost 12 inches in diameter. Flower stalks emerge from these basal clumps and bear clusters of buds at their tip, 1–2 feet above the basal leaves. Each flower is composed of 3 identically sized petals that vary greatly in color from white to extremely deep purple. Many color forms are propagated and sold commercially, but they do not breed true if mixed with more than one color form. Common spiderwort adds a great deal of color to a landscape over much of the year, but it also tends to spread to all corners of it over a short time and is difficult to weed out once established. If you introduce common spiderwort to your landscape, be prepared to have a lot of it over time and to thin it out of areas where it is not welcome.

Trillium Family—Trilliaceae

Trilliums (*Trillium* spp.) are native to the understories of deciduous woodlands in North Florida. They are one of the first wildflowers to make their appearance in the late winter and are well past blooming by the time the forest canopy leafs out. North of Florida, trillium species with large showy flowers are widely propagated and sold commercially for the home gardener; that is not the situation here, however. Florida has four species of native trillium. They are quite similar to each other and far less showy than species widely planted elsewhere. Recently, several nurseries have begun offering seed or tissue-cultured specimens for sale. Make sure you purchase these and not those dug from the wild.

Chattahoochee River trillium (*Trillium decipiens*).

Spotted trillium (*Trillium maculatum*).

Florida trilliums have a place in a deciduous woodland garden and add a lot of charm when used appropriately. Do not attempt them under live oaks or other evergreen canopy trees. Most species perform best only when grown in alkaline soils, and they require good fertility and a bit of extra moisture during the spring. Over time, trilliums produce side bulbs and slowly spread outward to form colonies. Our species all tend to have mottled 3-part leaves that rarely exceed 12 inches in height and maroon-colored flowers. I have kept several species for years in my Pinellas County woodland, but they are best attempted only in the northernmostern third of the state. Our species are Chattahoochee River trillium (*T. decipiens*) and lance-leaf trillium (*T. lancifolium*), both with very restricted ranges in and around the Chattahoochee and Apalachicola river basins, and spotted (*T. maculatum*) and long-bract trillium (*T. underwoodii*) from across much of North Florida. The latter two species are the best choices for most North Florida settings.

Verbena Family—Verbenaceae

The verbenas include a great many species, native and introduced, commonly used in the home landscape. They are often tough and dependable, and their heads of tubular flowers are often showy and excellent nectar sources for butterflies, bees, and other pollinators. Normally, verbenas have triangular-shaped leaves that are opposite each other on the stem. The most commonly available and showiest members of this family are described below.

Beach Verbena (*Glandularia maritima*)

Beach verbena occurs naturally in beach dunes along the east coast of Florida from Cape Canaveral to the Florida Keys. It has also been reported from a few west coast counties and is quite adaptable to most regions of the central and southern peninsula if given plenty of sun and well-drained soil. Beach verbena is endemic and has become quite rare as a result of the widespread development of our coastal dune habitat. It is easy to propagate, however, and available from a number of commercial sources. Beach verbena is evergreen in locations that do not experience excessive cold temperatures. It tends to sprawl in the landscape and rarely stands taller than 8 inches. Individuals spread across many square feet as they mature.

Beach verbena (*Glandularia maritima*).

The large circular heads of rich lavender flowers are produced during most months, and they are especially attractive to butterflies.

Beach verbena is an excellent choice for coastal dune plantings near walkways and leading edges where it can be most noticed. It also works well in inland settings, and I have seen it used effectively in the harsh environments created between sidewalks and roadways as well as in "easier" locations. If given too much shade and moisture, it will succumb to fungal diseases. Do not crowd this species with neighboring plants.

Tampa Verbena (*Glandularia tampensis*)

Tampa verbena is also endemic and quite rare in nature. Unlike its close cousin, it is an upright species and native to light gaps and disturbed openings in moist forested habitats of the north and central peninsula. It seems to be an exceedingly short-lived "perennial" in nature and reacts quickly to habitat disturbances caused by tree falls, wildlife rooting, and the creation of trails. Tampa verbena is easy to propagate, but difficult to maintain in a landscape. In all my attempts to grow this plant, I have never been successful in keeping it for more than just a few years. But its great beauty and butterfly value make it worth the effort to add it as necessary.

Plant Tampa verbena in the edges of a woodland planting where it will

receive filtered or partial sun. It will tolerate more sun if given additional water. Individual plants will reach 2 feet in height, with a spread of about 1 foot. Because of this, I like to plant them in small clusters on 18-inch centers and place them near walkways or in the front half of the planting area. Their rich lavender blooms are present during nearly every month from spring through fall.

Tampa verbena
(*Glandularia tampensis*).

Wild Sage (*Lantana involucrata*)

Wild sage is the only native lantana commonly sold by commercial nursery sources. Most other lantanas are not native, and most forms of common roadside lantana (*L. camara*) are exceptionally invasive and should not be used. Wild sage is cold sensitive and occurs naturally in coastal habitats in the southern half of the peninsula. It is not a good choice for areas that routinely freeze. This is an upright, narrow-crowned woody species that eventually reaches 5 feet in height and several feet across. Wild sage has small aromatic triangular leaves and grayish gnarly bark. Clusters of small white flowers are produced nearly year-round

Wild sage (*Lantana involucrata*) with nectaring Cassius blue.

except during periods of cool temperatures. The inside of each flower tube is pinkish to yellowish. Small magenta-colored fruit ripen about a month after the flowers. The flowers are very attractive to butterflies, while the fruit make an excellent food source for birds such as mockingbirds, cardinals, and catbirds. Wild sage is best used as a specimen plant in a coastal setting or as scattered specimens in a larger setting. Give it full sun and well-drained sand.

Blue Porterweed (*Stachytarpheta jamaicensis*)

Our native porterweed is found in coastal and near-coastal habitats in the southern half of the peninsula. It is not very cold tolerant and not a good choice for areas further north. Native blue porterweed is a low ground cover that rarely stands taller than about 8 inches and spreads rapidly across the ground. Upright forms are not native but have been widely sold as such in the past. They are actually a tropical species (*S. cayennensis*) now considered an invasive plant problem in South Florida. Blue porterweed has large triangular toothed leaves that enhance its value as a ground cover for open areas. The deep blue tubular flowers are produced during most months on numerous flower stalks close to the ground. These flowers are excellent nectar sources for butterflies. Because this species tends

Blue porterweed (*Stachytarpheta jamaicensis*).

to spread rapidly, a few will go a long way, and it often crowds out less aggressive wildflowers planted with it. Use it as a mass planting in large open areas where other species are difficult to grow. In coastal settings, it can be effectively mixed with a wide variety of other typically coastal grasses and wildflowers, such as dune sunflower and blanket flower. In inland locations, mix it with other robust species to confine it to only the open areas between other plants.

Violet Family—Violaceae

To me, there is no better sign of spring than a cluster of violets. Their colorful flowers, scattered throughout a semishady garden is something to rejoice, and I have been doing just that since childhood. Violets are relatively long-lived adaptable wildflowers that prefer shadier conditions than most. They will adapt to more sun if kept moister and tolerate occasionally droughty soils if protected a bit from the sun. Blooming occurs in the spring, and the flowers are pollinated by insects, mostly small bees. Violets do not require pollination to set seed, however, because they also produce self-pollinated (cleistogamous) buds, which never open, in the summer and fall. The seed capsules ripen in about a month, burst open with great force, and shoot the seeds many feet away from the parent plant. Several distinct species are native to Florida, though only a few are routinely propagated by commercial nurseries. The bog white violet (*Viola lanceolata*) is resident to wet soil habitats and is difficult to maintain in most home landscape settings unless given wetland conditions. Most others are easier and are described below.

Early Blue Violet (*V. palmata*)

Early blue violet is resident to much of Florida, except the extreme southern counties, and occurs in moist open pinelands, savannas, and woodlands. This species has been given several Latin names over the years, and most of those have recognized the tendency of its leaves to be deeply lobed and shaped something like a hand (i.e., palmate). The deep blue to purple flowers are produced in abundance in early spring. This is an adaptable species and can be used in a great many settings. Its best

performance, how-
ever, will occur in
semishade with a bit
of extra moisture.

Early blue violet
(*Viola palmata*).

Common White Violet (*V. primulifolia*)

Common white violet occurs throughout much of Florida, except in the
most southern counties, and inhabits a variety of semishady woodland
habitats. It has arrow-shaped to rounded basal leaves that lie close to the
ground and form a dense rosette. White flowers with some deep purple
streaking inside the lower petal
arise on long stalks in the early
spring. A great many flowers
may be open on any one plant,
and they stand several inches
above the basal leaves, making
well-grown specimens attractive. This species is extremely
adaptable and quickly spreads
throughout the landscape. Its
proliferation can be easily kept
in check by occasional weeding
if desired.

Common white violet (*Viola primulifolia*).

Common blue violet (*Viola sororia*).

Common Blue Violet (*V. sororia*)

Common blue violet is extremely difficult to distinguish from common white violet when the plants are not in bloom. Its leaves are often more round to heart shaped, but common blue violet is a highly variable species that some taxonomists split into multiple species. It shares similar traits and growing needs with the common white violet and can be grown successfully in the same conditions. I like to mix these two species. Over time, they will both move around the understory and form a more natural looking aspect in the landscape.

Walter's Violet (*V. walteri*)

This violet is a diminutive species found in alkaline woodlands and moist forest settings within the Florida Panhandle and the northern third of the peninsula. Where its needs are well met, it spreads slowly through the understory by runners—much the same as a strawberry plant. The small rounded leaves are often reticulated, with lines and netting along the leaf veins, and the ½-inch-tall flowers are normally a pale blue to light purple in color. Overall, these small plants, with their distinctive foliage and flowers, make a stunning show in the spring. I have had very poor success growing this plant as far south as Pinellas and do not recommend it for Central and South Florida. Give it good soil moisture and shade during the heat of summer and fall. Because of its size, plant it near the front of a woodland planting or along trails so it can be more easily admired.

Walter's violet (*Viola walteri*).

8 ∾∾∾∾∾∾∾∾∾∾∾∾∾∾∾∾∾∾∾∾∾∾∾

Landscape Approaches

Now that we have discussed the general concepts of native plant land-scaping and explored the plants in some detail, it is time to consider how to put this information together in a landscape plan. Landscaping is the purposeful combining of plants to achieve a conceptual goal. It is an art, and it requires an artist's touch to decide which species to introduce and how to combine them effectively. It is a visionary art because it requires us to see into the future and project what each area will look like once it has matured. Because most of us are working with a virtually clean slate, long cut off from any natural system, it is up to us to envision both the end point and the path to getting there. We may make a few mistakes along the way, but we can correct them. That is the challenge and the fun of any landscape project. Tinkering and making adjustments are part of the process. Once the process has begun, however, the endpoint is pretty well determined and difficult to substantially change, so we should have a clear vision of where we want to end up before we invest a lot of time, energy, and resources. We have many landscape styles from which to choose, so from the beginning it is very important to decide which of those we wish to adopt.

Some of these decisions will be based on what we have to work with. If our yard frequently floods after storm events, we will need to build a landscape that can adapt to both the wet and the dry times. If we live on top of a historic dune, it will be very difficult to successfully design a landscape that requires moisture. On limestone soils, we use plants adapted to high pH, and on acid soils, we use the opposite. These decisions go almost without saying. The more difficult decisions involve style more than substance.

In my own yard, those decisions involved whether we wanted a shady landscape or an open sunny one. There is a lot to be said for both. Shady areas help to cool us, and they provide a respite during the summer and fall when temperatures reach their peak. But, while shade has great value, it also limits the types of plants we can use. Most wildflowers, for example, do not tolerate too much shade, and without wildflowers you will not attract many butterflies, hummingbirds, and other pollinators. Sunny areas are best for those who wish to have these species nearby, but they don't do much to reduce our energy bills or provide an escape to sit and enjoy an afternoon with a good book.

It is possible to do both, but not necessarily in the same section of your landscape. Trying to cram both into a typical front or back yard usually makes everything look out of place. In using a more natural approach with native plants, it is best to design with an eye toward the types of landscapes found in nature, and the best approaches use larger swaths of these systems, not tiny patches. To effectively mix different landscape approaches requires us to create transition between them or to use a physical barrier such as a wall or fence to keep them separate. In our own landscape, Alexa and I have designed a woodland along the back of our home that extends to the side yard. As you open the gate beneath the hummingbird bower, you enter the sunnier front yard planted mostly with wildflowers and native grasses. Both areas are a bit hidden from each other, and they provide an element of discovery for Alexa and me, as well as for our visitors. Each time you open the gate, from either direction, you never quite know what you will see—new things in bloom or new wildlife flitting about. The front and back yards are distinctly different from each other, and this works because there is a separation that causes us to purposely enter one or the other.

Use nature to help direct you in selecting which types of plants to use together, and use your existing conditions to fine-tune your overall plan. If you are relatively new to Florida, take time to visit some of our finest parks and natural areas to get a feel of what natural Florida is all about. You don't need to be able to identify each and every plant you encounter, but you should absorb how the communities are structured. For example, if you choose to design a shady landscape, a closer look at nature will inform you that your understory will include a lot of ferns, with fewer choices of grasses and wildflowers. If wildflowers in your woodland are important to you, then it will be necessary to create some light gaps in the canopy or design a canopy that is mostly deciduous, or both, so your understory will get plenty of light in the winter and early spring. If you opt for an open sunny landscape style, you will not likely be using ferns, but you will have a great many decisions to make about which native grasses and wildflowers to combine.

Regardless of which general style you choose, you will then have to match it to the soil and moisture conditions of your site. Woodlands and

A gate can provide an effective transition between two widely different landscape styles. This gate separates the author's shady backyard woodland from his sunny front yard wildflower gardens.

meadows occur in every conceivable situation, from wet to dry and from alkaline to acid. Areas near the coast must also contend with salt spray or with occasional saltwater inundation. South Florida is a very different environment than the Panhandle. Therefore, it is necessary first to select a style and then to select plants adapted to your growing conditions.

Open landscapes can incorporate trees, but consideration needs to be given how much shade they will create. Large evergreen trees such as live oaks and southern magnolias will eventually create far too much shade to support an understory of native wildflowers and grasses. These are trees of shady forested hammocks, and it is best to use understory plants of this type of natural community beneath them if these trees are important to you. Pines are wonderful for filtering sun and allowing some of it to reach the ground. If you use pines, and they are not planted too close together, you will have enough sunlight to also use many of the wild-flowers and native grasses discussed in this book. Other narrow-crowned deciduous trees, such as turkey and bluejack oaks (*Quercus laevis* and *Q. incana*, respectively), can also be good, but space trees far enough apart to make sure the understory gets sunlight. After all, these trees are being used as accents within the landscape, not to create shade. The light shade they create, however, may allow you to use a few more wildflowers and grasses that do not tolerate full sun all day. Not every wildflower or native grass will respond well if left totally out in full sun, especially if the soils are droughty. By using widely scattered trees or shrubs that create small patches of shade for part of the day, you can often increase diversity in your landscape.

In the sections below, I attempt to define in more detail design consid-erations that are important and to list some of the best plants for each of the major settings you might encounter. The information in the lists that follow each subheading is intended to be general. Plants marked (A) are plants found throughout much of the state, (N) are plants best grown in the northern half of Florida, and (S) are plants best grown in the southern half. Soils are divided into categories that reflect their average moisture level. Moist to mesic soils are those that tend to hold a bit of extra mois-ture; droughty soils are those that are well drained. I have subdivided soils into three categories for sunny locations. Moist/wet soils are frequently saturated, mesic/average soils are typical of most landscape settings, and well-drained/droughty soils are deep sands. Coastal dunes are deep sands that also require plants to tolerate salt spray. The lists are not intended to be exhaustive, but informative. Most plants are adaptable and can be grown in more than one setting. I have placed them under the heading where I have found them to do best. Use the more detailed information I have provided for individual species to help you refine your own plant palette more accurately.

Shady Evergreen

The understories of woodlands that remain shady year-round are some of the most difficult landscape settings in which to design. In nature, these forests are mostly dominated by live oak, southern magnolia, red cedar (*Juniperus virginiana*), and cabbage palm in the northern two-thirds of Florida and by tropical hardwoods in the southern tiers of counties. Because little light reaches the forest floor, the understory is often very open and easy to walk in. Most of the vegetation is in the canopy, either as trees or as vines.

Understory species diversity increases with soil moisture. In evergreen forests where the soils remain moist, a much greater diversity of ferns develops. On dry sites, many ferns find it impossible to persist. In this setting, you will have to be content using just a few species of ground covers

An example of a shady woodland understory, Brooker Creek Preserve, Pinellas County.

and have it appear a bit less lush. It may be most effective to use shade-tolerant woody shrubs to provide the primary structure of your understory and mix in the few herbaceous plants adapted to such conditions. Good shrub choices for most of Florida would include Florida coontie (*Zamia pumila*) and wild coffees (*Psychotria* spp.). If your soil moisture is higher, these same shrubs can be used, but you will be able to create a more lush understory with ferns and other herbaceous ground covers.

Moist to Mesic Soils

Ferns
   Sword ferns (*Nephrolepis* spp.) (A)
   Shield ferns (*Thelypteris* spp) (A)
   Netted chain fern (*Woodwardia areolata*) (A)
   Virginia chain fern (*Woodwardia virginica*) (A)

Grasses
   Inland river oats (*Chasmanthium latifolium*) (N)
   Witch grass (*Dichanthelium* spp.) (A)
   Basketgrass (*Oplismenus hirtellus*) (A)

Wildflowers
   None

Droughty Soils

Ferns
   Sword ferns (*Nephrolepis* spp.) (A)
   Shield ferns (*Thelypteris* spp.) (A)

Grasses
   Witch grass (*Dichanthelium* spp.) (A)

Wildflowers
   None

Shady Deciduous

In designing woodland landscapes, I prefer to use deciduous trees. Deciduous forests provide good shade in the summer and fall, but they allow sunlight during the winter and early spring. This influx of solar power reduces heating bills and fuels the energy needed by understory plants to flower and set seed. A great many favorite understory trees and shrubs, species such as flowering dogwood (*Cornus florida*), redbud (*Cercis canadensis*), and native azaleas (*Rhododendron* spp.), are resident to deciduous forests, not evergreen ones. The same is true for many of the most beautiful woodland wildflowers, native grasses, and ferns. Of course, deciduous forests are not the norm for southernmost Florida.

If you already have a deciduous forest, increase the diversity of your understory by adding more species. Deciduous forests normally have many different plants in the understory, and it is far more interesting aesthetically and useful to wildlife if you take this approach. Start by planting your new additions in small clusters. Eventually, most will move around a bit and adopt a more natural look, but even in nature most plants appear in small patches. Use the more diminutive and ephemeral species near the front or along pathways so you can more easily admire them. The more robust species can then be used as accents or in masses in areas a bit further in. Don't be afraid of keeping this all in some sort of balance by weeding out plants that move into areas where they are not wanted. After all, you are now a land manager. During the early years while things are

An example of a deciduous woodland understory, Florida Caverns State Park, Jackson County.

getting established, it is best to label your deciduous plants to make sure you can remember where you planted them. Never add new plants until after everything has surfaced in the spring, and don't start weeding until your seedlings are large enough to distinguish them from each other.

If you are creating a deciduous woodland from scratch, you will need to keep a couple of things in mind. First, select your canopy carefully so your mature woodland is both diverse and its members compatible. You don't want them fighting each other for space, and it is best if they provide different wildlife values, fall color, and overall texture. Trunk size at maturity is a consideration, but even more important is the width of crown. Give each newly planted tree at least 10 feet of space in all directions; 20 feet or more if you want to want their crowns to reach their full potential.

The other major consideration is the timing of your understory planting efforts. Do not attempt to use most understory wildflowers, ferns, and native grasses until after the canopy has matured enough to provide summer shade. While you are waiting for it to develop, plant species better adapted to the existing conditions. In my own backyard, I used a variety of sun-loving wildflowers beneath an area of woodland I was expanding, knowing full well that in 5–10 years they would be shaded out and need to be replaced with something else. Be patient and let the canopy develop before you begin planting violets, Indian pinks, and the like.

Wildflowers such as this meadow-rue (*Thalictrum revolutum*) are impossible to add to a woodland planting until the canopy has developed.

Moist to Mesic Soils

Ferns

> Maidenhair ferns (*Adiantum* spp.) (A)
> Ebony spleenwort (*Asplenium platyneuron*) (N)
> Southern lady fern (*Athyrium felix-femina*) (N)
> Long strap fern (*Campyloneuron phyllitidis*) (S)
> Southern wood fern (*Dryopteris ludoviciana*) (N)
> Sword ferns (*Nephrolepis* spp.) (A)
> Sensitive fern (*Onoclea sensibilis*) (N)
> Cinnamon fern (*Osmunda cinnamomea*) (A)
> Royal fern (*Osmunda regalis*) (A)
> Christmas fern (*Polystichum acrostichoides*) (N)
> Shield ferns (*Thelypteris* spp.) (A)
> Netted chain fern (*Woodwardia areolata*) (A)
> Virginia chain fern (*Woodwardia virginica*) (A)

Grasses

> Inland river oats (*Chasmanthium latifolium*) (N)
> Witch grass (*Dichanthelium* spp.) (A)
> Basketgrass (*Oplismenus hirtellus*) (A)

Wildflowers

> Eastern blue star (*Amsonia tabernaemontana*) (N)
> Columbine (*Aquilegia canadensis*) (N)
> Jack-in-the-pulpit (*Arisaema triphyllum*) (N)
> Green dragon (*Arisaema dracontium*) (N)
> Wild ginger (*Asarum arifolium*) (N)
> Swamp leather flower (*Clematis crispa*) (N)
> Trilliums (*Trillium* spp.) (N)
> Violets (*Viola* spp.) (A, except *V. walteri*, N)

Droughty Soils

Ferns

> Sword ferns (*Nephrolepis* spp.) (A)
> Shield ferns (*Thelypteris* spp.) (A)

Grasses

    Witch grass (*Dichanthelium* spp.) (A)
    Basketgrass (*Oplismenus hirtellus*) (A)

Wildflowers

    Green-and-gold (*Chrysogonum virginianum*) (N)
    Cooley's waterwillow (*Justicia cooleyi*) (N)
    Woodland phlox (*Phlox divaricata*) (N)
    Lyre-leaved sage (*Salvia lyrata*) (A)
    Indian pink (*Spigelia marilandica*) (N)
    Violets (*Viola* spp., except *V. walteri*) (N)

Sunny

In nature, sunny areas have the most diverse understories. Well-drained sandy uplands known as sandhills, moist prairie systems near the Kissimmee River, and wet savannas in the Florida Panhandle have some of the highest plant diversities of any natural system in North America. Sunlight provides energy to the system and allows for greater complexity. We can model portions of our yards to mimic these systems and replace the monotony of singe-species turfgrasses with the diverse textures and colors of Florida's native wildflowers and grasses.

Expansive plantings of these species can be dramatic if done correctly and complete failures if not well planned. The dramatic ones incorporate the right balance of diversity and pattern, using many species but massing them in clusters so each gets noticed. They are also done with an understanding of the way they will look as the seasons change. It is always best to maximize the interest inherent in such landscapes by using species that will bloom at different times and for as long as possible. Grasses also provide most of the structure during the winter months when most wildflowers are dormant or deciduous. Widely scattered grasses, with no thought to form or location, will rarely add anything to the look of a winter wildflower garden. If the grasses are planted with an eye toward design, the same grasses will provide important winter aesthetics.

Creating diverse systems takes planning and management. In nature, natural forces such as fire and flooding rebalance the system from time to

An example of a longleaf pine sandhill understory, dominated by wiregrass and wildflowers, Riverside Island Tract, Ocala National Forest, Marion County.

time and create conditions that prevent a few species from outcompeting and dominating the others. Since few of us are lucky enough to live inside a naturally functioning system, we need to be careful not to use species that will dominate everything else, and we must be prepared to provide some management from time to time to keep the balance we designed.

Alexa discovered this need when she left her mostly native "cottage garden" of wildflowers to fend for itself while she returned to college to earn her nursing degree. After several years of very limited attention, her once diverse garden was reduced to essentially four species. The four "winners" in the battle for dominance were faring extremely well, but her garden had lost the aesthetic she desired.

Maintaining diversity in a garden of wildflowers and native grasses requires management. This management comes from weeding out both the "weeds" and the desirable species that have spread to areas where they are not wanted. Some species are simply better than others at reproducing. As they spread, make sure you do not allow them to crowd out other species. You will also need to prune or mow from time to time, especially the native grasses. Most grasses benefit from having their dead blades removed.

Over time, many develop large areas of dead material (i.e., thatch) that can actually encourage fungal problems and other diseases. In nature, this material would burn and fertilize the soil. In landscapes that don't burn, the dead blades are a problem. Take some time each winter to dethatch your grasses, or take a mower and cut them, making sure you mow no closer than 6 inches above ground.

There is nothing wrong with using wildflowers and native grasses in limited areas composed of just a few species. In doing so, you will not get the wildlife value inherent in a larger, more diverse setting, but replacing the traditional small bed of annuals or perennial non-natives with native species will usually improve nectaring opportunities for butterflies and native bees and reduce water and fertilizer needs. In smaller beds, do not try to use too many different species, and select your plants carefully to make sure you have something in bloom for as many months as possible. Wildflowers with very limited blooming seasons may not be your best choices in this situation unless you have just a few of them as accents to change things a bit at different times of the year.

Make sure you select species that all share similar growing requirements, otherwise they will always be at odds with each other, and eventually some will expire. Evaluate your site critically in assessing your soil

Areas dominated by grasses require regular management by fire or mowing to maintain their ecological health.

type and your normal soil moisture conditions. What is "normal" is likely to change over a typical annual cycle, so look at it carefully at different times of the year and gain some understanding of what happens during periods of high rainfall and drought. Then be prepared to tinker a bit. I have killed a good number of plants trying to find the "right spot" in the landscape. When I am unsure of how a new species will perform, I typically try it out in several locations at the same time. Once I understand it better, I add more in those areas where it seems to do best. Because my yard is such a hodgepodge of different fill and natural soils, it may be only a few feet difference between the "right spot" and the wrong one. Yours may be similar. In general, I have broken down the plant selections below by typical moisture requirements for some of the hardiest species. Do not be afraid of experimenting beyond this.

Moist/wet

Ferns

Giant leather fern (*Acrostichum danaeifolium*) (A)
Swamp fern (*Blechnum serrulatum*) (A)
Cinnamon fern (*Osmunda cinnamomea*) (A)
Royal fern (*Osmunda regalis*) (A)
Shield ferns (*Thelypteris* spp.) (A)

Grasses

Toothache grass (*Ctenium aromaticum*) (N)
Rush (*Juncus* spp.) (A)
Hairawn muhly (*Muhlenbergia capillis*) (A)
Maidencane (*Panicum hemitomon*) (A)
White-topped sedge (*Rhynchospora colorata*) (A)
Cordgrass (*Spartina* spp.) (A)
Fakahatchee grass (*Tripsacum dactyloides*) (A)

Wildflowers

False indigo (*Amorpha fruticosa*) (A)
Swamp rose milkweed (*Asclepias incarnata*) (A)
Swamp white milkweed (*Asclepias perennis*) (N)
Hyssop (*Bacopa* spp.) (A)

Yellow canna (*Canna flaccida*) (A)

Swamp lilies (*Crinum* spp.) (A)

Marsh rattlesnake master (*Eryngium aquaticum*) (A)

Joe-pye weed (*Eupatorium fistulosum*) (N)

Narrowleaf sunflower (*Helianthus angustifolius*) (A)

Hibiscus (*Hibiscus* spp.) (A, except *H. aculeatus* and *H. moscheutos*, N)

Spider lilies (*Hymenocallis* spp.) (A)

St. John's-worts (*Hypericum* spp., except *H. tenuifolium*)

Iris (*Iris* spp.) (A)

Blue jacquemontia (*Jacquemontia pentanthos*) (S)

Dense blazing star (*Liatris spicata*) (A)

Cardinal flower (*Lobelia cardinalis*) (N)

Water dropwort (*Oxypolis filiformis*) (A)

Obedient plant (*Physostegia virginiana*) (N)

Pickerelweed (*Pontederia cordata*) (A)

Meadow beauty (*Rhexia* spp.) (A)

Cutleaf coneflower (*Rudbeckia laciniata*) (N)

Shiny coneflower (*Rudbeckia nitida*) (N)

Marsh pinks (*Sabatia* spp.) (A)

Blue-eyed grass (*Sisyrinchium angustifolium*) (A)

Climbing aster (*Symphyotrichum carolinianum*) (A)

A ruddy daggerwing rests in a light gap within a South Florida wetland.

Mesic/average

Ferns

Bracken fern (*Pteridium aquilinum*) (A)

Bahama brake fern (*Pteris bahamensis*) (A)

Grasses

Bluestems (*Andropogon* spp.) (A)

Wiregrasses (*Aristida* spp.) (A)

Lovegrass (*Eragrostis* spp.) (A)
Hairawn muhly (*Muhlenbergia capillaris*) (A)
Little bluestem (*Schizachyrium scoparium*) (A)
Lop-sided Indiangrass (*Sorghastrum secundum*) (A)
Pinewoods dropseed (*Sporobolus junceus*) (A)
Dwarf Fakahatchee grass (*Tripsacum floridanum*) (S)

Wildflowers

Chaffheads (*Carphephorus* spp.) (A)
Lanceleaf tickseed (*Coreopsis lanceolata*) (N)
Common tickseed (*Coreopsis leavenworthii*) (A)
Twinflower (*Dyschoriste oblongifolia*) (A)
Purple coneflower (*Echinacea purpurea*) (N)
Rattlesnake master (*Eryngium yuccifolium*) (A)
Rayless sunflower (*Helianthus radula*) (A)
Woodland sunflower (*Helianthus strumosus*) (N)
Pineland heliotrope (*Heliotropum polyphyllum*) (S)
Garber's blazing star (*Liatris garberi*) (S)
Graceful blazing star (*Liatris gracilis*) (A)
Sunshine mimosa (*Mimosa strigillosa*) (N)
Dotted horsemint (*Monarda punctata*) (A)
Beardtongues (*Penstemon* spp.) (N)
False pennyroyal (*Piloblephis rigida*) (A)
Narrowleaf silkgrass (*Pityopsis graminifolia*) (A)
Yellow coneflower (*Ratibida pinnata*) (N)
Black-eyed susan (*Rudbeckia hirta*) (A)
Softhair coneflower (*Rudbeckia mollis*) (N)
Wild petunia (*Ruellia caroliniensis*) (A)
Red salvia (*Salvia coccinea*) (A)
Common skullcap (*Scutellaria integrifolia*) (A)
Starry rosinweed (*Silphium asteriscus*) (A)
Sweet goldenrod (*Solidago odora*) (A)
Stoke's aster (*Stokesia laevis*) (N)
Common spiderwort (*Tradescantia ohiensis*) (A)
Blue curls (*Trichostema dichotomum*) (A)
Ironweeds (*Vernonia* spp.) (N, except *V. blodgettii*, S)

A deltoid scarab beetle pollinating the flowers of a Florida paintbrush (*Carphephorus corymbosus*).

Atamasco rain lily (*Zephyranthes atamasca*) (N)
Simpson's rain lily (*Zephyranthes simpsonii*) (S)

Well-drained/droughty

Ferns

None

Grasses

Splitbeard bluestem (*Andropogon ternarius*) (A)
Lop-sided Indiangrass (*Sorghastrum secundum*) (A)
Wiregrasses (*Aristida* spp.) (A)

Wildflowers

Butterfly milkweed (*Asclepias tuberosa*) (A)
Yellow buttons (*Balduina angustifolia*) (A)
Soft greeneyes (*Berlandiera pumila*) (N)
Florida greeneyes (*Berlandiera subacaulis*) (A)
Calamints (*Calamintha* spp.) (N)
False rosemaries (*Conradina* spp.) (A)
Summer farewell (*Dalea pinnata*) (A)

Garberia (*Garberia heterophylla*) (A)
Resindot sunflower (*Helianthus resinosus*) (N)
Scrub St. John's-wort (*Hypericum tenuifolium*) (A)
Standing cypress (*Ipomopsis rubra*) (N)
Chapman's blazing star (*Liatris chapmanii*) (A)
Elegant blazing star (*Liatris elegans*) (N)
Scrub blazing star (*Liatris tenuifolia*) (A)
Palafoxias (*Palafoxia* spp.) (A)
Purple passionvine (*Passiflora incarnata*) (A)
Downy phlox (*Phlox pilosa*) (N)
Buckwheat family—Polygonaceae (A)
Sky blue salvia (*Salvia azurea*) (N)
Scrub blue-eyed grass (*Sisyrinchium xerophyllum*) (A)
Eastern silver aster (*Symphyotrichum concolor*) (A)

Coastal Dune

Ferns

None

Grasses

Bitter panic grass (*Panicum amarum*) (A)
Sea oats (*Uniola paniculata*) (A)

Wildflowers

Cottony goldenaster (*Chrysopsis gossypina*) (N)
False rosemary (*Conradina canescens*) (N)
Large-flowered false rosemary (*Conradina grandiflora*) (S)
Blanket flower (*Gaillardia pulchella*) (A)
Beach verbena (*Glandularia maritima*) (S)
Dune sunflower (*Helianthus debilis*) (A)
Seaside heliotrope (*Heliotropium curassavicum*) (A)
Beach morning glory (*Ipomoea imperati*) (A)
Railroad vine (*Ipomoea pes-caprae*) (A)
Beach jacquemontia (*Jacquemontia reclinata*) (S)
Seaside goldenrod (*Solidago sempervirens*) (A)
Blue porterweed (*Stachytarpheta jamaicensis*) (S)

Conclusions

The use of native wildflowers, ferns, and grasses in home landscapes is becoming more commonplace throughout much of North America. We are appreciating the fact that such landscapes can be beautiful as well as ecologically and economically superior to what we have come to accept as normal. Most of us yearn to some degree to be reconnected to the natural world. We will never succeed in the types of landscapes molded from plants of other continents.

The movement to landscape with native ground covers is in its early infancy in Florida. In a state founded largely on the tropical paradise myth, it is no wonder it has taken so long to realize that it is not and that Florida is special just the way it is. I hope that this book has helped you discover

Native ground covers nurture native wildlife in a way unequaled by non-natives. A ruby-throated hummingbird nectars from red salvia (*Salvia coccinea*). Photo by Christina Evans, with permission.

the many native plants possible in your home landscape and made you a bit more comfortable using them. Because it is a gardening book, I hope it helps direct you on a path to using these plants more successfully and that, over time, we all connect with each other's landscapes and with the natural world. We can make a difference. It starts with a trowel, a few plants, and the will to use them.

Resources

Online Native Plant Information
(Photographs and Information)

Flora of North America

http://www.fna.org/FNA

Lady Bird Johnson Wildflower Center

4801 LaCrosse Ave.
Austin, TX 78739
512-232-0100
http://www.wildflower.org

Florida Native Plant Society

P.O. Box 278
Melbourne, FL 32666-0434
321-271-6702
http://www.fnps.org

Florida Wildflower Foundation

Executive Director
P.O. Box 941066
Maitland, FL 32794-1066
407-353-6164
http://floridawildflowerfoundation.org

Florida Wildflowers

http://www.flwildflowers.com

Hawthorn Hill Wildflowers

http://hawthornhillwildflowers.blogspot.com

Institute for Regional Conservation

22601 SW 152nd Ave.
Miami, FL 33170
305-247-6547
http://www.regionalconservation.org

Institute for Systematic Botany

Department of Cell Biology, Microbiology, and Molecular Biology
University of South Florida
4202 East Fowler Ave., BSF 218
Tampa, FL 33620-5150
813-974-6238
http://www.florida.plantatlas.usf.edu

Panflora

http://www.gilnelson.com/PanFlora

The PLANTS Database

USDA, NRCS
National Plant Data Team
 Greensboro, NC 27401-4901
http://plants.usda.gov

Native Plant Nursery Sources

Florida Association of Native Nurseries

c/o JCM
P.O. Box 972
Melbourne, FL 32902-0972
321-917-1960
http://www.floridanativenurseries.org

Florida Gardener

http://floridagardener.com

Wildflower Seed And Plant Growers Association, Inc.

P.O. Box 776
Crescent City, FL 32112
352-988-8117
http://www.floridawildflowers.com

Online Plant Nurseries for Florida Gardens

Mail Order Natives

P.O. Box 9366
Lee, FL 32059
850-973-6830
http://www.mailordernatives.com

Niche Gardens

1111 Dawson Road
Chapel Hill, NC 27516
919-967-0078
www.nichegardens.com

Plant Delights

9241 Sauls Road
Raleigh, NC 27603
919-772-4794
www.plantdelights.com

Sunlight Gardens

174 Golden Lane
Andersonville, TN 37705
800-272-7396
www.sunlightgardens.com

Woodlanders, Inc.

1128 Colleton Avenue
Aiken, SC 29801
803-648-7522
http://www.woodlanders.net

Books

Field Guides

Ferns

Lakela, O., and R. W. Long. 1976. *Ferns of Florida: An Illustrated Manual and Identification Guide*. Miami: Banyan Books.
Nelson, G. 2000. *The Ferns of Florida: A Reference and Field Guide*. Sarasota: Pineapple Press.
Wunderlin, R. P., and B. F. Hansen. 2000. *Flora of Florida. Volume 1: Pteridophytes and Gymnosperms*. Gainesville: University Press of Florida.

Grasses

Taylor, W. K. 2009. *A Guide to Florida Grasses*. Gainesville: University Press of Florida.
Yarlett, L. L. 1996. *Common Grasses of Florida and the Southeast*. Spring Hill, Fla.: Florida Native Plant Society.

Wildflowers

Bell, C. R., and B. J. Taylor. 1982. *Florida Wildflowers and Roadside Plants*. Chapel Hill, N.C.: Laurel Hill Press.
Hammer, R. L. 2002. *Everglades Wildflowers*. Guilford, Conn.: Globe Pequot Press.
———. 2004. *Florida Keys Wildflowers*. Guilford, Conn.: Globe Pequot Press.
Nelson, G. 2005. *East Gulf Coastal Plain Wildflowers*. Guilford, Conn.: Globe Pequot Press.
———. 2006. *Atlantic Coastal Plain Wildflowers*. Guilford, Conn.: Globe Pequot Press.
Taylor, W. K. 1992. *The Guide to Florida Wildflowers*. Dallas: Taylor Publishing Company.
———. 1998. *Florida Wildflowers in Their Natural Communities*. Gainesville: University Press of Florida.

Gardening with Native Plants

Foster, F. Gordon. 1984. *Ferns to Know and Grow*. Portland, Ore.: Timber Press.

Haehle, R. G., and J. Brookwell. 1999. *Native Florida Plants: Low Maintenance Landscaping and Gardening*. Houston: Gulf Publishing Company.

Huegel, Craig N. 2010. *Native Plant Landscaping for Florida Wildlife*. Gainesville: University Press of Florida.

Jones, S. B., Jr., and L. E. Foote. 1990. *Gardening with Native Wild Flowers*. Portland, Ore.: Timber Press.

Nelson, G. 2003. *Florida's Best Native Landscape Plants*. Gainesville: University Press of Florida.

Osorio, R. 2001. *A Gardener's Guide to Florida's Native Plants*. Gainesville: University Press of Florida.

Wasowski, S., and A. Wasowski. 1994. *Gardening with Native Plants of the South*. Dallas: Taylor Publishing Company.

Index

Page numbers in **bold** refer to illustrations.

Craig Huegel is a wildlife biologist, ecological consultant, and lifelong gardener with a special interest in the relationship between plants and animals. He helped establish the Cooperative Urban Wildlife Program in 1987 at the University of Florida and has been deeply involved ever since in educating the public about Florida's native plants and wildlife. He is active in the Florida Native Plant Society and the Florida Wildflower Foundation, writes a blog devoted to wildflowers, and operates a small wildflower nursery that specializes in species not commonly grown by others. He has written another widely read book, *Native Plant Landscaping for Florida Wildlife* (2010).